FATHERS AND S

LITIMA*

— Masculine Energy

that violent emotion
— peculiar to the masculine part of things —
which is the source of
quarrels,
ruthless competition,
possessiveness,
power-drivenness and
brutality;

but also is the source of
independence,
courage,
upstandingness,
wildness (which is not savagery),
high emotions,
ideals,
the movement towards individuality and
the very source of the desire for initiation.

'If this is not honoured, it will take the brutal path.
Often, depression, reticence, hiding or lethargy is an actual — kind
of moral — decision not to erupt into the world and do damage to
oneself or others.'

Michael Meade

*From *Images of Initiation* (Audio Cassette), Oral Tradition Archives,
USA.

FATHERS
AND SONS

Compiled by
Tom Hyde

WOLFHOUND PRESS

Fathers and Sons is dedicated
with love and gratitude to
J.A. (Tony) Hyde 1907 –
whose son I became.

First published 1995 by
WOLFHOUND PRESS Ltd
68 Mountjoy Square
Dublin 1
and Wolfhound Press (UK)
18 Coleswood Rd
Harpenden
Herts AL5 1EQ

Wolfhound Press receives financial assistance from the Arts Council/
An Chomhairle Ealaíon, Dublin.
British Library Cataloguing in Publication Data
A catalogue record for this book is available from the British Library.

ISBN 0 86327 515 X

Typesetting: Wolfhound Press
Cover design: Joe Gervin
Photograph: Courtesy of Daniel De Chenu. Tom Duffy and Son's Circus provides the theme. David Duffy, son of Tom Duffy reflects generatons of Fathers and Sons with Benjamin Chipperfield Coles.
Printed by the Guernsey Press Co Ltd, Guernsey, Channel Isles.
Wolfhound Press and the author, in association with Oak Glen, will facilitate the planting of two trees for every one tree used in the manufacture of this book.

CONTENTS

'Thank You'

James Hillman and Michael Meade for conducting the 1992 Men's Gathering, the four Irishmen who organised it and the 'hundred men' who made it happen, and especially to Michael for returning and Malidoma Patrice Somé for coming with him; the contributors who make this book; Pauline for sharing the experience of parenting — Simon, Ruth and David for coming to us — and for her continuing affection in spite of our unpreparedness, Liz Sherry, for so much — including 'introducing me to men'; Noleen Slattery for her Chinese Medical care, and the invaluable Lodge, Aiseiri; my colleagues in the Men's Group whose interest in this book encouraged me to 'take the high-risk rather than the subsistence option'; Ciaran who followed-up a casual conversation by generously having a would-be 'writer-in-residence' in his home for six months; my VTOS colleagues — Joe, Leo, Mick and Willy — for their companionship and fun and the admirably encouraging teachers in Cabra Vocational School, especially Finolua Butler for dissolving my PC-phobia; Peter Sirr and Jacinta Douglas of the Irish Writers' Centre for their instant help and endless patience in the final stages of making this book, and to Ann Ingle for her similar support at the earlier stages; Wolfhound Press staff and especially Tom Turley without whose recognition it could not have happened; and to Dee, who 'saw' this book completed before I did, simply for being.

INTRODUCTION

Philip Kearney

'Old father, old artificer, stand me now and ever in good stead.'

James Joyce

When invited to speak of their fathers many men shrivel. Nothing better evokes the weaker and more vulnerable side of men than such an invitation. It takes a particular courage to speak tenderly (and publicly) of one's father and this is the achievement of those men who have contributed to this anthology. This book provides an opportunity for the voices of Irish sons to be expressed in a new way. Usually the father's version of events has pre-eminence. In this collection of stories and poems men retell their experiences as their father's sons and how that has shaped them and their lives.

This relationship has had less attention than other elements of the family in terms of careful analysis, although it has featured frequently in various artistic media, particularly the theatre. A brief review of recent Irish theatre elicits a recurrent theme of sons seeking connection with fathers. From *Philadelphia, Here I Come* through *Da* to *The Steward of Christendom* the plaintive cries of men in search of paternal acknowledgement or love may be discerned. *In The Name of the Father* echoes this refrain.

So prevalent is this image of father-son estrangement that a close, expressive, mutually-rewarding father-son relationship in adult life is seen as the rare exception. It has come to be accepted that many of these relationships will be fraught with difficulty and are irredeemable. The idea that intimacy might be possible between a son and a father before the latter reaches his death-bed, or even necessary for the emotional and spiritual health of both, is rarely mooted.

John McGahern's novel *Amongst Women* is a particularly graphic account of a family dominated by the oppressive and violent temperament of the father. This represents the extreme end of the spectrum but is by no means unique. Many of the stories in this collection are milder versions of this and reflect a continuing thread of acceptance of men as fathers who are emotionally inaccessible and, in some instances, physically violent. Not all are of this kind, of course. There is much here which honours and celebrates the father but the recurrent themes of disappointment and estrangement constitute the most significant patterns emerging in this anthology.

McGahern's work captures with subtle and damning force the oppressive power of the *paterfamilias*. It illustrates how the other family members are silenced and sidelined into roles of damage limitation, striving to pre-empt anything which might lead to an outburst. This progressively stifles much of the life-blood of the family in the service of the father's power. It might even be said that the family is organised to preserve the myths of the father's dominance and competence. This includes toleration of his outbursts and excesses. In its worst forms it ensures the preservation of secrets concerning violence and abuse. Taken alone McGahern's portrayal appears exaggerated, a caricature, and yet we have seen in recent years a series of such grotesque family stories emerge into the public domain. These travesties require that men's misuse of power in intimate human relations be scrutinised and challenged.

The degree to which the father-son relationship is the crucible for a man's construction of his own role as father merits attention. This book is a pertinent and timely contribution to that enquiry. It offers a different perspective in that it gathers the personal stories of many Irish men as sons. This has not been done before and the cumulative effect of assembling many voices on the same topic is a powerful testimony. There are almost fifty contributions from men from all parts of the island, from a wide range of backgrounds, some well known, some not published before. It provides a starting point from which to launch a re-evaluation of the strait-jacketed roles within which fathers and sons constrain themselves and each other in our society. It is an opportunity to reflect and rework some of the cultural premises and assumptions which underpin patriarchy.

This book is a gift for those who still have their fathers living, a comfort, perhaps, for those who have lost them and a seminal contribution to the regeneration of fatherhood. It gathers the dispersed shards of grief and joy scattered throughout our cultural landscape, the accumulated filial distress and devotion, much of which remains unrequited. It opens a conduit for the articulation and examination of a set of relationships of huge social significance which has largely been unaddressed.

It has no pretensions to be an academic study of the father-son relationship, rather it assembles, without commentary, a series of reflections, anecdotes and poems which invoke the paternal influence in the writer's life. Many are posthumous. Like all good wakes it is both a *caoineadh* and a celebration.

Regret And Grief

A number of patterns may be observed throughout the text. There is a recurrent theme of regret for opportunities missed, for questions unasked, for fathers remaining unknown behind unassailable emotional fortifications.

> I feel downcast that I can only remember my father like this as a figure, almost a type, rather than a person. His own inner private life is hidden from me completely. ... I do not want to think of my father as a Father. By being my father he is lost to me, as, for all I know, I am lost to my children. Perhaps I must accept the truth, miserably: that he, happily, lost himself in his children. It makes me feel so ungiving, so helpless, now that it is too late to explain to him that if he had been less good I might now admire him less and might have loved him more.
>
> *Sean O'Faolain*

> It was that typical Irish thing, a father and son not really speaking to each other, not really knowing each other. ... But was I close to him? No. I loved him and admired him, but I didn't really know him.
>
> *David Hanley*

Variations on this theme of the present but unknowable father abound in the book and no doubt will have strong echoes for many men. This is a loss for which there is usually no voice or understanding. At the Irish Men's Gatherings of 1992 and 1994 there were moments of intense communal grief which suggested a vast reservoir of unexpressed emotional energy. These moments were usually prompted by an individual man's story of loss. Through the medium of chanting a simple lament, some shared unfathomable loss was experienced. For some it was clear who was being mourned — often it was a father — for others the focus was unspecified but none the less intense for that. The well of collective grief expressed and experienced by men at these gatherings indicates the yearning for paternal nurturance which our culture does not appease.

The most powerful medium of fathers' communication with their children is often non-verbal. Many can recall the imperative power of father's glance, cough or gesture. The family is finely tuned to respond to or even predict such subtle cues. This is frequently reflected in contributions to this collection:

> A look, the tone of voice, the length of a caress, the precise weight of a slap — these tell me more than the words I play with.
>
> *Jack Houlahan*

Another of the recurrent themes is the prevalence of physical punishment in the experience of many of the writers. In both cases there is an acceptance that patriarchal dominance is a given, which must be sustained even in the face of great pain and disappointment.

Another Last Taboo?

Fathers and Sons raises some very profound questions about our culture, family roles in general and the father-son relationship in particular.

* Are we still raising our male children for the battlefield, actually or metaphorically?
* Can men with no paternal nurturing provide it for their own children?
* How will the configuration of relations in the family have to change to give fathers and sons greater access to each other?

My remarks are based on a premise that it is desirable for the father-son bond to be strengthened and become more intimate. Is this another great last taboo? It is not a view expressed explicitly by many of the authors in the text. To be fair they were asked to write about their own experience rather than how things should be. Thus there is much understanding of the limitations of the father, of him being a man of his time, of his devotion to duty, his excellence as a provider, in short much filial piety. There is relatively little challenge to the father's distance, emotional incapacity, or his use of physical forms of punishment.

When one considers the cruel conundrums in which many men find themselves the above is not surprising. To critique the father brings forth the violence and rejection which the son most wishes to avoid; to accept the father's distance and inaccessibility leaves the son incomplete and desolate. To reach across the father-son divide requires a trustworthy experience of fathering which is often not available in our culture; to cut the chord leaves the young man adrift in a world of equally aimless peers and charlatans.

The spiralling figures for young male suicides call for some explanations and the above conjectures may give us some direction for research. Of course there is no simple casual link but the hypothesis of young men increasingly bereft of mentors, meaning and manhood sliding into despair deserves closer scrutiny. Similar formulations may be considered in relation to other deviant and self-destructive activities of our alienated youth — from violence to crime to addiction.

Initiation and Mentoring

Some of the theorists writing about men would suggest that the lack of initiatory practices is at the heart of these social catastrophes. The phenomenon of young, anti-social males causing havoc for society and themselves and then being re-cycled through our prison system may be understood in terms of a search for the containment and challenge which would be provided in other cultures through initiatory experiences. Such rituals would assist them to make a transition to a meaningful adult role in the community. These are singularly lacking. This is a community responsibility rather than an exclusively paternal one. The constraints and obstacles surrounding the father-son relationship places fathers under excessive pressure to deliver in ways which are often beyond them. They are ill-equipped from their own experiences of being fathered, they lack any connection to an ancestral wisdom which could guide them and now there are expectations, often portrayed through the media, which they know they cannot fulfil.

Speaking of initiation can evoke images of scarifying and dangerous rituals — and in some cultures that is precisely what it entails. The popularity of piercing and tattooing can be seen as vestiges of these practices. Similarly the seeking for ecstasy or oblivion through chemical means may be a substitute for the challenge of the initiatory quest. Reinstating initiation does not require exotic rituals, however. The existing rites of passage can be invested with a new sense of significance whereby young people can be assisted to make the transition to adulthood.

Mentoring is another way in which the community can provide support to or a substitute for the father's role. It requires a cohort of elders who command respect and who can tell the stories which the young men (and women) need to hear. For those of us who have sought to establish a 'men's movement' in Ireland there has been a vacuum in this regard which is why we invited James Hillman, Michael Meade, Malidoma Somé and others to act as guides. The work of many of the older contributors to this volume may be seen in this light although they may not have perceived themselves as fulfilling such a role. Many of them are writing of their own fathers rather than offering guidance to their sons. The importance of this latter role and task needs acknowledgement. One of my hopes for this book is that it will inspire older men to articulate their roles as elders and mentors for the emerging generation of younger Irish men.

The Case for Separatism
There is a need for separate contexts for the evocation of maleness other than the pub, football pitch or battle field. Just as the transformative influence of the women's movement emerged out of extremism and separatism a similar phase is necessary for the men's movement to achieve a momentum which will overwhelm the status quo. For this reason it is vital that men meet separately, publish their own books and magazines such as this one and articulate their own voices in men-only gatherings. The call to submerge differences and seek a *rapprochement* with women because 'we are all human beings' is premature and misguided.

Much work of a radical nature still requires to be done. There are many changes already but these are largely cosmetic and transient. For example, the paternity leave which has been available for men in some Scandinavian countries has had a very slow uptake and the research shows that even with shared parenting arrangements the major bulk of the household work is still undertaken by women. At the same time there is substantial evidence that when men are the principal caretakers they are just as capable of nurturing children as women.

Valuing the Domestic Sphere

Until the work of maintaining the household and rearing and caring for children is valued, acknowledged and paid, the separation of the private and public domains will remain with all the biases, distortions and built-in constraints which cripple our gender relations today. Only such a shift can alter the power imbalances and reconfigure the father-son and other relationships within the family.

Conclusion

In collating these stories Tom Hyde is making a very substantial contribution to advancing the movement whereby men may come to a more life-enhancing view of themselves and their relationships, particularly as fathers and sons. He has assembled a catalogue of the ordinary and sacred — a kaleidoscope of a neglected domain of male intimacy. His inspiration for this is a product of his own experiences, catalysed by the Men's Gathering and supported by his men's group and other important friends. It began and remained as a vital personal journey of renewal and transformation and this is its enduring quality. Tom sought only to collect and retell men's stories. As with women, when men tell their heartfelt stories and are heard, the personal becomes political. This anthology will serve as a benchmark in the literature which will emerge on the experience of Irish men as they seek to reinvent themselves in a cultural landscape undergoing seismic shifts. It will offer inspiration to those who do not accept Sartre's admonition that 'the bond of paternity ... is rotten', but rather call for the reinstatement of its mythic and sacred significance.

> And you, my father, there on the sad height,
> Curse, bless, me now with your fierce tears, I pray.
> Do not go gentle into that good night.
> Rage, rage against the dying of the light.

Dylan Thomas

ABOUT THIS BOOK

I was unemployed, redundant for the third time in ten years, when the idea which resulted in this book came to me. Originally it was a simple idea which I thought would be of interest only to myself. Once I began to act on it however, it took on a life of its own and I was changed in the process. Being a fifty-one year old unemployed man in a country with a high level of unemployment and a large number of young people available, I faced a problem. On impulse I had rushed into a retraining opportunity in the west of Ireland. As usual I soon felt my impulsive mistake and began to wonder how to correct it. Uncharacteristically, and against all sensible rational advice, I abandoned the retraining, remained living in the ancient Clare countryside and took 'time out' — to rest, read, walk, reflect, listen to music, make new friends and generally behave in ways more appropriate to a person at the beginning of adult life. I read a lot, and I discovered that a few men's books had begun to appear on the 'Gender Studies' shelves in Irish bookshops.

As I read these, some poetry and the occasional work of history, I began to find the Father-Son relationship a theme of particular interest. A year previously I had participated in the first Men's Gathering in Ireland conducted by James Hillman and Michael Meade. Hillman is a Jungian psychoanalyst and Meade is a storytelling drummer. I thought of the other men who had been at the Gathering and that maybe some of them would have their own personal favourite, or personally meaningful, father-son poem, song or literary passage.

So I wrote to them all inviting them to share these with me, my book browsing habit became focused, and I raised the topic in conversation with men and women friends. Suddenly I found father-son stories, issues, griefs and triumphs everywhere. As I talked with male friends about their personal experiences as sons I was astonished by the range of reminiscences and the energy stimulated by their being invited to talk about it. Sometimes the most impressive reactions were the spontaneously joyful ones from men who had had good times with their fathers or who willingly spoke of reconciliation after a turbulent early-life period. But mostly the reaction was a forceful 'I don't want to talk about that'. When I spoke with female friends their responses were almost universally the same: *why* are father-son relationships as they are? Many women friends observed these relationships to be at least stressful if not outright violent in men's lives.

Then the replies to my letters began to come to me — some are included here — and my book browsing turned up all sorts of interesting stories, poems, autobiographies — some of which are also here. So I wondered about trying to collect accounts of experiences by Irish men as sons, with a view to publishing them in a book. I made a list of Irishmen whose experience interested me. These were men who in some way or another had touched my consciousness or curiosity over the previous half century of living in Ireland. Some I had met, or worked with for a time, but most of them 'wouldn't know me from Adam', and here I was asking them to share with me a part of their lives which my experience suggested might have ranged from peaceful coexistence to unending hostility!

I put together a leaflet (*ON FATHER*, See page 233) which I hoped would convey aspects of the father-son dynamic. This consisted of direct comments I'd heard repeatedly and quotations from some of my recent reading. With this leaflet enclosed I wrote to these men — strangers, vague acquaintances and also some friends. The results were interesting and revealing, and most importantly they accelerated a change within myself. Some of the responses are included here. A few men declined my invitation with courtesy, some with an explanation and encouragement. Others remained silent.

The silence, though disappointing from my collecting perspective, was not surprising. Authors of a number of the original items here included acknowledge the difficulty — even the pain — they experienced in writing of their experience as the junior partner in a father-son relationship. If the exercise was difficult for professional writers, how much more so for lay word-smiths? This was confirmed for me as copy-date approached. 'John' had attended the 1992 Gathering and therefore received my original request. He was one of the first to reply. He strongly welcomed an anthology on the theme, and when he heard I had such a goal he volunteered to write of his experience for inclusion. Now, nearly a year later, he has written '*I am finding it very painful to write about my father and doubt if I will be able to deliver another piece as talked about*'. At least he wrote of his difficulty — but then he is conscientiously working through the years of unconsciousness about his experience as a son — I can only wonder about the silence of other men. Some of them had been enthusiastic about my publication; some even spoke their promise to contribute to my collection, and some became less friendly or accessible to me in the past year. Can men's unfaced pain be such, that even to be invited to look at it evokes its symptoms? To somehow help the many other men who could follow 'John's' example is one of the reasons for this book.

This is not a representative or comprehensive expression of the variety of father-son experiences in Ireland. There are no personal recollections from sportsmen, 'pop-stars' or contemporary farmers and none of what are, to my mind unhappily and inaccurately, called 'new men' — men reared in the era of the women's movement and therefore different from the society in which nearly all of the men who've shared their experience here came into manhood. What is here is a collection of items which helped me in recent years to recognise and revalue *my experience* — by reminding me of forgotten love expressed in so many ways by my father, or by echoing somehow my soul's unrequited longing. As such it is not a book for cover-to-cover reading. The items came to me sporadically and over a time-scale which gave me time to reflect on each one and to talk about these separate glimpses into over forty sons' personal experiences of a unique aspect of the challenge of being a man — whether father or son, and sometimes both. To convey what each of the contributions means to me, or *why* these particular men, would take another volume. So this, in a way, is as it has been described by one of the contributors: 'Tom's story, with illustrations from other Irish sons'.

What I have included is only a selection of what resulted from my reading and all of the original reminiscences which I received in response to my unexpected invitation. Among the quotations I have collected in recent years is the advice of Chief Seattle that 'Fathers must teach their children that the ground beneath their feet is the ashes of their grandfathers'. So I have begun with Brendan Kennelly's powerful evocation of the Famine because I became really conscious of that horrific culture-destroying event only in recognising that my father was son of a man born and reared in its immediate aftermath.

I know that I'm a prisoner
To all my father held so dear
I know that I'm a hostage
To all his hopes and fears
I wish I could have told him
In the living years

So sings Mike Rutherford in his haunting lament *The Living Years*. To those sons who share this sense of regret this book provides a number of examples of how other sons came to review and honour their fathers' lives, hopes and fears — some in the living years.

Tom Hyde

THE FIRST FIFTY YEARS

Dad was a small town merchant. One of the two surviving sons in the 'C. Hyde & Sons' which was emblazoned across the shop front of the house in which I spent the first eighteen years of my life. The last four of these years were so full of turbulence that I almost tried to not think of the place as 'Home' after I left it. But I never actually managed to quite leave it mentally — or spiritually — for nearly the next thirty years. Growing up there, we heard that our mother was the eldest in her family of seven and Dad was the youngest of sixteen children born into his family. By the time I arrived there were only three of his brothers and four sisters remaining. Two of these uncles had died before I was ten. One of the survivors was my godmother. She, like my mother, was the eldest in her family. She was twenty-two years older than Dad and my eldest first cousin, her first-born, was only six or seven years younger than Dad. Thus my first cousins were spread over half a century! For me, growing up, this was somewhat confusing, especially as my eldest cousin was in the family business with Dad and his bachelor brother. Both my grandfathers and my father's mother had died before I was born. So the only living link to those generations was my mother's mother whose influence and presence was daily and dominant. Though only the same age as my godmother, Dad's sister, she seemed to me by her voice and manner to treat both my parents as if they were children. Their apparently submissive behaviour towards her was clearly the behaviour I assumed was expected of me in turn. 'Good children are seen and not heard' and 'speak when you're spoken to' were often spoken edicts. So my rebellion — or identity development — took the negative, covert, manipulative route from my earliest memories.

While my two brothers and sister who were older than me had spent a year at least in a Gaeltacht primary boarding school, I managed to avoid going to Ring until I spent a summer month there before my last year in secondary school. This was because of my apparently fragile health (I caught every annual sickness going in the schoolroom and playground, and more as well) and the fact that until my final year in primary school I occasionally wet the bed at night. As this was not appropriate behaviour for someone my age, and could not remain hidden in dormitory sleeping arrangements, I felt fairly confident about my not being 'sent to Ring' as long as it persisted, in spite of all the talk of my being able to bring a 'rubber sheet' (to protect the school mattress). But I cannot for certain say bed-wetting was either a conscious decision on my part or a determining factor in my parents making a family exception in my case. However, the bed wetting stopped when I shared a desk with a class-mate who smelled as I must have and I did not like it! My brothers were aged seven and six and my sister aged two when I was born. There followed a sister two and a half years after me, who died in infancy, and another sister two years after her. Then my mother had her womb removed. While I cannot imagine that at five or six years of age I had any knowledge of a hysterectomy, my strongest early childhood memories are of my mother being ill with such frequent nursing attendance that I could easily 'remember' a live-in nurse as well as Molly, our live-in maid. Though I was aware that going to boarding school and having a maid was not common among my pals, the other subtle manifestations of small town hierarchy (which were the basis of all my parents' child rearing practices) only slowly came through to me from the other boys themselves. And in this social consciousness, my parents were in every way the children of Granny, one of whose most easily remembered comments was 'tuppence ha'penny looking down on tuppence'. This characteristic ethos of my family origins was vividly evoked for me in recent months by Tony Farmar's *Ordinary Lives*.

C. Hyde and Sons was a Coal and Corn business started by my grandfather, Cornelius, after whom my second eldest brother was named. The eldest had been named after our maternal grandfather, Richard. Both names were abbreviated to Niall and Dick respectively. When my turn came it was to carry-on the name of one of my father's brothers. He had gone to Spain with O'Duffy to fight the Communists and protect the Church. He was killed within days by a similarly motivated group in that awful event. When the time came I too received a family nickname and one of my outstanding memories of achievement in childhood is of eliminating the use of that nickname. At around seven years of age I refused to listen to anyone who did not address me as 'Tom' and walked away (probably sulking) from anyone teasingly using the hated nickname. Later I look in awe at such effective persistence by a child in changing the behaviour of adults and other children. Clearly I had inherited my fair share of what Dad used call 'the Forrest stubbornness', and also my share of what he recognised when he used to say 'the Hydes were always moody'. While Dad was still a youth, his brothers had started a cinema, in addition to their father's business. And when Dad got married he bought an undertaking business and the house in which we were all reared — I uniquely so for eighteen years uninterrupted by the boarding school experience of the others. So what was life like for me behind the closed door on the Main Street a hundred yards from the family-owned cinema? The immediate image — or memory — is of endless tension relieved only by self-isolation in my own bedroom reading, or going three or four times a week to Dad's cinema. While I can in a general way recall Dad's high volume reprimands, injunctions and exhortations, I can only vaguely recall one occasion when he resorted to physical punishment. But I have always had an abiding sense of 'be quiet, Mammy (or someone) is sick', pervading my whole childhood. And everything was more highly charged once I reached adolescence. Even as a child, reading was an escape to such an extent that I clearly recall once rushing to return two books to the public library which I had read since borrowing them earlier that same day. The inconvenience for library administration of such speed reading was expressed but managed by Mr O'Leary, who long before I was old enough to do so allowed me to borrow books — highly vetted, no doubt — from the adult shelves.

From very early, the question 'What are you going to be when you grow up and leave school?' was easily answered: Dick was going into the business; Niall was going to university and 'Tom will be the priest in the family'. So little did I question this that when it seemed to me I might not be allowed to become a priest if I hadn't first been an altar boy, I asked to become one a year or two later than normal. Originally I was ill and I had been absent from class on the day when boys were selected to 'learn Latin' during school-time. When I returned, the Christian Brother who trained the altar boys invited me to join them, but I declined to leave Mr Carroll's end of day story-reading to 'learn Latin'. Requesting special treatment after I'd passed out of Mr Carroll's class was easy. By then I had learned of the fawning attitudes shown to my father in the small town hierarchy. One year, instead of a massed choir in the school fund-raising concert, a small choir was featured for which I was selected as an after-thought. Today, over forty years later, I can still remember being in the corridor putting on our coats after school, when one of the good singers came out to bring me back to join the concert choir practice. I knew there were better singers than I to fill the apex of the single line pyramid formation on the narrow stage of my father's cinema. So, asking to become an altar boy out of sequence was easy, when I imagined it to be a prerequisite for a 'Vocation' — a word which was exclusively used in connection with the priesthood, as if somehow individual choice did not enter into the process. But then, individual choice did not really exist in any area in spite of the phrase used by both my parents, 'All right, suit yourself', which really conveyed the opposite meaning to me. So after nightly family rosary, at school and other times, I fervently personalised the prayers for vocations, and believed my prayers were answered in the first ecstasy experience I had — when I heard the immortal words 'Come Follow Me' as I diligently said Prayers After Communion. Such ecstasy experiences, and more, were to follow: I was in my fourteenth year. Needless to say the only real physical knowledge I had about my body was the difference 'between the legs' of boy and girl. I had not noticed my older sister's body change shape in the previous two or three years and I used to wonder how the hero in a film felt with two bumps sticking into him when embracing the heroine — I didn't even know breasts were soft! The new mental and emotional experiences remained a secret, between myself and God. The return of nightly 'bed-wetting' went apparently unnoticed because I thought it was 'different and less than before'. Later my furtive interest in Dick's photography magazines was shared with no one — not even my pals.

By now Dick was living at home. Having finished school he had begun studying accountancy, but this was abandoned after he contracted meningitis through which he was nursed at home. Afterwards he began working in 'Ballinacurra' as the family business was called at home. Looking back later it became clear how much our family dynamics were dominated by the cult of the first-born, and how it determined roles, expectations and everything else that went on behind closed doors and in the public domain. Dick had everything and had everything going for him, as was said afterwards. I do not remember him very well as a real live human being — if indeed I ever knew him as such. But for me, between the age of ten and fourteen, in memory he seems to have been exactly what a boy requires of an older brother: athletic, sporting, creative and seemingly very much at home in the world. Though I was for decades haunted by — and trapped in — a short sequence of photographs he once took of me after a tea-time row, I do not remember many specifics of daily living in our home during his time there. I can remember being the number one member of his fan club — travelling to local athletics training and competitions with him, being the sole supporter on the touch-line for his Sunday morning rugby games, or watching the wonderful processes that gradually revealed pictures in his photographic dark room. But I cannot remember the sound of his voice, or if we went to early mass — or pretended to have gone to it — before Sunday rugby. By now my parents had begun to holiday abroad — the annual pilgrimage to Lourdes legitimising a stay in Spain or France which would otherwise be considered an extravagance I imagine. Shortly before my fourteenth birthday, Dad's nearest sister died, and soon after he and Mam went to Lourdes and Spain. When they returned Dick was in hospital with nephritis. Two months later he died. My world was not just turned upside down, it went into violent erratic orbit and did not begin to calm down for nearly twenty-five years. I still remember that day — being called home from playing next door. As I approached I noticed that the outer shop door had been closed and for some reason I checked the bedroom window curtains. They were closed also — though it was only early afternoon. Because he had been so ill, I had not been allowed to visit Dick in hospital. The family had as usual spent July in sea-side lodgings, though our parents had not come with us. The closed shop door and curtained windows told me, even before Dad spoke the words, that Dick was dead. There had been no preparation for this, except that he was very ill.

Growing up with the daily disruption of family life by funerals and removals, I knew that life *does* go on — but I knew nothing about grief or loss or mourning. Although not allowed to attend Dick's funeral (I was dispatched instead to an uncle's farm) I was about to experience through Dad a grief which was inconsolable. What an easy word — inconsolable — to link with grief. Like so many words which lose their precision or power to communicate by over use, grief in especially dramatic situations seems always to be described as 'inconsolable'. Dick's death was an inconsolable loss for my father — though then I was less sympathetic, being wrapped up in my own adolescent confusion and ignorance. And I was quickly trying to cope with the consequential changes in the family expectations of my own immediate and long-term responsibility.

The first effect of Dick's death on me was that having said goodbye to my local school two months previously, I returned to it two weeks after Dick's death instead of going to boarding school. I knew this was a decision based on my best interests, but for years and years I resented it. I imagined boarding school, even for a physical weakling and loner, could not have been worse than the environment which developed instead. Religious practice had always been a major characteristic of our family. Both Mam and Dad were daily massgoers and communicants — though Dad was noticeably slower out of bed in the mornings and mostly drove after Mam's early walking to church. My parents practised their belief in Fr Peyton's motto: 'The family that prays together, stays together', so we had the nightly family rosary. There was always the annual Lough Derg Pilgrimage — with the sweets and coffee brought home 'from across the border' — and the white gloved carrying of the canopy over the priest and monstrance in the Corpus Christi Procession. Lenten fast and abstinence regulations and Christmas and Easter duties were rigorously observed. There was a family trip to Knock during the Marian Year, and the Annual Lourdes Pilgrimage. I had already joined the weekly Men's Confraternity on a Monday night — with boys in the front of the church until after they had been confirmed. Then we were promoted to our fathers' section. It was all ordered, normal and somehow in keeping with the very frequent talk at home of priests having to be arranged for removals and funerals. As a result I felt as if Dad was some kind of almost-priest. But even priests say only one mass a day — except on Christmas Day and All Soul's Day. In the years following Dick's death, to assuage his grief Dad went to every mass he could manage every day — whether the daily parish mass, those in the hospital said by a retired priest living locally, masses said by off-duty curates or visiting priests, or funeral masses he happened to hear about, he went to them all. Every day of the week. And between masses, he spent most of every day in one church or another. I quickly learned that it was likely to be a long wait in the car if I went with him to mass, or even for a drive which required us to pass a church where mass or devotions were scheduled. The novelty of being now in the men's section of the Confraternity was far outweighed by the embarrassment of kneeling beside my father's heaving, sobbing body in a public place, and by being compelled to remain with him in the darkened church, long after the devotions had ended. Previously the focused ceremonials, music, ornaments and smells of the House of God had occasioned my private adolescent ecstatic experiences. Now it became a public source of disorientation and feelings of shame.

At the beginning of *Men and the Water of Life*, Michael Meade wrote: 'When I was in High School, the divisions between the adult world and the world that my friends and I inhabited were .... sharp, full of oppositions, and unexplained'. Apart from not having shared my world with friends, as Meade did, this exactly describes my experience at that time. The Jesus Stories were great to hear and read, but where were today's prophets and miracle workers like Him and the Apostles of nineteen hundred years ago? What had the two schoolboy-preying paedophiles who mildly molested this fair haired youth got to do with God? Having read of tribal youth's initiations to manhood in the encyclopaedias Mr O'Leary allowed me to borrow from the adult library, I felt being tapped on the cheek by the bishop at confirmation was a huge non-event — and as for receiving wisdom, understanding, counsel, fortitude, knowledge, piety and fear of the Lord ...! At the time I felt not even a hint of one of them had entered my being. Instead, I experienced total confusion and I retreated as quickly and as often as possible out of the presence of my father and other adults — to my bedroom, books and the solitary adolescent activity of masturbation which I had discovered. Three years later I learned from a book given me by my surviving brother Niall about the changes which had occurred in my body. Not even the schoolboy dirty jokes had made sense to me.

Meade goes on: 'On my own, I poured through books and newspapers looking for hints about these apparently parallel and separate worlds, searching for the links that connected them. I could find none'. Neither could I, Michael, neither could I — and to add to the confusion all talk of 'Tom going to be the priest in the family' ended. Now it was seen as inevitable that 'He's going into the business'. Niall was already halfway to becoming an architect, which had nothing to do with a corn and coal business, so obviously I would replace Dick and become the third male generation of 'Hydes in Ballinacurra'. It was simply the way things were done. Fifteen months later, Uncle Joe died. He had been the older brother and therefore presumably Dad's senior partner throughout his working life. Joe left a farm, which was amalgamated into the business, as Tom's cinema had been twenty years earlier. Now Dad had a new interest in life: a farm, which he grabbed with enthusiasm.

Dick's death had ended the golfing, rugby and the card nights that rotated between the players' homes for both my parents. Only the Saturday night Solo school survived, probably because it was Granny's main social activity. Now Dad had an interest which took him out of the house and out of the Church at least to some extent. Of course, he wanted to share it and I used to dread being told — it was never an invitation — 'Come on, we're going out to the farm'. I had never lived on a farm, knew nothing of farms except the smells and muck, and wasn't interested. This was no natural playground to share with children living there. Instead I used to stand around, incongruously dressed, listening to Dad, in a suit, talk to Ned who lived on the farm. So I used to stand embarrassed with him for a few minutes — and quickly return to sit and wait in the car. Finally one day I said I didn't want to go when summoned. I only had to refuse once. Dad was true to his reaction to my refusal: he never again asked me to go out to the farm with him that I can remember! There was no discussion. One did as one was told and never answered back. Obedience was the principle virtue. Obedience to God, through the church and its priests, followed by obedience to parents — and Granny — if one were still a child. Even at sixteen, seventeen or eighteen. There was no debate. The hint of refusal or even the suggestion of a preferred alternative was met with 'all right, suit yourself', leaving me trapped like Bull McCabe's son in the despairing cycle of escape and return, time after time, for years. Even decades.

Gradually the 'Vocation' evaporated, but I strongly believed that everyone had within them a vocation to something, if only they could find it or discover ways of expressing it from adults in their world. Stamp collecting had now become my most engaging pursuit, involving not only the potential for artistic arrangement of coloured pieces of paper on the album pages, but each stamp opened up imaginative explorations of geography and history. As a result of a meeting between my parents and some Australians in Lourdes, I received a gift of stamps from them on their return. The obligatory 'thank you' letter gave me the opportunity to express to complete strangers my tentative views about life-after-school — views which I obviously felt unable to voice to my parents. The reaction to their next letter to my parents drove me further into my surly unhappy rebellion. Niall tried to explain to me that he having been the original 'black sheep' to Dick's first-born pride of place, it was too much for Dad to cope with my becoming another black sheep.

Instead of going, as planned, a month after Dick's death to the boarding school which he and Niall — and Dad a generation earlier — had attended, I returned for a year to the local school and then travelled daily to a school in Cork which my father had also attended in his time.

For one who had been frightened of and awkward with hurley-sticks, in my new school I threw myself into the physical contact of rugby — no doubt hoping to emulate Dick's achievements and thereby replace him in Dad's evident pride in his prowess. I was then an eight or nine stone, six foot skeleton which in my second year prompted the concerned rugby coach to ask to meet my parents. As a result I was limited to the minimum togging-out required on Wednesday afternoons. I took years to forgive Brother Donovan for probably saving my life. I imagined it was a devious stratagem instigated by my parents to prevent me from trespassing on Dick's memory. Such was my confused perspective on what was going on at home.

The last school holidays I finally made it to Ring to learn Irish for the forthcoming Leaving Examination — but this 'going to Ring' I myself initiated so that I could innocently chase a girl I knew was going there. A decade earlier I had felt my sister's sadness the nights before she went to Ring. Now at sixteen I cried uncontrollably the night before I returned home from Ring. Approaching the Leaving examination was terror. A fluke result in science in the Intermediate had less to do with my knowledge or interest in the subject, or Dad's perennial exhortations about the importance of science, than with my accuracy in predicting the likely questions in that year's exam paper. As a result I had been streamed into chemistry and physics which were incomprehensible, instead of history and geography which could capture my imagination. What I would do after the Leaving was left up to me, but with the clear expectation that it would be on a path back into the business.

'Suiting myself' resulted in my choosing a Post Leaving Certificate commercial course which was novel and pioneering in its time. And for a brief time I was doing and enjoying something I had chosen myself and which met with my parents' approval. But I was also in love for the first time and within six months the armed truce at home had become nearly open warfare. As a result, after a brief few months actually in the family business, I proposed and it was agreed that I would join some friends working in London for the summer and go to university in the autumn! There was no relief in this for any of us and while the university course I had suggested could have been taken at the local university I was sent to Dublin. The pretext was that Niall was there and would help me settle into College. He did — by telling me of the new student Film Society and giving me my first taste of Guinness.

Coincidentally, the 'autumn sickness' which had so often previously caused my delayed return to school after summer holidays, occurred again as I arrived in university — though now it was my mother who was ill. She was in St Vincents Hospital, then within a hundred yards of University College. At the time we did not realise it but it was the first of a final series of hospitalisations for her. I remember being reprimanded by Niall for my unconcerned behaviour when visiting her, with the comment that 'Ma is never sick'. His view surprised me. It had not been my experience of living at home. Later — years later — I realised that the family tendency to minimise uncomfortable reality probably resulted in her letters to absent children being circumspect about her health and home-life.

The other significant memory I have of that time was seeing my father kiss my mother for the first time in my life; I was over eighteen. He kissed her lightly on the cheek. During the next two and a half years I again saw them share such discreet intimacy in hospital rooms, until finally he similarly kissed her before coffining her body, just weeks before my twenty-first birthday.

P J Kavanagh, writing of his experience in Oxford, described it as 'treading water in an eternally changing river of youth' and told of how he 'preferred to wander about and listen to the slow drip of my own boring, undiagnosable wound'. I certainly wandered about Earlsfort Terrace and the College of Science that first term. The only thing I learned was that whatever else I might become through being taught, it was unlikely to be an Agricultural Science graduate. So at Christmas I asked if I might change degree programmes to Commerce, which had been the subject of my previous year's schooling. After all Commerce was still compatible with my going into the family business, which remained on the agenda for when I 'got sense'. I was allowed to do so, proceeded to pass my end of year exams and returned the following year — not so much to college as to the Film Society — and failed that year's exams, and the autumn repeats. It was then I began to sense I was drowning in the river and began to really wallow in my wounds.

Before I finally graduated Mammy had died and the business had been sold, except for the farm and the undertaking. Apart from the fact that exams coincided with my early summer hay fever, I had always hated them, the expectations they carried for others and their unreal evaluation of my real self — whatever that was. The strain of my final exams resulted in my being sent by the family GP for neurological examination. Afterwards Dad continued to support me, idle in Dublin, for a whole year while eagerly trying to get me to live at home and take an arts degree in the local university.

Instead, I got a part-time job, managing a cinema and quickly fell in love with Pauline who worked there. Within three months we'd announced we were getting married — I sold my stamp collection to buy her engagement ring — and all hell broke loose. Apparently since my neurological examination the previous year Dad had been under the illusion I had been confirmed as having multiple sclerosis. His loving but misguided attempt to communicate this to my prospective parents-in-law ensured that no one could talk sense to me about my material or emotional unreadiness for marriage. While Pauline could have said 'No' or 'Let's wait', she too was in love and over the next fifteen years suffered the consequences of my immaturity.

Alcohol had been a dark secret in my childhood. Both my parents were abstainers and Dad was very proud of his silver — and later gold — Pioneer Pin. There was an aura of family shame on each side in relation to drink. Visitors would never be offered anything but tea or coffee. There was only a single occasion that I can remember hearing of Dad being in a pub — the night he sent a priest to explain that he was delayed in the golf club because he'd won a competition. Niall drank. Everyone except my parents drank. So I decided to drink too, but I would not get into drink-trouble, as I dimly perceived my uncles had. While a student on pints I was okay. I simply became drowsily bloated on the second pint — if I could finish it. My first taste I did not like, but I was told 'it's an acquired taste.' I diligently sought to acquire the taste. And twelve disintegrating years after we married I, in despair, tried to find out the secret of how people who had stopped drinking stayed stopped. Later I recognised that the despair which drove me to seek help from other people also made me willing for the first time in my life to accept help from other people. And I was blessed from the first, with the thousands of one-day-at-a-time sobriety since then.

Between my traumatic marriage and when I stopped drinking my attitude towards Dad was a mixture of blame and reliance on him to bail me out financially or help materially. This he always did — he with a certain mystification and I with ingratitude. Mercifully, my behaviour and eventually my attitude towards him changed with my new way of life in sobriety. But these were practically the only two areas of real improvement in my life, even after ten years of my not drinking. By which time I had become homeless — being estranged from Pauline and my children — unemployed and destitute. Then, through a friend I was introduced to a wonderful woman called Kay. 'God bless you Kay for all your work and thank you for the confrontations and gentle directions you then gave me'. I was forty-six and at last began to become a 'grown-up'. At the time Dad was in hospital, having a hip replaced. That I was unemployed, and not living with my wife must have been incomprehensible to him. Yet he was unintrusive and simple in his concern for me daily when I visited him. The following year when I phoned to tell him that I was returning from mini-cabbing in London to resume my career in Dublin, he broke down and handed the phone to my sister. Shortly after my return I was talking with Aunty Frank, my mother's only sister, about something which I saw to be unjust. She interjected while I was speaking to say: 'Of course Tony was always just'. It blew my mind and was one of the greatest insights I had received in my nearly fifty years.

'Tony' is my father. Frank's familiar use of his first name in voicing something about him which she saw in me and which I valued, blew away the cobwebs through which I had viewed him for decades.

Thank you Frank for helping me to begin to answer Blake Morrison's question: 'And when did you last see your father?' And thank you Dad for being there, for so long — loving me in your own way.

ANOTHER FIFTY BEGINS

When I returned to Dublin I set three goals for myself. The Lord of Life who had protected and sustained me during the isolated and frenetic lifestyle of driving a mini-cab in London, continued to support my efforts in two of the three goals. The job as Personnel Manager in a company's start-up, went well immediately. And within eighteen months, my now adult children to whom I had neither been a resident, or even at times accessible, father for the previous five years, gave me a framed photograph of themselves for my birthday. Receiving it from them in Bewley's Cafe, I 'made a show of them' (as I was later told) by bursting into tears.

But in the third goal I remained as incompetent as ever and blind to the obvious. I was, as always, completely ineffectual in the rebound-relationship which followed the end of my marriage. By the time the requirements of the job had eased somewhat Kay, who had earlier been such a help to me, had died and that was a huge loss. With a mixture of confusion, apprehension and resentment I finally 'did' an Assertiveness Workshop. My resentment stemmed from my perception that assertiveness training had been developed by and exclusively for women in the previous ten or fifteen years. How wrong I was! And for my need Liz was Kay's ideal successor.

So I began working, with her help, to learn to 'earlier recognise and better express my negative feelings', as I put it on our first meeting after the Workshop. At last I began to deal with my predispositioned or conditioned moodiness and stubbornness — to learn to choose how to react more effectively and use the energy of feelings in a more constructive way. Such that gradually more and more I moved towards living differently: towards living a life centred in itself, but interdependent also.

Then the 1992 Men's Gathering occurred. Though it powerfully affected other men when one man said 'Let's face it: we all hate our fathers', I really knew it wasn't true for me. Not now. Yet the Men's Gathering was a power-filled and empowering experience for me.

The only previous sense I had of men collectively was in the Confraternity or on the rugby terraces. Throughout my career my experience of men had been at best uncomfortable in that I always felt ill at ease with locker-room ribaldry and was neither a sportsman nor an avid spectator. So I tried to avoid such company, until eventually in my disintegration I sat alone in pubs with newspaper or book drinking myself into oblivion. Interestingly, as a mini-cab driver I had been aware of and enjoyed the masculine characteristics of the mini-cabbing and the curious solidarity which existed between drivers and our controller on the radio and with each other during our intermittent personal meetings on the job. At the Men's Gathering it was different. Here were a hundred men, all or probably most, strangers to each other. Listening to poetry, story telling and drumming. And in the process opening up and giving voice to their experiences as men: heterosexuals, homosexuals, priests and former priests, house-husbands, outdoor workers, professionally employed and unemployed men. There, just because we were men. To tell our stories, listen to each other and somehow, in some indescribable and positive way, to experience and celebrate masculinity.

Immediately after the Men's Gathering I returned to work and all the activity and direction of the previous three years of starting a new venture practically went into reverse. The commercial viability of the initiative had been exaggerated and within the three years the expected market had shrunk dramatically. Having completed what is euphemistically called a 'right-sizing' exercise, within six months I followed those who had left the company. For them it was temporary, but for me permanent and I went to Clare. When Dad had been having his hip replaced I recognised how easy and comfortable it was to share a conversation with him as long as it dealt with a confined agenda. Sadly, the less personal, the better or easier. One such topic which always animated him was his family tree: half of my ancestry. I had begun to get interested in it — recognising that he was the only living source of information available to me, he being the last of his brothers and sisters and cousins. So on my visits to him I began to collect his reminiscences while filtering his human biases which I felt I did not share. At the same time I was ordering books and audio tapes on men, masculinity and mythology from the Limbus catalogue in the US. Slowly my interest focused on the father-son nexus, its importance in the developing of a young male's sense of identity and his relationship with life and other people, men and women. I began to wonder had other men taken so long to come to terms with their fathers as I had. As Michael Meade suggested on one tape, 'Betrayal is of the essence of the father-son relationship'. Betrayal both ways. Did other men experience such disappointment with their fathers, or cause such disappointment to their fathers, as I had? So I began my letter writing and focused book browsing. The results partly, are this book. Two things happened which really brought my interest in the universality of the area into sharp consciousness for me. One was coming across Malidoma Somé and the other was picking up P J Kavanagh's account of his life: *A Perfect Stranger*.

Malidoma, with Meade and Hillman, had conducted a US Men's Gathering. The tape-recording of *Images of Initiation* took just as long to listen to as I took to drive from Clare to Dublin to attend the fortnightly meeting of a Men's Group which originated from the '92 Men's Gathering. Listening to it prompted me to read what else he had written and to get his tapes on his life as an initiated Dagara tribesman in Africa and in the West. One of the many challenging ideas I sensed from hearing and reading Malidoma Somé concerned the destructive effect of the western way of life on the father-son link in honouring and perpetuating the ancestors.

In a foreword to a 1991 edition of his book, which had been published six years earlier, Kavanagh explained how responding to the invitation to write a sequel had prompted him, as a man born in England of all-Irish forebears, to do something 'to clear (his) mind about this faith that the past continues in the present' and to go in search of his forebears, through his New Zealand born Irish father, Van Diemen's Land grandfather and back to Ireland itself. I was already 'doing something', didn't even have to leave the island; and my Father was a still living connection!

Because of Dad's longevity, and his father's age when he was born — and because of the coincidence of their each having been the last-born in their respective families — reaching back to Dad's grandfather encompassed nearly two centuries of life. And what life. What changes over three generations in a one mile radius around a parish boundary!

Not many people could be so lucky in trying to comprehend their father's life as I was. *Ordinary Lives* is a portrait of the Irish middle classes in three generations. The three individual years Tony Farmar chose to illustrate were: 1907, the year Dad was born into the middle class; 1932 the year his father died, and 1963, the year he became a widower at the age of fifty-six. Over the years I had often wondered why my father did such and such, didn't do something else, believed what he believed — loads of other aspects of his life and personality which were contrary to mine or to what I imagined I would have done in his circumstances. For a generation I had agreed with a character in a film who when his father said 'When I was your age ... ' interrupted with 'You were never my age.' For a generation I had sided with the son's adolescent self-centredness without recognising that the statement was equally real and could in fact have been validly made by the father to his son. Any father. My Father. To me.

As Farmar wrote: 'The world of 1907 is divided from us by more political, military, social and technological activity than had ever before split a century. A long series of revolutions, world wars, economic developments, and technological and ideological changes have destroyed a world that seemed in 1907 to most middle-class Europeans to be largely and comfortably fixed'. This was the ordered world into which my father was born. Farmar's 'snapshot' of it and the first twenty-five years of Dad's life made me wonder how I might have handled it any differently to him. Being born at such a time, and not just 'in Ballinacurra as the youngest of sixteen'. Now I see he was born to a man nearly old enough to be his grandfather, who had himself been an infant at the height of the post-famine deaths in the mid-nineteenth century. When Dad was born, he was separated by three sisters from his nearest brother who was already on the verge of puberty. Before Dad was eleven, his brothers had fought and one had died for King and Country in the war to end all wars. Before he was sixteen the brother who had survived that war and another one were fighting against the King's Forces in Ireland, and then against fellow Irishmen who refused to accept the partial freedom of the 1921 Treaty. Had I come of age, in Ireland of that time, would not I too most likely have committed myself to the mythology and promise of social order presented by the Catholic Church? A church which had throughout the previous hundreds of years presented itself as the church of the indigenous people now newly liberated; which celebrated that status spectacularly twice within five years before my mid-twenties? After all, hadn't I been affected, albeit briefly, in my own time by the Irish visit of *J.P.II Superstar*, as a *Time* magazine cover portrayed it!

The little history I had read and the genealogical research I had carried out while this book was unconsciously germinating gave me pictures of my ancestors and Dad's life which I had never seen before — and certainly never felt in my gut and wondered at as I've now done. The Forrest-side had always been more visible through Granny and through shared impressions about her life and origins. Now discovering I had a second cousin still living in the townland from which Dad's grandfather migrated to Midleton, was revealing. To visit Eadie in her three hundred year old home and for her to identify a similar now ruined cottage as 'Hyde's Farm' was a real joy. I dug into parish records and found numerous Hydes both in Midleton in my grandfather's time and in the adjoining parish from which his father came. I never knew of their existence and wonder how they lived and what happened to them all. Were any of the sixty Hydes who arrived in America from Ireland during the Famine years cousins of my grandfather? Or did he grow up knowing that, proportionately a quarter or a third of that number had died aboard the coffin-ships? I found out about Granny's childhood family and her mother's life, such that I feel enormous compassion for the life Gran had led long before I was to so fear and dislike her.

I discovered details about Dad's maternal grandfather (which had been around, but I'd never appreciated them before) including facts about his three families with three successive wives. My grandmother was of the second family and her step-mother was seemingly the source of the piety passed on to my father. Dad had three step-aunts from his grandfather's third family who became nuns — and a step-uncle who divorced his first wife! He had had an uncle who, in Dad's euphemism, 'left Cork' which meant he left his wife and four daughters. Dad had had another uncle who never married, was reputed to have had healing powers in his hands for children, and died leaving a debt-ridden pub for Dad's father to inherit and sort out. That grand-uncle of mine was named Tom, and in fact I was delighted to find 'Toms' in each generation and family group I have so far located.

So far I have been unable to locate documentary evidence about the early life or marriage of Dad's paternal grandfather John, who was — according to his gravestone and death certificate — born in 1803: a year after one and five years before two of my mother's *great*-grandfathers. But the search continues. In the meantime I wonder how people solemnised marriages before the Church and State administrative ceremonies were instituted, and speculate about people's feelings and sense of commitment when entering into marriage in those relatively recent times. Especially as I failed to succeed in remaining true to whatever form of words I assented to with Pauline — full of hope and good intentions but unaware of the unconscious currents flowing in my life that brought me to that wedding altar.

Genealogy was very important in Ireland before the destruction of the indigenous Irish culture in the seventeenth and eighteenth centuries. Pockets survived and to some extent, in the ever diminishing Gaeltacht areas, maybe still survive. Now Malidoma, who is still under forty years of age, tells us of his own experience in recent decades of indigenous lifestyle. He addresses the indigenous within each of us as the source for the next phase of our renewal. What survived the rape of Africa by the West, in less than a hundred years was still living in Malidoma's life-time and may not be too distant from us in Ireland today. It is accessible — by imagination at least — through our grandfathers, and their fathers, and by the living memories still in families of what they did. Not the self-aggrandising political military battles fought and rarely won completely — and which still blight the lives of men, their wives and children on this island — but the individual life of a soul's longing, which may have been expressed implicitly in something for which our grandfathers, or theirs, have been remembered through the generations in our families.

Digging back in the course of this book I learned that one set of my mother's grandparents (who both died less than ten years before I was born) used to talk to each other in Irish, and Dad's grandfather (who died more than a half century before them) was known to have translated a book of scripture from the Latin into Irish, as Dad always reports. I wonder about these near relatives of mine. About their lives and life-decisions. What prompted John Hyde to translate such a book into Irish? Why did his son, my grandfather, born into a majority Irish speaking area not pass on this way of being to his own family? Why were four of *his* sons to wear the military uniforms of four different countries including their own? The questions are endless and I delight in asking them and finding some answers. And Dad is still around to voice some memories or impressions of these near relatives who preceded and shaped me.

So at last, to answer Blake Morrison's question, I can now see my father — daily — and with understanding of the complex life he has had to live; the global and parish confusion in which his adolescence occurred; the hopes he has had smashed, and the inner demons he has fought and survived for nearly nine decades. Of course I can see his failings. They are human. They have been and can be anytime, mine. I can see his wisdom, understanding, counsel, fortitude, knowledge, piety and fear of the Lord. I do not share his faith in the myth he chose so long ago to obey and practise diligently for more years than I have shared the name and ancestry with him. But now I recognise how much the freedom and ability to search for other myths were part of his gifts to me. How his love, in his way, for me survived and transcended the mystification I repeatedly caused him. I hope that the myths I have been free to find and choose sustain me as long as his myths sustained him. I hope if near the end of my ninth decade a son comes to tell me he is doing something as previously unimaginable as when I told Dad about starting this book, that I can respond as appropriately as he did with the following story:

> There was a son and father — and this is a true
> story — who were always fighting and arguing. So
> much so that the son finally decided to leave home.
> When the day came and he was leaving, the father's
> last words to his son were: 'Well bad cess to you
> anyway leaving me. May you never have a day's luck
> and may the road be rocky for every step ahead of
> you.'
>   The son replied: 'I have only two wishes at this time:
> first, may your life be filled with everything
> you desire, and second, may our wishes to each other
> be reversed'.
>   And that's a true story. My grandfather told me.

As told by Tony Hyde, aged 87.

Brendan Kennelly

MY DARK FATHERS

My dark fathers lived the intolerable day
Committed always to the night of wrong,
Stiffened at the hearthstone, the woman lay,
Perished feet nailed to her man's breastbone.
Grim houses beckoned in the swelling gloom
Of Munster fields where the Atlantic night
Fettered the child within the pit of doom,
And everywhere a going down of light.

And yet upon the sandy Kerry shore
The woman once had danced at ebbing tide
Because she loved flute music — and still more
Because a lady wondered at the pride
Of one so humble. That was long before
The green plant withered by an evil chance;
When winds of hunger howled at every door
She heard the music dwindle and forgot the dance.

Such mercy as the wolf receives was hers
Whose dance became a rhythm in a grave,
Achieved beneath the thorny savage furze
That yellowed fiercely in a mountain cave.
Immune to pity, she, whose crime was love,
Crouched, shivered, searched the threatening sky,
Discovered ready signs, compelled to move
Her to her innocent appalling cry.

Skeletoned in darkness, my dark fathers lay
Unknown, and could not understand
The giant grief that trampled night and day,
The awful absence moping through the land.
Upon the headland, the encroaching sea
Left sand that hardened after tides of Spring,
No dancing feet disturbed its symmetry
And those who loved good music ceased to sing.

Since every moment of the clock
Accumulates to form a final name,
Since I am come of Kerry clay and rock,

I celebrate the darkness and the shame
That could compel a man to turn his face
Against the wall, withdrawn from light so strong
And undeceiving, spancelled in a place
Of unapplauding hands and broken song.

Hugh Leonard

THE STROKE OF A PEN

On my birth certificate, in the space designated 'Name of Father', there is a single pen-stroke. Blaise Pascal said that if Cleopatra's nose had been shorter, the whole face of the earth would have changed; well, if my mother had thought to invent a name for my father, my own life would certainly have been different.

My mother's name was given on the certificate as Annie Byrne, and, upon investigation, the address supplied proved to be what in those days was known as a 'common lodging house'. On a couple of occasions, while writing about my parentage, I have voiced the opinion that a person who would formally give her name as 'Annie' rather than 'Ann' or 'Anne' was probably uneducated and not wise in the ways of the world. This assumption was hotly disputed in letters from several well-educated and articulate Annies; nonetheless, it is the only theory I have, and so I stick to it.

And, since I have taken this road, I must go further along it. I have a deep-rooted belief that what I would describe as my maverick qualities must come from my father, who is for ever lost to me in time and space. I have always been a cuckoo in any and every Irish nest. I am by nature a loner who has never found his natural home; I detest nationalism and the waving of flags; my passions are not those of my countrymen or of the class in which I was raised. My only allegiance is to language and the world at large. I say this as a simple reality, not to boast or strike an attitude, and my father, whoever or of what race he was, simply must be the culprit.

I was adopted by Nicholas and Margaret Keyes, whom, with a fine display of double-think, I choose to regard as my rightful parents. They lived in a two-roomed cottage off Sorrento Road in Dalkey, and my father was a gardener at 'Enderly' — since renamed 'Santa Maria' — on Cunningham Road. His employers were Quakers: the Jacobs of Jacobs' biscuits. He went to work for them when he was fourteen at a wage of £1 a week and left fifty-nine years later, when the last of his employers died. By then, his wages had sky-rocketed to £4. 10. 0. a week, and he was given a pension of twenty-six pounds a year.

My mother had several children of her own, all stillborn, and was told that a further pregnancy would be fatal. In 1926, the procedure of adopting a child was not as complicated as it is today, and she set about the business of acquiring me without bothering to inform my father. The story is that she simply went into town and came home with me on the Number 8 tram. This was wholly in keeping with her regard for my father. I have written elsewhere that in every relationship there is the lover and the loved. My father doted on her. When she was seventeen she was walking out, as the expression went, with a B&I seaman named Ernie Moore. Meanwhile, my father, who was then twenty-one, approached her parents without her knowledge, telling them of his steady job with the Jacobs and that he had an offer of a cottage in The Square at a rent of half-crown a week. My mother, one of four children, was instructed to marry him; she did so, and, I suspect, never really forgave him.

This is not to say that their marriage was unhappy. They belonged to a time and class where survival was all that one could reasonably expect. My mother would staunchly declare that her husband was a 'good provider'. He did not drink except for a glass of whiskey, courtesy of his employers, at Christmas; his only extravagance was a shilling each-way bet at the bookies and a whist drive on Wednesday evenings. It was part of his nature to accept who and what he was, without complaint. My mother thought him soft and easy-going. She had a toughness that he lacked. She would drive a bargain down to the last ha'penny, whereas, rather than ask for his due, his code was 'Ah, whatever you say yourself'. She deferred to him in small matters, allowing him to believe that, as he would declare in his few moments of anger, he was the 'master of the house'. When it came to major decisions, such as adopting a ten-day-old child, she overrode him without a thought.

Part of her attitude towards him rubbed off on me. She made me her collaborator, and I have found it hard to forgive here. I do not know if a study has ever been made of the behavioural life patterns of adopted children. I have only lately come to know myself, to realise how much of my adult conduct might be traced back to what I subconsciously saw as an abandonment by my natural mother. Perhaps the hunger for acceptance was why my relationship with the 'Dalkey mother' was at my father's expense. When I was little, he and I went for walks together; he was my uttermost horizon and the fount of all wisdom. Later, I came to see that my mother's fondness for him, while undoubted, was grudging. She did not respect him as he deserved. The full thrust of her affection was lavished on me, and I began to see him through her eyes, as an amiable, hard-working man who did not amount to very much.

In time, I 'outgrew' them both. Actually, I was never half the man my father was in terms of honesty, honour and gentleness of nature; but my genes, whatever they were, came to assert themselves. I became hungry for a particular kind of life that was not my parents'. My mother came to see my first play, performed by amateurs, and her verdict, uttered with a bad-tempered sniff was: 'Too much old talk!' Usually, all her cygnets were swans, but she sensed that I was moving away from her into a world of my own. There was an unspoken agreement that I would not again give offence by asking her to see a play of mine. To my father, on the other hand, I was already remote. His comment on that first play was, simply: 'Oh, you're a comical boy'. I think that, if the truth was told, I carelessly assumed that he had no feelings to be hurt. My mother and I allowed him to do jobbing work on summer evenings and at weekends to pay for our extras, including my new suit or outings to the pictures or the Jimmy O'Dea pantomime every January. I did not think about this act of love, for that is what it was — and loving was an essential part of his nature — or look back on it until it was too late. To put it brutally, I never thanked him.

Years later, when he had been dead for six years, I wrote my play, *Da*. It was a way — my way — to have him remembered. As I worked on it, I discovered that at last I was beginning to know him. The son in the play rails at the old man: 'You were a sheep while you lived . . . you're still a sheep!' It was me raging at my father, but it was a hollow fury. Behind it was the knowledge that for all his forelock-tugging and his time-serving compliance, he was in some respects a better man than his smart-ass son.

There was a crowning irony. The play went on to achieve great success and to win awards. The actor, Barnard Hughes, on receiving his Tony, publicly thanked 'Nick Keyes . . . for having lived'. I thought that perhaps I too had, even if belatedly, thanked the old man for all the love I had never returned. Then it came to me that without him there would have been no play, no awards and all that went with them. I had put myself more in his debt than ever.

Brian Smeaton

MY FATHER AND I

Daddy, William Alexander Smeaton, was born on 14 November 1911 in Rathdowney, County Laois. His mother was Isabella Sutherland, from around about John O'Groats in Scotland, a Sutherland from Sutherlandshire. His father, William Smeaton, was born in Glasgow's Govan, and was employed in Perry's Brewery, Rathdowney, as a cooper. That was the family trade. Three generations of Smeatons were coopers. The Smeatons were Presbyterians, but Daddy had a connection with the Church of Ireland without ever undergoing the ritual of Confirmation.

My grandfather had been involved in the Boer War, and my granny always maintained that his arthritic leg was the result of injuries he had received, but the British War Office disagreed and refused the claims for compensation.

Daddy, Liam Smeaton, or 'Sonny, as he was called by many, grew up in a town which supported all kinds of sports. Although he had a slight disability which required thick-lensed glasses, he was wonderfully well coordinated and all forms of sport came easily to him, especially tennis and hockey. His younger brother Herbert ('Buster') played hurling for Laois and later soccer for the Luton Brewery team. In his subsequent army career as a paratrooper he was also a regimental boxing champion. Liam went to train as a teacher to Saint Mobhi's — the institution set up by the government of the fledgling state to ensure Protestant teachers could be proficient in Irish. He was expelled from that place after an argument with a teacher about a misunderstanding over an exercise which she said he had not done properly. He simply walked out of the place and refused to go back. Later the principal fixed him up with a junior teaching post in a Protestant secondary school in the Republic. Liam found himself dealing with young men of almost his own age, which at the time he found difficult. He maintained his interest in sports and a local newspaper report records him scoring seventeen goals in a school versus town match.

On 28 September 1935 he and Dora Alexander, a woman from Leitrim whom he had met during the teacher training, were married. They settled in the Schoolhouse at Windgates, Co. Wicklow, where my mother Dora, had the job of principal in that rural one-teacher national school.

Liam had been doing odd jobs here and there. I have an early memory of him behind the counter in a clothing shop in Bray. Another early memory is of him going off to join the British army in late 1939 or early 1940. The picture in my mind is of this man disappearing over a hill with a little bag on his back. I have vague memories of him being home on leave and once giving me a sharp crack on the head for some alleged misdemeanour. It was a kind of a flick with the back of the hand to my ear or thereabouts.

He was tall, slim, wiry, with a shock of brown hair, something over six foot, and the ever present glasses. I don't remember him paying much attention to me. I do know from my mother, and from him that around the time of my birth he was in fact very involved in caring for me. At five days old it was discovered that I had a white rash, so the nurse in the nursing home where I was born decided to send my mother home and keep me in. Then the nurse decided to circumcise me. I always thought that this was something to do with my mother's religious principles. Much later I learned that the nurse who ran the nursing home had married late in life and her husband had developed problems with his penis which necessitated circumcision. Not long after he died, I think as a result of the operation. It was because of her tragic experience that the nurse decided that all youngsters needed to be circumcised. During my recovery from the circumcision operation it was Daddy who visited me regularly. I remember asking him not long before he died about the circumcision. His answer was that it was good to have it done because, as he said, 'Babies don't feel it'. I smiled at him and thought 'That's what you think'.

I remember the night he arrived home from the war. It was in 1946. Years later I was with him and Mammy and Sandra, my partner, and he suddenly said 'You know its forty years to the day since I left Piraeus Harbour to come home'. We literally fell into each others' arms and cried. Mammy got real upset at the sight of her son and her husband clinging to each other and bawling their heads off. Luckily Sandra was able to intervene and head her off so that we were able to enjoy a little bit at least of the years of isolation. The night he arrived home from the war we were living in the Schoolhouse in Templemore, Co. Tipperary, where my mother had moved after Windgates. The two of them stood clasped together in the dimly lit hall of the house, and I slunk off to my room and wound up the old record player my mother had bought in an auction and cried myself to sleep to the sounds of 'Little man you're tired/you've had a busy day ...' It was difficult for both of us. I was nine years of age and he was back after six years in the North African desert, Sicily, Italy and Greece. He could not take the cold and would sit hunched over the fire shivering in his shoes. The local Church of Ireland clergyman persuaded him to invest his army gratuity, £600, in a small shop almost across the road from the regular Templemore newsagent and sweet emporium. On fair days the bullocks used to wander into the shop and glare over the counter at Daddy. He was miserable. He always rose early in the morning, at six or thereabouts, and he'd smoke six or seven fags with as many cups of tea before opening the shop. That was one of his 'demob' prizes, about five thousand cigarettes loose in long boxes.

Not long after he arrived home my mother got pregnant. Nobody told me about this. What they did do was arrange for me to go to relatives in Manchester for the duration of the pregnancy. *Sin sceil eile* as is said. In the heel of the hunt I arrived back from a seven or eight month stay in Manchester to find a baby in the house — a big surprise, I can tell you. Then the matter of schooling came up and various boarding establishments were mentioned. Eventually it was decided that I would go to Wilson's Hospital, Multyfarnham, eight miles the far side of Mullingar, a fair trip from Templemore. I made that journey in the back of Young's car convinced that somehow I wasn't wanted at home. Liam Smeaton was a shadowy figure in the background of all this. It was a further dagger in the wound of being separated from my mother at five days of age, and it was as if Daddy simply wasn't there.

After that it was boarding school, summer holidays of catching odd glimpses of him in between time off from the job he had with a firm called 'Anti-pest Services Ltd' set up by a retired British army colonel, a decent man, with very little capital. Or at least, if he had capital, he didn't put much of it into the business, because Daddy had this brown Ford van which was a devil to start. There were mornings when Mammy and myself would push the van past the church in Rath-molyon, County Meath, where we were then living, and down around the corner for a mile or so sometimes until the engine at last sputtered into life and Daddy would be gone for another day or two. Once he took me with him to Dundalk where he was doing a job on McArdles' Brewery. I remember the big vats and the beery smell. Daddy was a life long teetotaller. He did not like alcohol in any shape or form and Granny told me once when he was about sixteen he had poured a bottle of whiskey down the sink after deciding that his father had too much to drink. They said that even the 'smell of a cork' affected my grandfather, and he would get his anger out on my granny when he was inebriated. She was well able for him, and could put him in his place very quickly.

On the way back from Dundalk, Daddy took me to see Newgrange. Then it was a mound in the middle of a field with little or no publicity or tourist infrastructure. We had a real good time together that day wondering over the amazing nature of the sun trap. There was only ourselves and a guide there.

During the time in Rathmolyon Daddy got very sick. I remember him rolling around in the bed and shouting with the pain in his stomach. The doctor, a locum from England, diagnosed a stoppage in the gut and prescribed castor oil. At the same time he was injecting liberal doses of painkiller. I remember cycling a couple of miles to contact the doctor. There was a lot of panic around and Daddy was obviously getting weaker. He was sent to Navan Hospital where he lay for a few more days, until Mammy contacted the local landlord, Colonel Fowler of Rahinston, who used his influence to get Daddy transferred to Baggot Street Hospital, in Dublin. There they quickly discovered that the scar of his youthful appendix operation had stuck to his intestines and was causing massive infection. He was rushed to theatre and in the ensuing operation about forty feet of his large intestine was removed. He recovered fairly quickly, and I was delighted to see him regaining his smiling wit and his physical good shape.

He didn't socialise. He liked sitting by the fire and talking to the cats. There were always cats, and he loved to stroke and talk to them. You'd swear they were answering him back. We hadn't much time for each other, him working, and me at school.

I remember him meeting me in Dame Street on the morning I was due to go for an interview with the directors of the Royal Bank of Ireland Ltd, in Foster Place in Dublin. He was telling me to sit up straight and be myself. It was good; he was taking an interest and that was good. The interview was a blur — in a big room with a bevy of glowering men behind a long table, with me sitting uncomfortably on a lone chair about twenty feet from them. Did I open my mouth? I don't know.

Then I was working and he was working. We both drifted around each other, like ships in a fog. Sandra arrived on the scene. And Granny died. Mammy was down in the kitchen of the flat on the North Circular Road dispensing cooking sherry in cups and Daddy was up in the sitting room holding court with his mates. It was a fraught occasion. I was working in the bank and they had prevailed on Sandra to telephone me with the news of Granny's demise. I think he might have cried at some stage.

The wedding was interesting. For the first and only time in his life my Da donned a morning suit. He looked real good in it; very handsome. He lent us the car for the honeymoon. Not long before I had shunted into another vehicle on the Sunday afternoon of an All Ireland football final, and when I came back to report the damage he was up a ladder with a hammer doing some minor repairs to the flat. I thought he was going to hit me with the hammer when I made an announcement. He loved that car, a Morris Minor '1000' — GYI 84.

He had driven tanks in the desert, and he always had a love of cars. The first one I remember him with was a 1938 Morris, LI 4242, in which he allowed me to practise around the school yard in Tullamore, another of my mother's teaching situations. The car was always a bone of contention. I was firmly convinced that it was the passport out of the isolation I felt, an entry into the world of women and dances. My Da did not see it quite like that, but I always got to use it with the assistance of my mother. She never learned to drive.

Daddy never carried money. Mammy dealt with the bills, and he used to get the money for petrol and his lunch when he was working in Dublin as a book-keeper in a Rathmines garage. We were living in Balbriggan at that time. It was there my brother broke his leg in a confrontation with a cyclist not far from our front door. I remember my Dad carrying my brother with his leg in plaster into the local cinema for a night's entertainment.

Another important element of his personal integrity was his abhorrence of any of us playing games on a Sunday. He always went to church on a Sunday, and although I was swimming a lot at one stage, he refused to give me his blessing to go to swimming galas which were held on a Sunday in various midland venues. That was hard for me. Church was a regular part of our life. It was a personal commitment of Mammy and Daddy, and also because she being the teacher it was expected of her, and Daddy gave her his complete support in her occupation.

After I got married and the children were born he was a regular visitor. He was very good with the children. Once when Susie got pneumonia as a two-year-old he was distraught. On another occasion he came to watch me playing cricket and he was so incensed with the state of my cricket gear (I used to stuff it all into a bag from one match to the next) he came to the house, hoked it out of the bag and put it into the bin. I felt very angry about that.

When we went to Belfast he was understanding of the kind of feelings I had about the church and my view that class oppression had taken over the religious dimension in Ireland. They both visited Belfast during the 1970s, something which not everyone wanted to do. He was proud of the fact that I had been ordained a priest in the Church of Ireland, and enjoyed hearing how I was getting on. Although he was committed to the church his view of the class dimension was not in any way diluted. He did not like any hint of pulling rank. He had refused to accept a commission in the army for that reason, and he gave up attending Masonic meetings at a very early stage in his life, partly because of his dislike of alcohol, but also because he reckoned that it was a secret society with questionable aims and objectives.

Two incidents marked major turning points in our relationship. One was an illness he had about twenty years before he died. Mammy and he were both retired and living in Tullamore. One evening he suffered a kind of epileptic attack which left him in an uncontrollable state for ten or fifteen minutes. Mammy went to get help and three or four men could not hold him. Afterwards he did not remember what had happened, and intensive examinations by a number of doctors revealed no definite cause. He recovered very well. During the time of his recovery I got very close to Mammy and she told me lots about my early life and Liam's involvement in it, all the information about my circumcision, and the weekly letters he had sent her during the war which she had safely kept in an old tin trunk. I think I began to understand him a little better after this.

They left Tullamore and moved back to Dublin and there Mammy had what is generally called a 'nervous breakdown' which necessitated a stay in St Patrick's Hospital for a period. It was during that time I got close to Daddy and on occasions he would have a good cry while talking about his fears and grief. Once he rang up and I knew by his voice that he was feeling something. He didn't often ring up like that. So I asked him how he felt and he simply burst into tears and cried for twenty minutes while I just listened and encouraged him.

He never stopped smoking fags. Once or twice he tried cigarettes substitutes, but the regular routine of seven cups of tea and seven fags before nine o'clock in the morning never really ceased, so eventually emphysema destroyed his lungs. It was sad. He had spent time in hospital, away from the place he shared with my mother, in an all male establishment. He did not like that. None of us did. Looking back on it now I think we did the very best we could, although it might have been better had I simply decided to make him the priority and nurse him myself. At the time it never entered my head. I was caught up in the business of letting other people — professionals, good people whom I had been taught 'knew better' — get on with the job. What was really powerful for me was the opportunity to give the address at his funeral, which amounted to my appreciation of him as a father, a friend and one good man.

What I now know is that he did the very best he could with the information he had, despite the conditioning he had received. In his own way he tried his best to be my friend, and I certainly learned in the latter years how to be his friend. It is good to write this down, because it makes me confident that it is possible to interrupt the age old process, handing on of the oppression from parents to children. The present revelations of the extent of child sexual abuse, which is one aspect of the general abuse of children, affirms my belief that the abuse of children is at the heart of all our later difficulties with relationships. My hope is that future generations will look back on the 1990s and say 'That was when our forbears realised the nonsense of abusing children and started really listening and caring'.

Somewhere, somehow I know my Da is about now, hearing all this stuff. I'm conscious of his presence — there's a bond between us that nothing can break, and I appreciate that.

William Trevor

FIELD OF BATTLE

My father was a big, healthy-looking man with a brown bald head and brown tobacco fingers. He liked to tell stories rather than jokes — stories about people or events that amused him. He smoked Sweet Aftons, drank anything he was offered, and had a flair for picking winners, always turning first to the sports pages of the *Irish Times* and the *Cork Examiner*. As he advanced in his career as a bank official he became skilled at guessing which farmers to lend money to. He was popular with the townspeople he lived among, popular with country people because he understood them.

My mother was tiny, capricious and beautiful, firm of purpose, fiery and aloof, with a sharp tongue, and an eccentric sense of humour that often took you by surprise. She had a faint Northern Irish accent, and used to say she supported the North when in the South and the South (the Free State as it was then called) when in the North. She was a great reader: Philip Gibbs, Francis Brett Young, A.J. Cronin, Robert Hichens. In the succession of small towns where we lived she borrowed their books, in brown-paper jackets from the nuns at the convent, or from a branch of the Argosy circulating library, usually to be found at the back of a sweetshop. She had a weakness for Fred Astaire and Ginger Rogers.

My father hardly read at all and although he willingly accompanied my mother to *Top Hat* and *The Story of Vernon and Irene Castle*, his preference was for gangster adventures featuring Edward G. Robinson or James Cagney. They agreed about the Thin Man series, but to their three children it often seemed that they agreed about little else. Accord was short-lived, increasingly so as the years went by.

What children of a marriage rarely witness is the nature of the love that brought the whole thing — themselves included — into being in the first place. The marriage of parents is almost always mysterious: the sensual elements scarcely bear thinking about, the romantic past can only be guessed at, and all such curiosity invariably comes too late.

What inadequately fills the vacuum now is a sun-browned photograph of a young man in plus-fours with hair brushed straight back. He stands by a motor cycle and there's a misty image of the girl in the side-car, her face mostly turned away. She disliked being photo-graphed — an odd distaste in a beautiful woman. He didn't mind: in other snapshots he is at the wheel of an open-hooded Morris Cowley; striding across the square in Mountbellew; lighting a cigarette. They are together, newly engaged, two in a family group: his white-bearded father and upright handsome mother, his brothers and sis-ters and unidentified friends, all sitting on the grass at Millbrook, the County Roscommon farm which due to some misfortune was soon to slip out of the family's grasp. Honeymooning, they are together again, strolling on the promenade at Bray.

They met in Dundalk, he a bank clerk in the Bank of Ireland, she the first 'lady clerk' ever to be employed by the Ulster Bank. Their backgrounds were not dissimilar: she, too, came of farming stock, from the apple country of Armagh, a small farm near the village of Loughgall. There wasn't much money on either side, none at all to spare for this marriage, for any kind of dowry or for a few sticks of furniture: love and optimism were all it had.

Both were charming in different ways, and all their lives remained so. But their charming of one another, their pride in one another, their pleasing of one another: in later years it was hard to believe any of that had ever been there. What had lasted was a kind of rivalry that once, perhaps, was playful. Otherwise no effort was made, there was no give and take. Speculation charts a marital progression: from being lovers to becoming enemies in love, and then that rivalry turning sour.

The cold facts, all that is known, tell nothing: what happened, or did not happen, is private territory, a disappointment guarded in life and death. They made no bones about their shattered relationship, yet in all the quarrels that exploded, in all the accusations and recrimi-nations, in all the brooding silences, there never was a clue to the truth that lay at the root of its failure.

In the places where they lived together, shackled within convention — in Dundalk, Mountbellew, Mitchelstown, Youghal, Skibbereen, Tipperary, Enniscorthy, Portlaoise, Galway — indifference drifted into irritation, into hatred in the end. Yet now and again, as though in mockery, there were faint echoes of what had once so briefly been, hints at least of a companionship, if never of the passion that had burnt away. Once in a while, not often, there was a visit to a race-meet-ing together, a variation of the Saturday-afternoon journey to one of the cinemas in Cork. Parties were attended in one another's company, and parties given. One summer the family spent four or five weeks in a remote bay along the Waterford coast, he making the daily journey back to the bank in Youghal when his own holiday came to an end. Tents, including a marquee, were hired, and erected in a field on a cliff. Chests of drawers and dressing-tables, beds, chairs, oil stove and wireless set, were conveyed in a borrowed lorry to the cliff-top site. Camping wasn't common in those days, and had a pioneering feel to it. Milk had to be fetched from a distant farmhouse, and baskets of potatoes and peas, and water from a spring There was a sense of enjoyment about the adventure, which stretched a skin over whatever wounds there were, and while that summer lasted there was a fragile harmony.

In the evenings the big paraffin lamps were lit in the marquee and a record played on the wind-up gramophone: *Red Sails in The Sunset, The Isle of Capri*. He set snares for rabbits and never caught any; she laughed at him and he didn't take offence, getting his own back by trying to take a photograph of her. But even so they never addressed one another with endearments, or by their Christian names. And suddenly, out of nowhere, something would go wrong and silence would cut the chatter short. Halcyon days could not be counted on. Nothing could.

The divide widened: the last good family memories are of that cliff-top habitation and the sea below. In the bleakness that possessed the marriage all the love was given to its children, who would happily have settled for less. Only they were optimistic now, hoping without encouragement that miraculously everything would change, that when a silence of months came to an end the communication that replaced it would not be short-lived. But it always was.

The autumn following that last summer dragged by, then winter and spring. Morosely, he worked the hand-pump in the yard, twice a day conveying water to the tanks in the loft. On Sunday mornings he carried tea to her in bed, but no word was exchanged. Gregariously he went about his business, and frequented more bars than once he had. She took up leather-work.

Their spirit was not broken. Both laughed a lot, but differently, and not in one another's company. Both were clever, but in different ways. Both were perceptive, but did not share the nature of their perception. Perhaps she was too complicated for a simple man, he too undemanding for a demanding woman. Yet all this might have been overcome, and often is in marriage. What could not be was that she had borne three children and was left with no further purpose. He was making his way: for her, as he did so, there was the claustrophobia of small-town existence. Her frustration was that she was the victim of circumstance, his that he could do nothing about it.

In September 1939, soon after the war broke out, there was the move from Skibereen to Tipperary, and life became even more confined. The cinemas of Cork, where she had eased her mind, were no longer within reach. Gone, too, were its clothes shops, which she loved, and late-night suppers while the voices of Nelson Eddy and Jeanette MacDonald still echoed. Without petrol, there was no escape, without love no release.

He strolled down the street to Dobbin's Hotel and to the club next door where he played cards. When he returned in the middle of the night the sound of quarrelling would begin in their children's dreams and then become real. He joined the Local Defence Force and would disappear into the Galtee mountains on manoeuvres. Another excuse for drinking, she said.

Christmas was a time when the fragments of the family uneasily came together. He still sent to Switzer's in Dublin for scents and cosmetics he had seen advertised in their catalogue, and these would be waiting for her at breakfast on Christmas morning. She still bought him things herself, scarves and ties mainly, sometimes a pullover. Gratitude for these gifts would be conveyed in a roundabout way, through admiration for the articles received. But as the years went on all that broke down: Christmas became a bad time because of the nature of the occasion, because of the extra drink or two in Dobbin's and because, for her, the Argosy Library wasn't up to much, restricted in what it could offer because of the war, not enough to see her through those empty festive days. There was a dearth of social life. Tipperary's one small cinema burnt down.

She took to creating drama out of unpromising splinters of everyday life. One of these was a love-affair between a clergyman and a lady doctor, both of them middle-aged and married to other people. They had met when the former was summoned to administer the last rites at a deathbed, the latter having already done what she could. Waiting in the house for the inevitable death, the erring couple fell in love, and the rest had to do with the rector's car being observed late at night in places where it should not be. The town now was Enniscorthy, and County Wexford tongues — Catholic as well as Protestant — joyfully wagged. The respectable caught with their dirty linen in disarray — medicine and the Church canoodling in the back of a Ford V-8 — was relished with a vengeance. The unfortunate cleric's church wardens carted him around the parish, from house to house, urging his parishioners to give him a talking to. 'As good as the pictures,' my mother remarked. As good as 'Warwick Deeping'. But such real-life drama was rare, and as time went on and removal vans came again

49

and again, this rootless life increasingly took a toll on its own account. For almost half a lifetime new friends hadn't had a chance to become old ones; there'd been endless adjustment to different houses and surroundings, yet another wearying beginning in place after place. Behind the lace curtains that had been altered to fit windows all over the south of Ireland life stumbled on, until it stumbled to a halt.

Abruptly they separated and did not ever meet again. They had stayed together for the sake of the children, and the children were now grown up. It might have been better had they not done so, but in retrospect there is something gallant about their efforts to hold together the family their one-time love had brought into existence. Their perseverance was full of a self-sacrifice that was not apparent while they were making it; and there was a courageous honesty in their refusal to hide from their children the plight their marriage had become. They did not cover up; there was no hypocrisy.

My mother died a crippled and unhappy woman, in 1965. On a freezing snowy day her body was conveyed from Dublin to County Armagh and buried beside her father's in the small Church of Ireland graveyard at Loughall. All the way along the route, eighty or so miles, people crossed themselves as the hearse went by, and since Catholics had always respected the firm Protestant she'd been it seemed apt enough. Apt, too, that the husband she had married forty-four years ago wasn't there.

He died ten years later, of a heart attack while he was drying his hands. He was eighty-four and still attending race meetings.

'It was all my fault,' she said in a vague moment towards the end of her life. He might have said the same, but I doubt that that was where the truth lay. They were victims of their innocence when chance threw them together and passion beguiled them, leaving them to live with a mistake and to watch their field of battle expanding with each day that passed. They gave their love to their children and were loved in return, fiercely, unwaveringly. But not for a moment could that heal the wounds they carried to their graves.

Michael D. Higgins

THE BETRAYAL
A Poem for my Father

This man is seriously ill,
The doctor had said a week before,
Calling for a wheelchair.
It was
After they rang me
To come down
And persuade you
To go in
Condemned to remember your eyes
As they met mine in that moment
Before they wheeled you away.
It was one of my final tasks
To persuade you to go in,
A Judas chosen not by Apostles
But by others more broken;
And I was, in part,
Relieved when they wheeled you from me,
Down that corridor, confused,
Without a backward glance
And when I had done it,
I cried, out on the road,
Hitching a lift to Galway and away
From the trouble of your
Cantankerous old age
And rage too,
At all that had in recent years
Befallen you.

All week I waited to visit you
But when I called, you had been moved
To where those dying too slowly
Were sent,
A poorhouse, no longer known but that name,
But in the liberated era of Lemass,
Given a saint's name, 'St Joseph's'.

Was he Christ's father,
Patron saint of the Worker,
The mad choice of some pietistic politician?
You never cared.

Nor did you speak too much.
You had broken an attendant's glasses,
The holy nurse told me,
When you were admitted.
Your father is a very difficult man,
As you must know. And Social Welfare is slow
And if you would pay for the glasses,
I would appreciate it.
It was 1964, just after optical benefit
Was rejected by De Valera for poorer classes
In his Republic, who could not afford,
As he did
to travel to Zurich
For their regular tests and their
Rimless glasses.

It was decades earlier
You had brought me to see him
 Pass through Newmarket-on-Fergus
As the brass and reed band struck up,
Cheeks red and distended to the point
Where a child's wonder was as to whether
They would burst as they blew
Their trombones.
The Sacred Heart Procession and De Valera,
You told me, were the only occasions
When their instruments were taken
From the rusting, galvanised shed
Where they stored them in anticipation
Of the requirements of Church and State.

Long before that, you had slept,
In ditches and dug-outs,
Prayed in terror at ambushes
With others who later debated
Whether De Valera was lucky or brilliant
In getting the British to remember
That he was an American.
And that debate had not lasted long

In concentration camps in Newbridge
And the Curragh, where mattresses were burned,
As the gombeens decided that the new State
Was a good thing,
Even for business.

In the dining-room of St Joseph's
The potatoes were left in the middle of the table
In a dish, towards which
You and many other Republicans
Stretched feeble hands that shook.
Your eyes were bent as you peeled
With the long thumb-nail I had often watched
Scrape a pattern on the leather you had toughened for our shoes,
Your eyes when you looked at me
Were a thousand miles away,
Now totally broken,
Unlike those times even
Of rejection, when you went at sixty
For jobs you never got,
Too frail to load vans, or manage
The demands of selling.
And I remember
When you came back to me,
Your regular companion of such occasions,
And said, They think that I'm too old
For the job. I said I was fifty-eight
But they knew that I was past sixty.

A body ready for transportation,
Fit only for a coffin, that made you
Too awkward
For death at home.
The shame of a coffin exit
Through a window sent you here,
Where my mother told me you asked
Only for her to place her cool hand
Under your neck.
And I was there when they asked
Would they give you a Republican funeral,
In that month when you died,
Between the end of the First Programme for Economic Expansion
And the Second.

I look at your photo now,
Taken in the beginning of bad days,
With your surviving mates
In Limerick.
Your face haunts me as do these memories;
And all these things have been scraped
In my heart,
And I can never hope to forget
What was, after all,
A betrayal.

Garret FitzGerald

ALL IN A LIFE

When I went ahead with the Aer Lingus job he refused to speak to me. Given his precarious state of health at the time, this was very painful for me. I attempted to overcome his objections by calling in aid the Jesuit who at school had aroused my political ambitions, Ronnie Burke-Savage. He argued my case with my father, but with no effect. Happily, however, after a little while my father began to recognise from my enthusiasm, and from the way my work obviously stimulated me, that my interest in air transport was genuine. In mid-March 1947 he relented. Our relationship was restored, to my immense delight. It was a timely reconciliation, for on the morning of 9 April my mother, returning to their bedroom after an early breakfast, called me frantically. He was dead of a heart attack on the floor beside his bed, at the early age of fifty-nine.

It was a devastating blow for us all but above all for Mother. She never really recovered. In the eleven years that followed before her own death she certainly derived pleasure from her children and grand children, but never hid from us the fact that she longed to re-join my father as soon as possible.

My brothers and I shared her sense of loss. All of us had loved, admired and respected our father, and had found enormous stimulation in his company — drawing in different degrees according to our individual interests on his literary, philosophical and political talents, but all enjoying equally his company, his irrepressible sense of humour and his extraordinary fund of anecdotes. To live up to his standards of integrity, emulate fully his patriotism and sense of public service, or replicate the combination of physical and moral courage for which he was so highly regarded by many of his contemporaries would be impossible; but at least these qualities gave us something to which to aspire.

Lest this seem unduly hagiographical it should be added that there were other sides to his character also. He never succeeded — indeed I do not think he even seriously tried — to be objective about the 1921 Treaty, or the Civil War or its aftermath. While capable of warm friendship with people who had differed politically from him at the time, he never lost his bitterness about those events, and, like many of his contemporaries, was often reluctant to accept the good faith of some of the major political figures on the other side, tending to ascribe base motives to people who at worst may have had mixed motivations and many of whom had in fact acted with the same good faith as himself. He had little sympathy with, or understanding of, many aspects of Irish life, and suffered neither fools nor people with less elevated cultural interests than his own very gladly.

I felt his death particularly because of my age; I had enjoyed his company for a shorter period than my brothers, and although our relationship had been fully restored a few weeks before his death, it had been clouded in the preceding year or two by his opposition to my proposed marriage and to my choice of career. I was conscious also that I had missed an opportunity to get to know him better by trying to break through his reticence about his childhood and youth, which was characteristic of many people of his generation.

Peter Sheridan

BRENDAN'S WEDDING DAY
(from a draft screen-play)

In a taxi
Brendan and Beatrice, heading from Clogher Road towards the Behan household. Brendan is wearing a suit and tie, and Beatrice is also in a two piece.

Beatrice	I'm scared, Brendan.
Brendan	Relax. You'll love me Ma.

Inside Behan house

Brendan	Come on Ma. You never get out of the house. And there's someone I want you to meet. Someone special.
Kathleen	What about your father's dinner?
Brendan	Don't mind me Da. Let him fend for himself for once.
Kathleen	Fend for himself! Da can't boil an egg.
Brendan	It's never too late to learn. Come on, Mother, you're coming out with me.

In the taxi
Kathleen, still trying to put her overcoat on, is being pushed out the hall door by Brendan. Beatrice blesses herself and starts to pray quietly. Brendan opens the door of the taxi and Kathleen enters.

Kathleen	God bless us and save us they hang the wrong fella in that play of his.
Beatrice	How do you do, Mrs Behan?
Kathleen	Well, I was grand til five minutes, ago, Alannah.
Brendan	The Bailey public house. (*To the driver*) Ma, I'd like you to meet my wife, Beatrice. (*To Kathleen*)
Kathleen	You're married? (*To Brendan*) (Brendan nods). To him? (*To Beatrice*) (Beatrice nods).

Kathleen leans her head back on the seat.

In a taxi — night time
All three are in high spirits. The driver also. They are drinking in the
car. Brown paper bags of take-outs line the back seat.

Kathleen   It's not the men who marry the women, daughter.
            It's the women who marry the men. (*To Beatrice*)
Brendan   True for you, mother, true for you.
Kathleen (sings)
            It was down by Anna Liffey
            My love and I did stray
            Where in the good old slushing mud
            The children sport and play,
            We got the whiff of ray and chips
            And Beatrice softly sighed
            Arrah Brendan come along for a one and one
            Down by the Liffey side.

Stephen at the window, pulls back the curtains. He is not amused.
Kathleen knocks at the front door, followed by Brendan laden down
with drink and Beatrice likewise. Kathleen knocks again.

Stephen   Where were you all day, missus? (Opening the door)
Kathleen   Out celebrating your son's marriage. (She enters the house)
Brendan   Da, this is Beatrice, my wife. Beatrice this is Stephen, me
            Da.
Beatrice   Pleased to meet you, Mr Behan.
Stephen   The pleasure's all mine. (Sarcastically)
            Where are you going with that drink? (*To Brendan*)
Brendan   Where do you think I'm going?
Stephen   I think you're going home, where you should be
            at this hour, with your good wife.
Beatrice   Come on, Brendan, it's far too late to be keeping your
            father up.
Brendan   Jesus. I'm not going to be turned away from me own
            home. And that's an end to that.

Brendan pushes past Stephen and into the house. The physical contact
between them a harbinger.

In the living room
Brendan pulling a few bottles and passing around. To Kathleen. To
Beatrice. Looks to his father.
Brendan   Are you having a stout?

Stephen	I don't want no stout, no.
Brendan	You're just going to sit there are you?
Kathleen	Have a bottle, Da. It'll cheer you up . . .
Stephen	I'll do as I please in my own home.
Kathleen	We had a lovely hour today, hadn't we daughter?
Stephen	I'm delighted for yous.
Kathleen	So here's to you both. *Slainte agus fad saol.* (Health and long life).
Brendan	*Agus go mbeimid go leir beo ag an am seo aris.* (May we all be alive this time next year)
Stephen	I wish you luck in your marriage, Beatrice, I think you're going to need it.
Brendan	Well, I won't chain her to the kitchen sink which is more than I can say about my mother's predicament.
Kathleen	Can we not just have a nice quiet drink? And a song?
Stephen	You can have what you like. But I demand a little respect in my own home. I demand it from those that were kept here.
Brendan	You had to keep us. It's against the law to starve your children.
Beatrice	I think we should go home, Brendan.
Stephen	You were all reared properly.
Brendan	I didn't mean that the way it sounded.
Stephen	I worked me fingers to the bone to put food in your bellies and clothes on your back. I treated you all as equals. You all stood the same before this judge.
Kathleen	And what are you saying Da, that I had favourites?
Stephen	You reared him a pet. That's the truth.
Kathleen	I treated Brendan the same as the others.
Stephen	Signs on it he hasn't an ounce of gratitude in his bones.
Brendan	And where's the rest of the family, tell me? They've gone. Gone because they had to get out.
Stephen	They left because they couldn't find work in this country.
Brendan	They left because they couldn't stick it here with you. Who could?
Stephen	You know where the front door is?
Kathleen	You stay where you are, son.
Stephen	Take his part against me, you always do.
Beatrice	You're so alike, you two. You're like twins. I just wish you could see yourselves.
Stephen	We're alike in some ways, Beatrice. If I had a death

	sentence laying over me I'd pray for a reprieve. Your husband now, he'd prefer to be shot.
Kathleen	You saved Brendan's life that time, I'll grant you that.
Brendan	You had no business interfering in IRA affairs. (Extremely agitated)
Stephen	Gratitude.
Brendan	Meddling in what didn't concern you.
Stephen	The first time I saw you was through the bars of a prison.
Brendan	I know. I've been listening to it since I could crawl. I'm really glad you had the time to father me before they caught you. I don't needyou to remind me of how grateful I should be. I'm glad to be alive. I don't need you to tell me how should love. If if I should love at all. I can decide all that for myself. Understood? I should have known not to come back here. You don't respect me, that's all. You don't respect my talent, you don't respect my politics. You don't . . . . I've had it. I'm not going to set foot in this house ever again. I'm not going to have you looking at me like . . . like I owe you something.

Brendan walks out.

Stephen	Brendan come back.

Beatrice follows him out.

Outside Behan house — night
Brendan on the pavement outside. Beatrice joins him. Arms around one another. Brendan hails a taxi and they get in. As they pull away, Brendan looks back to see his mother standing at the door, and his father looking out the window.

Brendan (V. O.)
> Somebody once asked me how I felt about my father. I love my father. Of course I do, and the less I see of him, the more I love him.

John D. Nugent

MY FATHER AND I

A kaleidoscope of images. Contradictory fragments of memories. I have never been asked to write anything I found so difficult. Truth keeps slipping away. Part of truth is that doing a piece like this imposes a constraint. Judge not. If you must judge, you must be prepared to stand alongside the prisoner in the dock. You cannot be more merciful to yourself than you are to the accused.

My father was as all men: complex. So am I. Very. Strange, isn't it? Despite my best efforts to be my own man I should end up like him. Stranger still, that I should ponder these questions in my sixtieth year — the same year he died; very probably thinking out the same things.

My father had a bad side. He specialised in the silent treatment. If you did anything you weren't spoken to. At times it seemed to me that the drains in the house were blocked and the smell was distinctly coming from me. That was cruel of him, of course; it caused me endless problems in later life. But that's another story. I resented him most savagely, times when I plotted murder. But then when I grew up — rather late in life, I'm afraid — I saw that most sons resent their fathers to some extent and the trick is to forgive them first and then to come to see that there is nothing to forgive.

He was very loyal. He was truth. He had integrity. And he could be fun to be with, especially when my mother was alive. I remember being gently trapped between his knees, his eyes looking earnestly into mine and his voice insistently demanding whether I had told a lie or not. I was very small. I had some idea that a lie was one of those pieces of ivy which grew on our front wall. But that first lesson stuck; a respect for truth. To this day I do have a contempt for shabby dealing. I find politicians of all colours a particularly disgusting breed.

And he had guts. By the bucket. I could boast of him for hours. Never the man for great exploits and feats of derring do on land and sea; but the steady determination to hang in hard when nobody knew and there was no reward. The best kind of guts. And that became important to me too. He had a pal, a solicitor in the UK who became unstuck and was sent to prison. After he got out, my Dad invited him over, slapped a big cigar in his mouth and took him to dine at his club. That was the kind of thing he'd do.

It was after his heart attack at age forty-three that he became successful at the Bar. He went to the courts every day, there to fight the various legal battles of his time. Around the Four Courts he became alive — vibrant. If you met him there he was eminently approachable, the quintessence of the good guy; warm and friendly which is how his contemporaries remember him. When he died a judge, paying tribute to his memory, said that he would pass into history as a true friend; of inflexible courage and fearless integrity. What the judge said is unimportant; what is important is that I know it to be true. But when he came home in the evening it was different.

He withdrew into himself, a tired and wounded man. Like most boys — wise before their time — I quickly learned the difference and had I to approach him about anything I would make it my business to do so in the Four Courts where you would be certain of a fair and sympathetic hearing. But you never, but never, bearded the lion in his den.

It was my own children who finally got me to understand him. Both my marriages ended in failure and whatever else they may have overlooked, I don't think the children have ever forgiven me that. My son has told me of times when he could have done mayhem to me. My daughter has told me of a burning rage against me. All at once I saw myself and my father in both encounters and at last I understood. I said to my son; don't hit me please. Or one day you will find your blows raining on yourself. My daughter told me: the shit stops here! I'll not make the mistakes that you did. I smiled. It doesn't, I said. It never does. How often did I make the same vow myself? I would never allow my own children to grow up with such indifference. And I didn't. I made other mistakes. With precisely the same result. The shit goes on. That's the curse of our humanity. It is the business of every child to overcome it and to see that fathers particularly are always human, and prey to all the fallibility, wrong headedness and bloody mindedness of the human condition. Mothers, curiously enough, seem to escape this. God knows they have enough to put up with; including the men they marry.

I thought that my alcoholism was my father's doing — what a dreadful legacy to leave a son! (A good alcoholic will always find somebody to blame for his condition.) Furiously I raged against his memory. Until one day one of my fellows pointed out that resentment killed more alcoholics than drink. What will I do, I asked; a self pitying bundle of resentments against the whole world and my father most of all. List them out, every one of them, analyse them — and most of all, find out the part you played in causing them. Then pray for him.

And keep it up. Night and day. What a dreadful sentence! What if the prayers were answered? The alcoholic's prayer for those we resents runs: I hope that son of a bitch is given everything he wants! But I did what I was told and after a short time found that I could scarcely remember what the resentments were about. I came to recognise how false my own *perceptions* of being unloved and unwanted had been.

All life is a disease of the perceptions. We perceive; but often wrongly. We place interpretations — often fallacious. We have a lamentable tendency to get it wrong. We believe the lie. But we all love our children. For me they have been the greatest high speed and technicolour of my life. The love of my wives, bless them, I can about limp on without — there's somebody else now — but not my children. We are always human. To love somebody as a human being, be it a child, a lover, spouse, parent, or friend is to let them down at times; to fail to come through. My Dad was the very same. How very human! How misunderstood. He loved me. And damn near wrecked me in his efforts. Growing up was never easy. It doesn't matter now. His memory rests gently with me. Maybe I will meet him again. I don't know. The hereafter has yet to be proved, not to mention the chance of our being in the same place. Admiration, pride and gratitude, yes; but love? Well, what do you think.

Sam McAughtry

FATHER'S CHRISTMAS PARTY

My father first went to sea as a boy, in 1897. He made his final voyage in 1951, and in all those fifty-four years he was only twice home for Christmas. The first time was during World War One, when, according to Mother, Tiger's Bay, where we lived, became noisier than the Western Front. He was a sergeant major in the army then, and if I'm asked how a donkeyman greaser in the merchant service came to be a sergeant major I'm bound to say that I'm not too sure. His own explanation was that he worked in the Cunarder *Olympic* at the time: it was a troopship under army command, and as donkeyman greaser my dad claimed that he automatically assumed army rank in keeping with his position as leading hand in the engine room. This could be true, but my dad was a bit of a character in his straight-faced way. For all I know he could have been impersonating a sergeant major. In any case, I wish I'd seen him in the uniform, he was only five feet four and about as wide as your finger. I'll bet the genuine soldiers stopped in their tracks and scratched their heads when they saw him in the street, with his Western Ocean roll, and the hands jammed into his pockets.

Well anyway, apart from the faces that Mother made when that wartime Christmas at home was mentioned, I knew nothing more, and the older I got the more I used to sympathise with Dad as one Christmas after another came around, and his present was dispatched to him by parcel post weeks before the date. 'Merry Xmas, Daddy,' we used to write, round about the 4th of December. It seemed such a shame.

He wasn't a man much given to talking yet he did plenty of talking about that: 'I'm going to miss Christmas again, sweetheart,' he used to say to Mother, and she would say aye, it's awful isn't it, but away in behind her sorrowful glance I used to imagine I could see the ghost of a glint of gratitude, almost thanksgiving.

Now when I was a young man, I was, of all the family, the one who spent most time in Dad's company when he was at home. This is not because I had any more special relationship than the other brothers had with him: no, it was because the brothers had things to do outside of drinking pints, and I hadn't, and when Dad was at home he became unsettled and nervous if he had to sit around the house for any length of time. 'Throw on your coat and come on', he would say to me in the mornings, and in the afternoons and in the evenings. 'Where are we going?' I would ask. 'We'll take a bit of a dander and get the fresh air', he would say. About a minute and a half later the two of us would discover, to our surprise, that we had landed up outside Jimmy McGrane's pub in Spamount Street, and in we would go, to get out of the cold. It was only to be expected therefore that Dad's second Christmas at home should leave its mark on me, more so than anybody else.

It was 1950, a year before I was married, and a year before Dad died and was buried in Cuba. There were just the three brothers, the sister and myself at home, for Mother was four years dead then. Father's ship tied up in Immingham in Yorkshire a week before Christmas, and he wasn't due to sail until the 27th. 'Right Sam', he said, the minute he hit Belfast off the Liverpool boat, 'you and me have to stock up for the Christmas party. 'Where are we having it?' I asked. 'In the parlour', he said. We called in for a jar on the way home from the boat, and when I left I was humping a dozen of stout, the first of the special party stock. After the sister had coaxed him into eating a wee pick of fried ham and a cup of milky tea, round to Jimmy McGrane's we went: 'I'm going to be home for Christmas', Dad said to all his cronies, 'and I'm throwing a party'.

At first I wrote down the names of the acceptors, but no paper could have held out to it. 'We're going to need some drink for *this* party', I told him. 'Right then', he said, 'go up to the bar and get some', and with that he thrust a handful of mint-fresh notes at me. On the 22nd, 23rd and 24th of December our parlour began to look more and more like Jimmy McGrane's. There was drink everywhere. The sister wasn't too sure what to do about it all. For all our lives we'd been used to Dad just going round for a mouthful, and coming back like a gentleman — sometimes an unsteady gentleman, but well under control for all that — and now things seemed to be heading for an unmerciful binge, and in the parlour too, a place reserved for the clergyman, or maybe the insurance man, if he was paying out on a policy.

'Do the parlour up a bit', Dad said, 'make it look like a bar.' So I put a lick of paint on it, and rigged up a makeshift bar out of a sideboard and a china cabinet, covered with curtain material.

'Right', I said to Dad on Christmas Eve morning, 'the bar's all ready, we've enough drink for the First Battalion of the Rifles: what time does the party start?'

'Midnight', he said. I gaped at him. 'Well', says he, 'the pubs'll be open till ten, and we usually bring a carry-out, don't we? So it'll be midnight before we finish our normal drinking. I've told the guests to arrive at twelve, and to prepare for an all-night session.' 'How old are you now?' I asked him. 'Sixty-eight', he said. 'Excuse me for asking', I said, 'but what did your mother feed you on?' 'I don't see what you're driving at', he said, and so help me God he didn't.

They came from far and near to Dad's Christmas party, and every blessed guest brought a bottle. Standing behind the bar, I tried desperately to get them to take the drink we'd left in, but the stock actually grew larger as the morning wore on. I heard Dad reminisce with old pals he hadn't seen for years upon years. 'Do you mind the time we rolled the hundredweight of cheese down the gangway at one in the morning?' one old seadog said. 'Aye, I do', Dad said, 'that was in Cork. We sold it to a publican for a bottle of whiskey.'

It was a lovely party: a delightful party. They were standing on top of each other, singing songs, and weeping and shaking hands. When it finally came to an end at dawn, seven or eight of the guests had to be carried and laid out on sofas or beds. And Dad was as steady as a rock. And as happy as he could be without my mother.

On Boxing Night I left him down to the Liverpool boat. 'What on earth am I going to do with all that liquor in the parlour?' I asked him as we shook hands.

'What do you usually do with liquor?' he asked, 'you drink it, don't you?'

And away he went to sea, at sixty-eight years of age. Five feet four, and seven stone ten. The quart into a pint pot champion of the world.

Brendan Kennelly

I SEE YOU DANCING, FATHER

No sooner downstairs after the night's rest
And in the door
Than you started to dance a step
In the middle of the kitchen floor.

And as you danced
You whistled.
You made your own music
Always in tune with yourself.

Well, nearly always, anyway.
You're buried now.
In Lislaughtin Abbey
And whenever I think of you

I go back beyond the old man
Mind and body broken
To find the unbroken man.
It is the moment before the dance begins.

Your lips are enjoying themselves
Whistling in the air.
Whatever happens or can not happen
In the time I have to spare
I see you dancing, Father.

Des Wilson

MY FATHER

I did not have an ambition to be like my father. I did not have an ambition to be unlike him either. I admired him. Good humoured, hardworking, successful, he told us that if you were sweeping the streets you should aim to be the best sweeper in the district.

He could have gone in for politics but my Mother was against it. They were different from each other in so many ways. I remember the two of them processing to Mass on weekdays. Processing because that is the way the pair of them advanced, well dressed, happy looking, assured in their own minds that they really had made a go of it. And weekdays — because on weekdays it was possible to meet men down holes.

Men were often digging holes along their route, something to do with gas, or water, or other mysterious doings under the south Belfast streets. Smells arose from the holes, as the thick brown clay on which that part of the city is built was shovelled out of them. Most important from my father's point of view, men sometimes arose from the holes as well. His attitude to men in holes was one of easy comradeship. He wanted to stop and talk to them, to ask them where they came from — hoping they came, as he did, from Co. Cavan. He would peer down a hole, hard hat on his head, gold chain swinging out from his ample front, his four foot something in height dangerously close to a shift in his centre of gravity as he leaned nearer and nearer to the hole diggers.

Seeing this manoeuvring my mother processed on her way, unwilling to converse with the hole diggers, my father almost caressing pipes and red clay in his anxiety to hear what the men were saying to him. It was typical of him and of one great difference between them. They lived in harmony, with occasional outbursts of disagreement, both determined to succeed, but my father totally lacking a false dignity which could well have teetered on the edge of pomposity. For my Mother, teetering on the edge of pomposity might well be marginally better than teetering on the edge of a hole dug by the Corporation.

Determined, able and good, and completely without pomp. He did have pride though, and often told the four brothers and myself how he had faced the parish priest and told him he knew more about running parochial dances than the parish priest did. Which was probably true and certainly earned for him the admiration of ourselves and sundry parishioners, and the respect of the parish priest. He should have been anti-clerical but escaped it by sheer good nature.

When I saw him on the putting green giving his opponent something to aim at by standing almost over the hole on the eighteenth or heard him shouting 'bogues' (his affectionate name for a golfing score he seldom attained) in the pompous atmosphere of a south Belfast golf club in the thirties, I understood that my father was without either pomposity or needless inhibition. He liked talking to workmen digging corporation holes and giving an opponent a helping foot to fill a golfing one. He did not have to lecture us about such things. He did not even have to tell us to watch him at it. He just did it, and we realised that because he did it, it was right. He never had to tell us he did it because it was right. That would mean sermonising. The fact that he did it showed it was right, and that meant trust.

He enjoyed relating to people like Sir Dawson Bates, Stormont Minister of Home Affairs, a feat which must have earned him automatic entry into heaven and a high place in it. Bates was anti-Catholic, anti-democratic and arrogant, the complete opposite of my father. So my father never bothered to instruct us to love our enemies. He just showed us how not to bother having any.

I never liked flute bands, or even flutes, until James Galway arrived and showed that music from the flute could be wonderful — music which seemed not so much played on the flute, as coming from the flute, like some diabolical exhalation of its own wicked accord tormenting us like country and western in enclosed spaces. The reason for my dislike was flute bands in Belfast hired out for the day by Orange secret societies to play tunes whose words were as offensive as anything I have ever heard anywhere. The tendency of most of us was to avoid flute bands as one would the plague and to welcome the approaching sound of a flute with the same enthusiasm as one would the visitation of a banshee. My father not only stopped to listen but even went to listen to them. My attitude was like Dr Johnston's to the Giants' Causeway: 'Sir, it is worth seeing, but not worth going to see', but my father would leave the warmth of his own home to watch the Orangemen marching in the dismal street. 'Come on and see the Brethren', he would say.

And because we recognised that if he did it, it must have some redeeming features, we made the sacrifice and went. He would stop the car — we were among the fortunates who had one — when the Brethren came along the road during the long marching season, not just to let them pass but to listen to them, while the rest of the family chafed with impatience and recoiled with distaste. 'Here's the Brethren', he would say, and our hearts sank as he slowed the car and stopped.

He would also remark mischievously that his name had probably been worth a couple of thousand a year in extra business — being called William Wilson tended to enhance takings in the Belfast of the thirties and forties. But successful as he was, he was not a good business man in the sense that, say, Tony O'Reilly or Robert Maxwell would have understood the term. One day when very young we were brought to visit him during business hours. Instead of serving customers we found him standing with his back to the gas fire reading the *Irish Press* (he maintained that de Valera was all right, but it was the people surrounding him. . . An excuse I have heard many times from liberal people who refuse to believe the party leaders of their choice could possibly be failures after all) and generally enjoying his idleness. He looked over the top of his glasses, smiled broadly, probably offered us a penny each, and said, 'I hope no more customers come in today, I want to read a bit and then go and talk to John Maguire'.

It was from him principally that I learned the triple lesson that reading is a good thing for the brain, that there is much knowledge contained in the heads of your friends and that friends are more important than profits. John Maguire was a crony from the same part of the country as he was, with whom and with a select few others he used to walk and talk and discuss *Labour in Irish History* and suchlike works. Like many of his friends my father had come through an appalling apprenticeship in the liquor trade, he became spokesman for barmen looking for better wages and working conditions, got his own business and eventually became spokesman for proprietors in negotiations with people like Dawson Bates.

That is not the way he meant it to be, which brings me back to why he should have been anti-clerical and wasn't, and why he always made clear to us that we shouldn't necessarily follow him into business but should make up our own minds about what we wanted to do and then go for it.

When he finished primary school in his home parish in Cavan he meant to become a teacher. In those days you did this by serving an apprenticeship as a monitor, and then you went on to teacher training. He was accepted and looked forward to doing what he wanted to do and would have been very good at. But then the local parish priest, a canon, came along one day and told him that a different person had been chosen for the monitorship and teacher training. He was aghast, the more so because the selected person was a niece of the canon. There was not room on the small farm for more than one inheritor, so his sister went to America and he went to Belfast.

I never heard that story from himself, because both he and my mother protected the good name of the clergy and the church with a faith that was firm and fair though not at all subservient. So, far from being anti-clerical, he always taught us to be respectful to clergy, but then he taught us to be respectful to everybody. He read prodigiously, especially works of history and politics and would quote Dickens at us long before his example had convinced us Dickens was worth reading. We did not realise how humorous he was until it was too late — he died when he was fifty-nine and I was sixteen. Many of the things he said in fun still seemed funny even after the hundredth time he had repeated them. It was always funny when he mimicked Mrs L who was the perfect snob, or John McD who proclaimed himself on a crusade against the hypocrites of the town (a task which would have kept him occupied for life even had he conquered one a month and lived to be a hundred), or the lady next door who maintained that if she were not the sweetest tempered woman in Belfast she could not have lived with her husband. He could capture for us the essence of a personality and bring it home with him as surely as my mother could capture the essence of elegance in dress and bring that home with her in a bag at a bargain price.

Being the youngest in the family I never had a single confidential conversation with him. I didn't feel the need of it. We were observers of life, his life as well as other's lives, not doers of important deeds ourselves. Parents were dependable but often uncommunicative and while they did not necessarily know best, they were best obeyed for all that. Dependable, and immensely protective. I can still see my Father on his knees, facing into the fire, my Mother standing at his left shoulder and him hastily stuffing that evening's *Belfast Telegraph* into the flames. We made sure to find out what was so awful in the paper as to deserve burning. It was just a divorce story. Nothing salacious, nothing crude, just a divorce case.

It was not prudery but rather a sense of decency, which did not approve trailing the ills of the world in front of children who would learn about them for themselves soon enough. Too decent, too protective, in a sense too innocent with an innocence I could never imitate and really would not want to.

Whatever he saw of the evils of the world, it sat lightly on him. In spite of the indigestion and the worries he must have had about business, especially in the thirties, there was scarcely a day when he was not capable of coming down the stairs proclaiming his awful version of Shakespeare's, Hamlet, 'I am thy father's gimlet . . . ' or even though he hadn't two notes in his head to put together in civilised sequence, trying to sing, 'I love a Lassy, a Bonny Hi'land Lassy'. He had a great affection for the music hall in his early days, which is possibly one reason why I enjoy the theatre as much as I do.

Of course performers had to be decent. One evening he arrived home with my mother from the cinema having seen the latest Laurel and Hardy film, and both agreed that when all was said and done, they were 'only a couple of wastrels'. We made it our business to find out why this awful judgement had fallen on two of the world's most brilliant comedians. It was because in this latest — and perhaps tired — offering, the pair were filmed in company with scantily clad females. Of course standards were stricter in those days but the film was mediocre anyway and this gimmick did not improve it.

And he mortified us when we had visitors by asking us — he who could not sing a note — to perform on the piano, reminding us that it's a poor musician who can't play 'Donal Abu'. I never learned how to do it, and did not want to then, but now I wish I had. Somehow it did not seem important to please people then. You might follow them, you might obey them, you might imitate them, but you did not necessarily have to please them, have to help them experience pleasure. This was perhaps the worst effect of living in a puritanical society.

There was compensation when visitors were escorted through the house on a tour of inspection which included a visit to our bedrooms where we were supposed to be asleep. As we lay seemingly unconcerned with the fancy food, the brightness and the warmth downstairs and presumed to be fast asleep, we heard him say things to the visitors which showed how proud he was of the whole lot of us.

I never told him I was thinking of being a priest. While he was alive I was not thinking that way. He had a lot to do with it when it happened, however, although he never pushed me in one direction or another as far as my future was concerned. He had brought us downtown in the mid thirties to show us the barricades in Belfast streets dividing citizen from citizen. In the early forties there were air raids during which father and mother and the whole family showed courage they never gave themselves credit for. Then when I was sixteen and he was fifty-nine he went to the doctor, was diagnosed as having cancer, was opened up, closed up again and died.

We went into mourning for a year and wished we had listened more to him.

I thought that being a priest I could help make the world a better place than the one he scarcely talked about and never condemned but from which he always protected us. I am sorry we never did talk about it because now I wonder whether, knowing as much about the world and the church as he did, he would have agreed that my becoming a priest would help.

He would have said, 'If you believe in it, do it'. He certainly would have said that. I learned that lesson from him and it was the best gift he ever gave me.

Sean Haughey

MY FATHER, CJH

An Irish family will never wash its dirty linen in public and certainly a political Irish family would never engage in such activity. If there is a problem at home a family will close ranks as far as the outside world is concerned. In this respect, I have no reservations about writing on my relationship with my father. In short my relationship with my father is a good one.

Nevertheless, the task of committing to paper the details of this relationship is a daunting one. There's no tradition of men talking about their fathers in this country. Women speak the language of love, intimacy and sharing of self, with consummate fluency. Men are no good at it at all. To bring out all the implicit details of this interaction is a challenge and something that I have never thought about before. In most traditional Irish families the word love is rarely mentioned openly in the home.

CJH's father was an army officer and died of multiple sclerosis when he was forty-eight years of age. I have never heard my father talk about him. His life and early death must have had a profound effect on my father but I can only suspect that they were close.

To the Irish people, CJH was definitely the head of the household in the tradition of things. My father loves his four children. He has never said this explicitly but has displayed it in so many different ways. He has always seen the good in us and never the bad, is positive about us and never negative. However, he loves his four children equally and if he has any favourites he has never shown it. I can therefore boldly state that my father loves me and I love him!

Like most Irish families, my mother reared the children. My father freely admits that he was unable to take an interest in me until I was seven years of age or more. It must seem very unfair to my mother, therefore, that even at an early age, the most exciting time of the day was when Father returned home.

Every child has an inherent desire to look up to his or her father. In my case however this was very easy indeed. My father's occupation is listed on my birth certificate as Minister for Justice. From an early age I knew he was important. He was exciting and my fascination with him was total. His sense of adventure captivated me. I once watched him, at sixty years of age, leap from one moving boat to another in the middle of the turbulent Blasket Sound. The previous week he survived unscathed in a plane crash in Farranfore Airport. The following week his boat sank off the Mizen Head. His irresponsible side always surprised me. It could be said that my father loves life.

One of my earliest memories of him is when he brought a glass of milk up to me in the middle of the night to ease a persistent cough. I recall too him bringing me and my older brother to the St Patrick's Day Parade. I stood to attention behind him for the National Anthem and was then ushered to a seat in the front row of the review stand. Like any other child I enjoyed the parade immensely.

My father once took my brother and I to an agricultural show in Paris. It was a real adventure travelling by aeroplane and I was allowed pick what I wanted from the menu. The visit was official but I was well behaved and was fascinated by the different animals on display. In addition, staying in a big hotel with elevators and room service was exciting, exciting for any child. We all had to dip our feet in disinfectant on our return home to prevent the spread of foot and mouth disease. That gave me something to talk about for weeks. On another trip to a political function in Donegal, I remember my father being pleased with me and my older brother when we sang with feeling a rebel song to the assembled crowd.

My father too took me for regular walks. When walking with him I felt I should stay three paces behind as he always seemed to be in deep thought. Sometimes I watched him tap each newly planted tree gently in order to encourage it to grow. On another occasion he stopped the car in the middle of the road and got out to talk to a cow, in order to ask it to move out of the way. On the same journey he pretended to get lost on a roundabout and had me believe that he was unable to exit from it. He has a very real sense of fun.

My father will now say that he only really got to know his children during holidays on Inis Mhicileain and the reverse is also true. He totally relaxes on the Blasket Islands, but in a very energetic way. He becomes absorbed in Island living and I have many fond memories spending the day with him fishing lobster, flying kites, lamping rabbits, bird watching, deer spotting, swimming or simply listening to another verse of Yeats' poetry. The evenings are spent drinking and telling stories. On many occasions I recall being in awe at his depth of knowledge and classical education as the stories continued into the early hours, by the fireside on foggy wet nights.

Later on I remember very clearly also how he visited me in my study every evening prior to the Leaving Cert exam. I did well in the exams and know that this would not have been the case were it not for the encouragement of a father. He always knew what to do in every situation. If I was worried about something and then talked to him, I would end up wondering what on earth I was worried about in the first place. A positive, decisive father can solve all problems. He had a sixth sense about his children's financial needs and often would offer to help out before we even realised we had a problem at all.

I recall also how everyone craved the attention of CJH. I was no different. If he was in a working frame of mind, you could be nervous going into his study to talk to him. On these occasions, he has no time to waste and unless your case was presented clearly, you found the meeting was over before you had even started. My father never struck me or gave out to me. If, however, he was annoyed with me, I would soon find out about it. To be met with that intense stare or a dismissive sigh, can be just as effective.

Inevitably, politics is at the very centre of my relationship with my father. As a child, general elections were very exciting events and I was delighted to help in my father's campaigns — putting up posters, delivering leaflets and so on. In the early 1980s, Fianna Fail was a very disciplined party. Issues were presented in black and white terms and members of the party were either for or against the leadership. I, of course, as a member of the organisation in my father's constituency was totally behind the party leader and defended the party tooth and nail. In those times loyalty was everything.

My decision to enter politics was my own, influenced as I was by a strong family tradition of public service. My father never sought to influence my initial decision one way or another but has been supportive ever since.

My first election was to Dublin City Council in 1985. Ever since then, people suggest that 'I am a chip off the old block' and point out that 'if I'm half the man my father was I will be fine'. I am always delighted to agree with them and have no 'hang-ups' whatsoever in this regard given that I have no expectation of ever being the same success he was. Once this was accepted by me, I could get on with my own life and political career.

In 1987 an independent committee of the National Executive recommended that Alderman Sean Haughey should be added to the Fianna Fail ticket in Dublin North East. As President of the National Executive, CJH ultimately had to ratify this decision and I will always be grateful to him for accepting the recommendation of the committee, despite the allegations of political favouritism which this generated. Some years later, I realised that in order to win a seat in the Dail,

I should wait for my father to retire from politics and then contest his seat in the following general election. History is full of examples of sons waiting in the background to succeed their fathers in the political world. Indeed Alexander the Great went as far as to assassinate his own father. Nevertheless, the retirement of my father as Taoiseach was a very emotional experience for me, my family and all those close to him. The realisation then that a vacancy now existed for me which would fulfil my ambition seemed unimportant.

My father never gave me any formal lessons in politics but I have always observed him closely. From time to time he does offer some tips and suggestions which of course are always appreciated. In 1992 however, following his retirement from Dail Eireann, he did throw himself enthusiastically into my general election campaign and even canvassed door to door for the first time in many years. During the campaign I was happy to be the pupil and man enough to realise that here was a true professional at work.

When my father retired as leader of Fianna Fail, I felt an enormous sense of independence and now felt free to speak out on many issues under a new regime. It was in fact a liberation. I could now emerge from the shadow even though I had never any problem with being in that shadow previously. And I feel closer to my father than ever before. Whereas before we never discussed politics, now we can discuss the issues at length. He has more time and is more relaxed, and I am more mature.

I always have great difficulty in buying my father a Christmas or birthday present. He is after all 'the man who has everything'. Some years I have been successful and other years I have not. However the birth of my son and his first grandchild was the greatest present of all. It was only then that I realised that my father could display emotion. His friends of course always knew this.

CJH is the classic father. If this is all too good to be true, well so be it. He has had a profound influence on me. At an official function in the Mansion House to unveil my portrait as Lord Mayor of Dublin, he informed those gathered that he had been 'unveiling Sean for a long time now.' I didn't pay too much attention to the remark at the time, but as the years go by, I often reflect on the truth of his simple statement.

Gay Byrne

THE TIME OF MY LIFE

My father and mother had met before the war on the Dargle Road near Bray. He and his brothers would come into the seaside town, some in a pony and trap, some walking alongside. They were big, strapping six-footers, handsome men who caught the eye of any girls they met along the road; and since they timed their incursions to coincide with May devotions or the other pious rituals that attracted the town girls, they were quite successful. My mother, Annie, and her four sisters were one group that came to their attention, and a sedate courtship began. As it happened, two of the sisters, Annie and Kathleen, married two of the brothers, Edward — who became my father — and Dick. Annie worked as a clerk in the Dargle and Bray Laundry with two of her sisters, but when war broke out and their young men left for the front they all decided that life would be more adventurous elsewhere than in Bray. They went north and took jobs in the Monarch Laundry in Belfast, where the pay was better.

In 1917 my father came home on two weeks' leave from the trenches to marry his Annie in Belfast, and then he went back to war. She made a private vow to God that if he returned safely from the war she would go to mass and communion every day for the rest of her life.

He did, and she did. I remember only one or two days when she was just too ill to drag herself out of bed; otherwise every single day until she died, even after Da died, she fulfilled her promise. (In fact she regularly attended two daily masses, both eight o'clock and ten o'clock.) Like ninety-five per cent of the men who served in that appalling war, it never crossed my father's mind when safely at home on leave to do a bunk and stay put, safe and sound, even though they knew that back in the trenches their life expectancy was a matter of weeks — with luck. To desert would have been an act of cowardice and treachery to their comrades. Apart from which, if they'd been caught they would have been shot.

The family connection with Guinness's brewery started right after the war when three of the brothers, including my father, got jobs there. The jobs were known in our neighbourhood around the South Circular Road as 'jobs fit for heroes', because of the policy of the Guinness organisation, which went out of its way to offer jobs to soldiers returning victorious from the fight 'for the freedom of small nations'. They were labouring jobs, six days a week, with a fortnight's annual holiday, but the conditions were very humane for the times that were in it, with a free pint of Guinness thrown in morning and evening.

My father, Edward, worked on the barges — or lighters, as they were sometimes called — that plied the Liffey. These were lovely, sturdy craft, with the 'chuff-chuffing' sound from the big steam engines, a sound that boomed excitingly as the slow craft passed under the archways of the Dublin bridges of stone. Da's run was from the brewery at James's Gate, where he loaded the heavy wooden casks, down to the ships at the North Wall. His talk at home was always of weather and east winds, driving rain and sunshine. He worked hard, and loved his job.

People in our area who worked in Guinness's always had a special status, and this spanned the era of our family involvement, from the early twenties up until the present day. The company had a long and distinguished connection with the City of Dublin. For instance, in 1865 Benjamin Guinness paid for the restoration of St Patrick's Cathedral. A few years later, Arthur, Lord Ardilaun, presented the city with a tract of land, once a medieval common, which was landscaped and opened to the public as St Stephen's Green in 1880. Edward Cecil Guinness established the Guinness and Iveagh Trusts, to provide housing for the poorer working class of Dublin, and built the Iveagh Market.

There were also unofficial perks for the employees, like the days during the years of the Second World War on which Da managed to secure for us some of the lovely soft white loaves of bread that were brought in from Liverpool on the Guinness cargo ships. During those years, we in Ireland ate chewy indigestible bread, which as time passed became blacker and blacker and more and more unappetising. The 'Emergency', as it was so cutely called in Ireland for most people who did not have friends or relatives actually involved, meant very little except dietary inconvenience. Only those lucky families with sons who were serving with the RAF in sunny climates like Egypt's ever saw a citrus fruit. We all re-used our tea-leaves, spreading them out to dry again and again until they were like specks of dust; and most children of that era developed a sweet tooth because the biggest treat afforded us was bread dipped in milk and spread with sugar.

When one of the Guinness ships, the *Carrowdore* or the *Clarecastle*, was arriving home from Liverpool, she sounded her siren as she came slowly up the Liffey. Da, alert for the signal, no matter what hour of the night or day it was, got up on his bicycle and cycled down to meet her at the North Wall. The crew gave him this beautiful soft white bread for our mother, who could not, she claimed, digest the awful black stuff. It was the sort of bread, tiny white loaves with the consistency of cotton wool, that today's nutritionists would throw down the nearest septic tank, but how we drooled at the sight and smell of them! Needless to remark, the smell was all we got. This bread was for Ma and that was that.

Eventually Da became a barge skipper, a Paycock captain in charge of his own little domain, and he was endlessly patient with the gurriers who, when he was lowering the funnel for passage under O'Connell Bridge, would line the parapet to amuse themselves by shouting remarks like 'Bring us back a parrot!' It was tidal work, and depending on the tides, he left for work and came home at strange hours. It was just normal to all of us children that he would go to work sometimes at two in the morning, sometimes at four in the afternoon.

He was a man of few words and little education. He left school at the age of twelve. I was never very close to him, nor, I believe, were any of his sons. (Our sister, Mary, remembers him differently. To her he was strong, quiet and loving, whereas to us he was strong, silent and strict.) Yet I think we all knew that if there were any external threat to any of us he would fight to the death for us. Every Thursday he came home and handed to my mother his unopened pay packet of £3.10s. (£3.50 in today's less elegant coinage). She gave him some pocket money out of it for his cigarettes. Since he got the free daily Guinness he needed no money for drink, or indeed for much else.

In fact ours was a very temperate household. There was somewhere, under lock and key in a sideboard, a small bottle of spirits, whiskey or brandy, which was hardly ever produced except for Very Important Visitors or for medicinal purposes, or later to add to Gay's egg-flip, the story of which was blown on the 'Late Late Show' special programme on New Year's Eve of 1987/88. Young Gaybo was always thought of by his fond mother as being 'dawny' — delicate — and she presented him with an egg-flip every morning to build up his strength. The story is quite true. I *was* about thirty years old before I realised that all along she had been putting increasing amounts of whiskey into the egg-flip to try to disguise the taste of the egg, which I did not like, and I *was* thirty-two before I realised that egg-flips did not automatically taste the way my mother's had!

My mother had a curious attitude to drink. If you were important enough to be offered a drink and you asked for a whiskey or a brandy, you would get a tumblerful, filled to the brim. Just like reverend mothers in convent parlours all over the country who sent priests reeling into the night after their tea, she had no idea what constituted a measure. But if you asked for a bottle of stout you were immediately under suspicion as a drunkard. In later years, when Mary was pregnant and visiting home she would be offered a glass of Gilbey's invalid port, along with an admonishment that she was not to enjoy it: it was purely for the purposes of keeping her strength up. Yet, like a lot of Dublin women her age, Mam, if she was feeling a bit 'dawny', would indulge in a snipe — a miniature bottle — of Guinness mixed with milk and sugar.

In later years I once went on holiday with both of my parents, a driving holiday, which we grandly called 'touring'. Each day, once a day, we would stop outside a pub and Ma would allow Da to go inside for a pint while she and I sat outside and waited in the car. The poor man must have had to open his throat and literally pour the pint into it, because Ma was not disposed to wait too long.

Her word was absolute law with him, and whereas he never lifted a finger to us on his own behalf, if she complained to him about our behaviour he belted us unquestioningly, even to the extent of waking us out of a deep sleep to hand out a clip on the ear. There was one occasion — and only one as far as I remember — when he went further than that. I had given 'lip' to my mother one morning, refusing to go to mass in most uncivil terms. I was simply fed up with being expected to go to mass and communion every morning as she did. I made the fatal mistake of pretending that I had actually been in the church all along and she was meeting me coming back, as it were. As always, she recognised the lie, and began to harangue me. I cannot remember quite what I said, but it was something that in her terms was particularly nasty, like 'Sod off and get off my back with this bloody nonsense about mass'.

She simply said quietly: 'Your father will hear about this'. I knew he would, and spent a most uncomfortable day in school in anticipation of what lay ahead of me. For that day, the Synge Street Brother and his andramartins was only in the ha'penny place.

When Da came home from work, I was in the front room. There was an uncharacteristic silence and tension in the house. He went down to Ma in the kitchen as usual, and then I heard the dreaded footsteps coming towards the front room. He came in and closed the door, and then beat me unmercifully — not for not going to mass but for the way I had treated my mother. His hands were large and like leather, as tough as the barrels he handled, and I received a real battering. Afterwards I had to go down to the kitchen to apologise to my mother.

We all believed, and still do, that our Da did not like being a disciplinarian, but that he felt very strongly that he had to support my mother at all costs in her efforts to stay on top of us. He was quite gentle at the back of it all. I never had the opportunity to get close to him, since he died before I left school, and in the era in which we lived the only chance to get to know your father was later, in adult life, when you could approach him as an adult. One of my pals, Clive Culliton, has two sons, Simon and Peter. All their lives, but particularly from the time they were fifteen or sixteen years old, they were pals with their father. The three of them lend cigarettes to each other and buy pints for each other and go around with each other as equals. It is not that I envy the relationship, it is that I cannot fathom it. Just imagine, having a father that you could be close to and would call you 'pal'. . . .

My father was someone I avoided as far as possible, because I regarded him as someone who would knock your block off. It was not that he was uncultured, or stupid: he was a big labouring man who thought he was fulfilling his proper role as a father. He was popular with his workmates and quite close to one of his brothers, but by and large, in my vision of him, he was a big, lone man. I suppose it boils down to the fact that he had not time for kids: that was women's work. But I am very sorry that he died before I had the opportunity to sit with him on a bar stool, to buy a pint and to shoot the breeze. None of his sons ever had that opportunity: I was too young, Al was totally preoccupied with his studies, and Ernest and Raysie were away. My school pals who called around to our house remember him only as a big, quiet presence in our kitchen, clad in his dark Guinness jersey, but always silent. He was, simply, a man of his generation.

Although they were not particularly physically affectionate with one another — at least in front of us, in that I never saw them cuddling or with their arms around one another — there is no doubt in my mind that Ma and Da loved one another. We all kissed each other good-night and so on, and he showed his love for her by working around the house for her, washing dishes and cleaning, polishing all the shoes. I was brought up to do the same. It was only in later life that I discovered that all Irish men, all fathers, did not automatically make beds, chop logs, clean out fires.

All of us remember being woken up in the middle of the night by what we called 'Da's little turns'. In the dead silence, the air would suddenly be rent by the most appallingly violent screaming. The whole street was woken: the screaming was so loud and we all lived so closely together. I believe now it was *petit mal*, that mild form of epilepsy — but my mother was always convinced that Da's 'turns' had been caused by his experiences in the trenches of the First World War. She would say that at the height of the thrashing around and sweating he would be screaming about something coming in on top of him and smothering him, or trying to escape from something, or people being killed or dying all around him.

And always, after the shouting and thrashing around, he lapsed into a coma. No-one, not even the doctor when he was called, could wake him when he was going through one of these horrendous experiences. He would just have to be left in peace until he woke naturally some time during the following day. He never spoke about it and seemed to have no conscious memory of what might have caused it. Even if he had, he would never have spoken about it. He was obviously in huge distress and would be agitated for quite a while after he came out of one of these episodes, but this was in the days when men were supposed to be 'manly' and to keep feelings and fears to themselves. Many years later, while making a documentary about the war memorial at Islandbridge, I discovered that many men who had fought in the First World War had similar recurring nightmares, visiting terror upon them at regular intervals throughout their lives.

The sad outcome of Da's 'turns' was that he had one at work one day, when he was loading his barge at Custom House Quay. And from then on, he was never allowed handle a barge again, but was given an indoor job. He was thought to be too big a risk.

Guinness's had a benevolent policy towards its employees. Those who became ill while still on the payroll were given whatever type of work they could still do comfortably. So Da became a sort of glorified dogsbody, rolling the odd cask around the vast warehouse, or taking messages from one part of the huge complex to another, or even going into town on his bicycle on an errand for one of the staff. He was only fifty-one at the time, and I believe that after the freedom and dignity, even status, of his labouring job, which he had loved, it must have upset him greatly.

He had been going hoarse from the time I was about thirteen. He never investigated it, because he was not in pain, nor did he feel sick. His voice simply got fainter and fainter. When it had at last faded completely and was merely a whisper, he went down to Dr Steevens' Hospital, where they discovered he had throat cancer.

He was treated with radium and everything that medicine could offer at the time, but it was already too late. He lingered on for about eighteen months and in terrible pain until he died. He had to have his larynx removed and a tracheotomy tube inserted in his throat, through which he breathed, each breath rattling horribly. Before he was removed to hospital he spent some time in bed in our back bedroom, lying quietly and uncomplainingly in the depths of his appalling misery and suffering. All of us, I am afraid, are pretty finicky about blood and pain and sickness; but it was Al who overcame this and took it upon himself to perform the distasteful but loving task of changing and cleaning the tube. I think Al was superb at that time in dealing with a hateful job.

When Da was removed for the last time to Dr Steevens', a grim, forbidding building dating from the early eighteenth century, I found it extremely depressing each time I managed to pull myself together enough to go in to see him. One evening in July 1953 the four of us — Ma, Mary, Al and I — went in to see him. He was visibly failing. The telephone rang in the house at two the following morning. It was the hospital, calling us to come back as Da's end was near.

I had never been out on cold streets before at that time of the deserted night. We drove along the canal and down Steevens' Lane in the family Morris Minor, and the journey was far too short. I was full of conflicting emotions: terror at what I might see in the hospital; terror if he was still alive and that I would see him die; terror that he might already be dead; relief that he was at last going to be out of misery; relief that I would not have to witness this misery any more; guilt that I felt such relief.

Da had died by the time we reached the hospital. I remember very little of the funeral, out to Little Bray, and, as I remember, there was very little fuss made about my bereavement at school. I was absent for a day or two and then came back and life resumed.

Whatever about the manner of his death, which was slow and prolonged and hard, looking back on it now I often think that my father had a ferociously harder life than any of us. He worked very hard for Guinness's, long hours with comparatively little pay. And as far as I am aware from my observation of him, he got very little enjoyment out of life. Now I have no doubt that Mary and Al would say that he was a happy man, contented with his lot: but I am simply comparing the life that he had with the life we have, and especially my own. Our life-styles are so incomparably different; my regret is that he wasn't a younger man and that he did not live a bit longer to join us when the better times came, so we could have spoiled him a bit.

Again I regret that I never got close to him. We never went together to a football match, because he wasn't interested. We never went fishing, because he didn't fish. I cannot recall ever going anywhere with him as father and son.

The only time we were ever in any way close was when I tried to teach him to drive. I learned to drive when I was about fourteen, because I was mad about cars and made it my business to ingratiate myself with a few older fellows locally who had bangers. I made sure to get myself into their driving seats. And when we eventually got a car, Dad wanted to drive — but he never made a very good fist of it. I keep on thinking: poor Da, he missed out on so much.

Desmond Egan

from *A SONG FOR MY FATHER*

I.
I chanced on a photo

my father in shirtsleeves
standing by the greenhouse

on so relaxed a summer's day
no one bothered to pose
least of all the dandelions

and my mother saying something to Kate
who wonders with the yellow roses

the privet hedge we cut down since looks lovely
a doll lies forever in the sun

and I can almost smell the dinner
see our folding chairs and table the
other side of my camera

the red serviettes blowing

II.
the heart monitor   *out of the exile of age I*
jigged up   *rediscovered him as you do your youth*
down
its small screen   *we got closer than ever*
     thick as thieves

we were afraid   *until it came his turn to leave*
to look   *after the American Wake of*
and not to   *those last years*

his life jerked along   *and when time was up*
out of control now   *I would sit by the locker*
     holding that hand

zig zagged through
all conversation

as that graph
plotted everyone's
utter fragility

until
Wednesday 17 April
20 past 9 it
thinned
out

gave one last kick
before
nurse switched it off

gone gaunt now sunken as his eyes
and blotchy from needles from suffering
but soft and warm as I always loved
and vulnerable as his father's hands
protecting him in a Communion portrait
still hanging near the desk and books
in my old room

Patrick Moloney

CHILDHOOD DAYS — 1925-39

I was born on the tenth of July, 1925, the seventh child in a family of eighteen births. The house was a semi-detached cottage in Knocksouna, County Limerick, Eire. On looking back I wonder how so large a family, seven boys and six girls, survived, through an era of poverty, lacking in food, clothing, warmth and love. We had no proper sleeping arrangements, and a total lack of parental love which is every child's right. Any compassion or love we experienced was derived from each other, which accounts for the fact that we developed into a very closely knit family through some very hard times.

My parents were not to blame, their background and environment equipped them only to survive, but I cannot help feeling, their basic intelligence should have warned them against bringing so many children into a world with nothing to offer. Unfortunately their religion on the other hand encouraged this, and provided them with a clear conscience.

My father worked on the so-called second class roads, repairing and mending pot-holes and providing drainage. When he was out of work he scratched a living out of our acre of ground by digging, quarrying and breaking stones. The council then bought these for ten shillings a load, for repairing roads; needless to say, as soon as we boys could swing a hammer, we quarried and broke our quota of stones. My father was a great athlete in his younger days, especially in the local game of hurling. On the strength of this he was Kilmallock's pride and joy in all the pubs. He was also a good song and dance man who could play the melodeon, plus having a great flair for backing losers.

As a boy, I can remember looking forward to his drinking bouts, because when he returned at night, he would start cooking what he considered to be 'Irish stew'. This stew meant anything he could lay his hands on, from potatoes, turnips, cabbage, bread, eggs, lard, etc. He would throw it all into a frying pan and stew it up. Meantime he never noticed the queue of hungry faces peering from the stair banisters, waiting for the left-overs. Father never seemed to mind that it was late at night, in fact he was almost kind to us. Despite all, he was the idol of us boys, nobody could fish and poach like him. He could charm the trout out of the local river either by home-made fly, by hand, or an unconventional net. A salmon coming up the river to spawn stood no chance with him, he would use every cunning trick in the book — if there was a book — to get them on to the bank of the river.

Once I watched him putting cinders inside his trousers, from the knee down to his boots. When I enquired why, he said he was off trapping otters for their skins. He said if he was unfortunate enough to get bitten, the otters would immediately let go if they heard the cinders crackle, if not they would hang on until they heard the bones crack. He also laid night lines for the bigger trout; the only snag was, we had to be there at the crack of dawn to fish them out before the cranes got to them. This we did not mind, as it was a great thrill to see the white bellies of the trout, and the chance of getting the tail or the head for breakfast. ...

Besides teaching us all the tricks and thrills of the poaching trade, Dad would have us children sitting goggle-eyed listening to his ghost stories. Our favourite was the one about his lady-friend ghost, who when he was late-night fishing, used to join him at a certain point on the river bank and disappear at another point a mile further on. He was a great story-teller. Another of Father's pastimes was to keep thrushes and linnets as songbirds, often using crude and cruel methods to catch them. He would spread bird lime on trees, which acted as a form of glue. Sometimes he would locate a bird's nest as far as three miles from home and when the chicks hatched out, he would transfer the nest into a suitable small cage and hide it near to the nest. Every day he would move it closer and closer to home, until eventually he had the cage in a little outhouse, with the parents still feeding their young. I will always remember being amused when one of his best singing linnets died: he said it died because of a crack in the wooden roof of the cage, the bird kept squinting up at the rays of light and had died of the noodle-noodles (whatever that was).

My mother literally slaved from dawn to dusk. I cannot ever remember her being ill, or taking a rest, except when she was having a baby. Her day consisted of getting my father off to work, and getting all the children off to school, milking the goats, collecting firewood, baking bread over an open fire that had to be continually stoked and bellowed. Water had to be fetched from a well over a mile away. She was for ever patching already over-patched clothes, or converting flour bags, etc., into shirts or dresses, or dashing into the garden to dig potatoes or cut cabbage. She also spent a lot of time knitting thick black stockings for my sisters. Mum would visit the town of Killmallock, about three and a half miles away, with a donkey and cart once a fortnight. Here she would buy a ten stone bag of flour, plus a few essential groceries and, if she had enough money, a hundredweight of coal. At night she would round up her brood and, one after another, stand them in a tin bath of water and scrub off the day's dirt, and patch up the cut knees, and often broken toes too. She would dispense first-aid to boils and blisters. We would all kneel and say the family rosary; this done she would get the belt off the bellows, and the last one up the stairs had a red arse. After dispatching the children she would tend to my father's needs, he was the only one who received two cooked meals a day, and he always ate on his own, except on Sundays and Christmas Day, if he decided to come home from the pub. ...

One of our main household problems was fuel, no so much for warmth as for baking and cooking. The result was all we children were experts in raiding the local countryside for sticks and wood of any description. It was commonplace to see a youngster carrying what we called a 'bart' of sticks tied with a rope for four or five miles, dodging the farmers and finding the easiest route home. On some occasions we would take a hand-saw and prune quite a few trees, cutting the wood up into short pieces. We would then conceal it all and all traces of our work, and return back at night to fetch the wood home. We needed very little persuasion to maintain a good supply, it was a case of no firewood — no bread. Weather conditions did not make any difference. Another source of fuel in the autumn, was cow dung which, over a large area of grazing land, we would visit and expertly turn upside down to dry, to be collected a few days later. This used to burn better than peat. Needless to say, the farmers did not approve of us depriving them of such a good fertiliser from their lands. ...

I visited the old cottage recently with my family, and was amazed how small it is. It consisted of two bedrooms and a living-room downstairs. Upstairs was just a loft where we all slept, with the exception of our parents, who occupied the downstairs bedroom. This room contained what might be termed the only decent bed in the house. It also contained the all-important cupboard, or press as it was called in Ireland. This cupboard was locked and it held all the tea, sugar and bread, etc, and woe betide anybody who went near it. My mother guarded the key of the press like the crown jewels. We used to swear she kept the key in her red flannel drawers. Of importance, were all the racing papers kept under the mattress on Dad's side of the bed from which he studied form.

The living-room-come kitchen, come bathroom, come everything else, was about fifteen feet by nine feet. It had an open fireplace, which had a swinging arm, where hung the boiling and baking pots. The kitchen also contained three wooden chairs, a wooden table, an oil lamp and a sacred heart picture on the wall. It had a concrete floor, a main door, and a half door. In one corner under the stairs was the coal hole, which also served as a punishment cell. On either side of the fire were the two hobs; those were the most popular seats, on the occasional get-together round the fire, when there was a ghost story to be listened to. I can still recall when going up the stairs after the stories, seeing my brothers' and sisters' eyes large with fright, petrified, and seeing ghosts everywhere. ...

On rare occasions in the summer-time we would go as a whole family for a walk along the river bank. On one of these walks my father stopped and called us together near a very deep pool with a steep bank. Without any warning or further ado he threw three of us boys in the water. This threw my mother into a wild panic; she called all the saints in heaven to save us from drowning. The only consoling words Father gave her were, 'Will you hold your whist, they will learn to swim before they go down for the third time!' and we did! With a pat on the back, 'Ah, you are handy lads,' the walk was resumed....

All our toys were mainly home-made. For guns we shaped pieces of wood, and brass corners of a lady's old-fashioned purse we called revolvers. Easter and Christmas were outstanding occasions. Easter, because we got two or more hen's eggs to ourselves, and Christmas because my mother made a special effort and we got at least one toy each. It was not much, mainly a toy car for each boy and dolls for the girls. There was no hanging up of stockings, as there were no stockings to hang up, and Santa Claus was someone who visited the more well-to-do children. Christmas dinner was also a great treat, as it meant a really square meal. It usually consisted of a goose and the sacrifice of a few precious ducks, and this would be followed by a currant cake and a few sweets. Father would be in good form in the evening. He would play the melodeon, sing to us and entertain us with tap-dancing at which he excelled. I can recall he could play any musical instrument on which he could lay his hands. He would hear a tune sung, whistled or played and when he came home, would demand a paper and pencil and immediately write down the music he had heard. He was obviously a born musician.

Family feuds were another form of excitement. The venom and hatred displayed over the most childish and ridiculous issues, were a source of amazement to me, even as a boy. I must have expressed my views, because I was often cast in the role of a disloyal rogue. Where did Christianity begin and religion end? We would all be down on our knees saying the rosary one minute and wishing fire and brimstone on our neighbours the next!

As a young boy, I recall, I very seldom had a good night's sleep. I used to be frightened , lying there in a cold sweat, hallucinating about apparitions passing by my bed. Daylight was a blessing, with the terror of darkness past. In retrospect, I suppose, it was my child's mind reacting to the threats of the 'bogey man', ghost stories, and insecurity through a lack of reassuring love, fear of God and fear of the devil. Religion was instilled through fear and damnation by priests and missionaries who would make Hitler's Gestapo look like choirboys. I never really understood religion. I went to mass every Sunday, but I did not have a clue what it was all about. I accepted it and reacted to it like you would to military discipline. ...

For some reason unknown to me, my father hated his brother Mick, and hostilities permeated through both families. I heard it said that it all started because Mick cheated my father out of a legacy of £800 left by a relative from the USA. Mick at this stage had a grown up family of six boys, whom I never got to know very well. It all started with a slanging match of taunts and threats by Dad, who was spoiling for a fight. Eventually Mick supported by four of his sons appeared at the cross. Dad, supported only by James, my elder brother, advanced upon them and fists flew in all directions. Dad and James eventually returned home, bloodied but satisfied that honour had been restored. ...

I cannot remember whether it was when the twelfth or thirteenth child was born, but I can recall one of our neighbours saying to my father, 'Jim, isn't it time you stopped? The poor woman cannot stand it!' Father replied, and a tear actually appeared in his eye, 'What can one do, when you share the same bed together?' I piped up in all innocence that Father could have my corner of the big bed upstairs. Needless to say, I received an Irish brogue on the backside which elevated me over a small wall, and into the only bit of flower garden we had. I received another belting then for breaking the flowers.

On one occasion when we were fishing in the big flood he hooked a big trout; in the excitement that ensued, I fell into the river. To my amazement he continued to play the trout leaving me to flounder and force my way to safety.

When I told him I could easily have drowned, all he said was, 'God blast you — go home out of my way, I nearly lost that trout over you!' As an afterthought he added, 'He put up a great fight'. ...

As time marched on the elder members of the family reached their teens, and went out to service with farmers. This work resembled a slave market, the farmers and parents of those eligible for work would congregate in the town of Kilmallock just after Christmas, and the deals were clinched on a twelve month basis. The young worker would then be told to whom he was assigned and the conditions to which they were subject; these differed, depending on whether the worker was a boy or a girl. A boy would be told how much he was hired for, not that it made any difference what his opinions were; it was out of his control and he had no say in the matter. The boy was also instructed how he was to behave and that he should do everything that his employer would ask of him. The girls had more severe instructions and left for their future employment locked up in mental chastity belts, and if the material chastity belts were missing, their clogs, thick black stockings and frumpish clothes were a good substitute. There were no such luxuries in the young working life as holidays or time off. It was seven days a week from dawn to dusk with a few hours off to go to church on Sundays. If the girls had wanted to misbehave they could not do so, they just did not have the time. How they ever managed to maintain their femininity is a miracle. I remember by eldest sister cleaning her teeth, and my father's remark was, 'Look at the hussy — what next, she will be painting her arse black and going mad'. If the girls tried to pretty themselves up, they were ridiculed and suspected of foul play immediately, and so were the boys for that matter, basic hygiene like teeth cleaning was frowned upon.

The family had now begun to break into groups, mainly because of age differences. One such group was Michael who was two years older than myself and Tommy, who was one year younger than me, and of course myself. The older members were planning to break away from the slavery which stared them in the face for the rest of their lives. My eldest sister was the first to head across the Irish Sea for London. This was no doubt prompted by a gallant attempt by my father to marry her off to a dim-witted middle-aged peasant, because he was the owner of a very, very small holding. He was the type who wore a cloth cap pulled down over one ear, thin as a bean pole and thought he was God's gift to all women in his cycle clips. My sister was young, very attractive, with a bubbling personality. I can still hear her derisive laughter when, in all seriousness, my parents promised her a new bicycle if she would go through with it. It is difficult to understand their logic. The sentiment of love did not enter into it, she might as well have gone to bed with a hedgehog!

So Kitty set the pattern, the emigration and scatter was about to begin. I remember the third youngest sister putting out tentative feelers about going to England, and my father swearing black and blue, she would never see Euston Station: but she did and was followed by others. ...

As I approached my thirteenth birthday, my father decided I had enough schooling and much to my delight took me away from school to put me to work full-time in the 'pit', breaking stones. This state of affairs did not last long as the law soon reminded my parents that I had to continue school until I was fourteen years of age, and most reluctantly and sulking I returned and completed another year, to leave not very much more the wiser.

In summing up, all that could be said for my six years of school was that I could read and write.

Pat Boran

HOUSE

Water clanks from the tap
like a chain — a lifetime

since anything has moved here
but rats and birds. I see

the last inhabitants as a father
and son, the father

sending the son off to the city
with a handshake and a pocket

of old pound notes.
He might as well be sending him

to bring home the time
without a watch to carry it.

Paddy The Cope

MY STORY

When I could not save any money to send home I stopped writing. Then I began to get letters from my sister Annie, appealing to me to come home, saying my mother and father would go out of their wits if I did not write by return.

I would then make up my mind to write home on Saturday and send a £1 or perhaps £2. We were paid every Friday but when we got washed and dressed all the boys went to McCormick's if the evening was wet (we had no other place to go) and began to drink beer, it was cheap — then only 1/- a half gallon. Next day, Saturday, instead of writing home I went with the lads to see Celtic play. On Monday I had no £1 to send home. I had not the courage to send an empty letter, this went on for a long time.

On a Thursday when I came in from the pit I saw my father sitting in the kitchen. He did not know me. I was as black as soot. It was a dirty, dusty pit and all the colliers were as black as niggers, coming home. Well, God forgive me, I did not like to see my father. However, I went up to him and said, 'Father' and caught his hand. He looked at me for a long time and held my hand tightly, and then said, 'It's you, Paddy', the tears flowing from his eyes.

When I got washed and all the lodgers welcomed my father, I went out to Mrs McCormick's and got a bottle of whiskey on tick. I gave the first glass to my father and I shoved the rest around the house. After we had our dinner, Willy Laffy said, 'Come boys, it is not everyday that Paddy's father will be here, come with me'. We all followed Willy to Mrs McCormick's. He ordered a half gallon of beer, a lot of the other colliers gathered in, and many a half gallon of beer was ordered. Spud Murphy got up and sang 'The Bonny Banks of Loch Lomond'. Heavens, he was no sooner sitting than my father got up and sang 'Come Back to Erin'. I think I hear the applause still, although I was crying. O! Such a night!

He slept in my bed that night; although he had a good few in him he prayed for a long time. I said a few wee ones too. When we were in bed he said, 'Paddy, if we were at home, your mother would be angry with us for going to bed without saying the Rosary. We will go home tomorrow; your mother is waiting hard for us'. I said, 'Father,

I can't go home now. I promise you sure I'll go at Christmas'. He said, 'Well Paddy, your mother told me not to come back without you, and I'm not going to, I'll look for a job in the morning and will wait until Christmas, and then in God's name, we will go home together. God, but your mother and the children will be glad for us'. We soon fell asleep.

On Friday morning, I told the Pit Manager I was leaving and would like to get my 'lying time', that my father came from Ireland for me and wanted me to go home. He said, 'All right,' so I picked up my 'greath' (tools) and called at the office. I had £2. 12s. 6d. for the week and £2. 15s. lying time. Before I went to the lodging I went into McCormick's and paid for the bottle of whiskey. Mrs McCormick filled up a glass for me. I did not take it. I was fully determined to be away somewhere early on Saturday morning before my father would rise so that he could not trace me.

We are all in McCormick's on Friday night. No one, not even Willie Laffy could make me put anything to my lips. My father took a few but if you killed him he would not sing for them. We went home early as I wanted to be up early next morning.

My father said, 'Paddy, we will say the Rosary'. We popped on our knees and said the Rosary. When we finished I said my three Hail Mary's, and went to bed, none of us spoke for a long time. Suddenly, I said 'Father, I have no money, but I am going home with you'. He lifted up his hand and said, 'Thank you God for hearing Nancy's (my mother) prayers'. He then put his arms around me and did not say another word. I am sure if I were offered the pit and all Scotland, aye, and Ireland, to hide on my father next morning, I could not do it.

Malachi Horan Remembers

There is no doubt but my father was the hard-working man. All the same, when he was not working he liked to show himself off. He was a fine figure of a man. Anyone would have thought that to have seen him on the Mass-path beyond of a Sunday. When he dressed himself he would wear the felt half-tall hat which was known here as 'a nailer's chimney'. He would wear a 'trusty', or, as you would call it, a cotamore — the name the people had on it hereabout was a 'bang up'. This was a frieze coat that reached the ankles and which had attached to it a cape to the wrists. It was heavy but very warm — a first rate protection when driving. Beneath the coat he wore corduroy or moleskin breeches above grey stockings . ...

The Mass-paths? They were the start of half the rights-of-way in the country. They were often the start of trouble, too. The landlords hated them. They were just short cuts for the people and they going to Mass. There is one by the door here that runs from Killenarden to Callaghan's Bridge, nigh on Bohernabreena. In my father's time the landlord here — McGrane it was — tried to close the way. He was a sore man on the tenants. But my father and some of the neighbours got the law of it. They were advised to pull down every fence he put on the path, and that when he took away the stepping-stones over the stream to put them back at once. This they did time and again. After many a row they won their way. McGrane was beat. There was a poet — Frank Sheridan — who lived on the hill here and who wrote a ballad on the head of it. I have only one verse of it now:

Success to Pat Horan and likewise Miley Keogh
Who never flinched a single inch
But travelled to and fro.
Some went round the limekiln way,
More went by Bradley's Lane;
And some of them they stayed at home
For fear they'd vex McGrane.

It was at the head of this path that my father was near put to the loss of his life by the Whitefeet. ... They were a secret society with the same ideas about tenant-right as the Ribbonmen. I could never see a difference between the two. Both societies had about half-and-half members around here and Tallaght.

My father was always a hard-working man, but a man of spirit too. Perhaps he would have died as readily for the country as any man. But he was never ready to take orders from every gang who took it on themselves to lead the people. He just minded his own business and let the leaders of the land mind theirs. Some of the Whitefeet were angry with him either for standing apart, or perhaps they were like many another, just land-grabbers itching to have him out of the way. Howsomever, they made up their minds to think that he had been acting the informer against them. That is what they gave out, anyway.

I remember well him telling as how it was a dark November evening when he struck up the Mass-path for Killenarden. The wind had rain in it, and the cold struck into his sides like spurs. The weather had put every soul indoors before him. Suddenly, as he came to Ballamallick, a dozen men stepped out from the back of a ditch. One said:

'We want you, Horan. You know us! We're the Whitefeet. So you would inform on us, would you? Well, let me tell you this, you have earned your last blood-money.'

My father knew every man-jack of them, but he had never seen this look in their faces before. It spoke death to him. He saw they were all armed, but he faced up to them, and answered:

'And why should I inform on you? And what have I to inform? I know every one of you and you me. If one of you did me an injury, would I not have a short way with you, answer me that? If I sold you, wouldn't every man of you know as soon as myself I had money about my place, tell me that? Would you send me to my God without showing proof or facing me with my accuser? Are ye men at all, at all, or what are ye?'

At this they looked at each other a bit foolish. But one of them — Billy Moore it was — persisted: 'Oh, he'd heard this and he'd seen that and he knew the other.' But the rest stood fast; they said 'No', they would give him trial.

They marched my father back of the dyke where they would not be seen. He was told to choose a jury, and he picked six. One of the others, decent man, offered to act in his defence. Billy Moore set himself to prosecute. Their leader was made judge by him standing on a stone with his back to the dyke.

It was a shocking time for my father, standing there watching while the dying light showed the anger in their faces and the arms in their hands. They argued the case and fought with each other like the hedge-lawyers they were, but my father had really won when he first showed them that he was a true man. The judge found in his favour, and told him to go home. As he went he heard them warn him not to open his grave with his mouth.

A short while after, my father hired Billy Moore to work about the farm here. He was the one, you remember, who had wanted to shoot my father

One day, after asking me could I hold my tongue, he told me all about Moore and of what happened of Ballamallick Hill. God save us, what a fright he gave me! I asked him how could he have such a man in the place and him craving his death. My father answered quietly:

'Let you remember, Malachi, if you have an enemy and him free to harm you, contrive it that your eye is never off him. Put him, if you can, where his daily bread will depend on you. Keep him closer nor a friend. You will be safe as long as you can so keep him.'

One night we were sitting in the kitchen here. My father was where I am sitting; Moore there, where you are, and I beyond by the churn. We were saying nothing, just waiting for the supper. Whether it was the comfort of the fire or the safe feeling of a house, or that his memory had got a jog by something through the day, at any rate my father turned on the minute to Moore, and said:

'Well for you, William Moore, that you are not sitting there to-night with blood on your hands and its sin on your soul. You have hate in you yet. It is a wonder what saved you that night on Ballamallick Hill beyond!'

'Ah, Mr. Horan,' growled Moore, 'sure, will you let bygones be bygones. Why would you be remembering trifles?' *He* was a *right* one, was Billy Moore.

The next morning as he was hedging up there at the back of the haggard I went up to him and said:

'If you had served me as you tried to serve my father you would not be labouring this farm to-day, or perhaps any other farm.' I thought he would strike me with the slasher, but, instead, he just looked at me very knowingly.

'Maybe and maybe not,' he answered. 'But I'll tell you this: *you* will never be the man your father is. Maybe some day you'll wear his shoes, but you'll never have the head to fill his hat.'

Maybe it was what he did to my father, and maybe it was what he thought of me; what everway it was, I never spoke to him from that to the day he died. I was only a chap when all that happened. ...

Patrick Campbell

MY LIFE AND EASY TIMES

My mother said to me on the telephone from Dublin, 'I don't want to talk too loudly because I think he can hear me, but you'd better come over. He had a bad night and he's very feeble'.

I said I'd come at once.

I found I was neither shocked nor sad, but only excited. My father, Lord Glenavy, was going to die. It would be an event of some importance in Dublin and I, as the inheritor of the title, would be playing a leading part in it.

At this moment it wasn't possible to guess what the effect of his death would be. Death to me was an unknown quantity.

My sister had been killed in a flying bomb towards the end of the war in London, but we hadn't seen one another for a long time. The only emotion I could remember was a disgruntled feeling of waste. Her husband was killed at the same time and they hadn't been married long enough to have any children, so that one of the things I wasn't going to be was an uncle. But behind this familiar selfishness was the grey melancholy of knowing I'd never see my sister again.

I supposed I'd feel the same kind of thing about the Lord if, indeed, he was going to die. He'd already made, at the age of seventy-eight, an astonishing recovery from a major abdominal operation and when I'd last seen him a couple of months ago he'd been talking about playing golf again and buying a small boat.

No one ever spoke of the reason for the operation. The Lord himself called it, with a cheerful good humour that didn't look faked, 'Just straightening out the guts'. Perhaps he really didn't know, but everyone else could only believe it was cancer. The Old Lord had died of it, too, although he was eighty-eight.

They were always known in the family, and to the few close friends who ventured into it, as the Lord and the Old Lord. My mother, however, referred to my father as Gordon and his sister called him Charlie, while my brother and I spoke to him as Lordship. His infrequent letters to us were signed in the same way.

I know, for my part, that this use of 'the Lord' and 'Lordship' in place of 'my father' or 'Daddy' was to relieve us of an intimacy that would have been embarrassing to both. The Lord liked to keep everyone at a safe distance from him and particularly those that he didn't know well. Whenever I brought new friends to the house he'd refer to them for months afterwards as 'the Paul' or 'the David', de-personalising them for curious reasons of his own. Once the 'the' was dropped they were in.

And now it seemed that he was dying, and I was going to have to face the fact of his death. But all that I had at this moment was the feeling of excitement, of much to be done, of taking over the leadership of the family. ...

Hundreds of people all over Ireland — businessmen, farmers, trades union officials, cattle dealers, industrialists, politicians — all of them certainly knew more about my father's commercial capabilities than I did.

All that I knew of his working life had been what I'd read in my mother's voluminous scrap books, cuttings of every kind which she'd kept since the first war.

I knew that he'd been a barrister in London before 1914, and during the war had worked under Churchill in the Ministry of Munitions. I knew, like his father, who'd become Lord Chancellor of Ireland and later Chairman of the first Irish Senate, that he could have had what is always called a brilliant career at the English bar, but that he'd given it up and come home to Ireland to do what he could to assist the first Irish Government under President Cosgrave. In this he became Parliamentary Secretary to the Ministry of Industry and Commerce, a job he held until Cosgrave lost the election to de Valera.

This return to Ireland had always seemed to me to be a strange sacrifice for a man who liked being successful and who had enjoyed in the literary life of London the serious, cultivated kind of discussion that he never really found in sufficient measure in Dublin.

In fact, he frequently railed against 'the cretinous slobs who pass for people of intelligence in Ireland'. Once, when I asked him, 'Why did you come back here, then?' he shook his head — an instinctive gesture that said the question was out of order.

The truth was, of course, that he'd come back to Ireland because he loved Ireland, and loved the idea of taking part in the formation of what he thought of, romantically, as being a new and ideal Free State. One of the first tastes he got of the new and ideal Free State was when the IRA burnt down our house on Christmas Eve, 1922, and it seemed for a long half hour that they were going to execute him on his own front lawn.

I never knew how he made the transition from politics to business. I must have been at school in England when it happened, or at Oxford or in Germany, but when I came home again the Lord was a director of the Bank of Ireland, Chairman of the Great Northern Railway and of the Royal Hibernian Insurance Company, and on the board of a number of other companies he never mentioned.

I formed the idea — and literally formed it, almost out of nothing, because I had to have one — that he was a kind of financial mystic or seer, the kind of genius who can be shown the balance sheet of an unknown company and can diagnose its ills an hour later.

Mysterious figures from the world of international finance would occasionally come to the house on Sunday evenings. Large, weighty Swedes or silent Englishmen with big foreheads. More often than not my mother, by her own passionate enthusiasm, would draw them into some discussion of painting or the theatre in which everyone except the Lord would join.

With increasing frequency he'd sit by himself at the window, looking bored and more and more resentful of what he'd come to describe as 'women's kitchen gossip'. Soon, we were able to identify 'kitchen gossip' as any form of emotional communication, any expression of subjective opinion that was not based upon knowledge or reasoned thought.

Once, trying to compensate the Lord for a particularly bitter and silent evening, I asked him, 'Why do all these experts from the World Bank or whatever it is come all the way to Dublin to see you?' He gave the self-deprecating grin that wasn't deprecatory at all and said, 'They come to get straightened out'.

Probably much of his time in the Bank of Ireland was spent in wondering whether to allow a farmer in Mullingar to increase his overdraft by another £1000 or in trying to talk the bank clerk's leaders out of another strike, but I do believe he had a visionary sense of money. It was his form of art, a desire to see money irrigating the affairs of individuals or companies to the best possible effect. In exchange for this service, however, he never seemed to receive very much of it for himself.

For as long as I can remember the family lived in considerable comfort — on the very edge of bankruptcy. An unnecessary shovelful of coal on the fire, or the stove left on in an empty bedroom, would bring on the Lord's grim look and the statement, 'You people simply don't understand the value of money'. My mother often said, 'The Lord's always telling me I'll be scrubbing floors in the workhouse but I wouldn't mind at all. I've been scrubbing floors all my life.

'This refusal to be depressed by the constant threats of bankruptcy seemed to the Lord to be the essence of feeble-mindedness and irresponsibility, and then he'd go to the races or buy a new, if modest, car.

We never knew where we were, and the Lord's certainty that we were incapable of understanding the fearful position we were in meant that he never took the trouble to explain it in any realistic detail.

In this he was abetted by Archie Robinson, who'd been the family solicitor for as long as anyone could remember. But Archie was more than a solicitor. He was the silent, dedicated guardian of the lifeblood of the family. It always seemed to me that the whole of his working day, every day, must have been concerned exclusively with our affairs, whatever they might be. In this, he and the Lord were one, and particularly in the belief that there was no point in inviting interest or understanding on the part of the rest of us.

The only other person I knew of who had the Lord's confidence in matters of money was Willy Ganly, despite the fact that Willy was at least twenty years younger.

He was one of a huge family of Ganlys, most of whom were in the cattle business in Dublin. He'd first come into the Lord's life as a friend of mine and particularly as a friend of my sister, Biddy.

Willy was direct and forceful and a very astute businessman. Like my father, he loved fishing and any kind of outdoor life. He was also incorruptibly honest, a quality that the Lord admired, in business, above all others. Before long, he took Willy into the Bank of Ireland as the youngest director the Bank had ever had. In one day Willy said of my father, 'He's the only completely incorruptible banker I've ever known', and my father said of Willy, 'You could trust him with your very last shilling'.

Though Willy and I were close friends I never learnt anything from him about the hidden, commercial side of my father's life. It was as though he had complete respect for the Lord's certainty that his wife and children were incurable imbeciles where money was concerned. And I have no doubt that this unquestioning respect, as much as Willy's outstanding qualities, went a long way to warm the Lord towards him. Unquestioning respect was not one of the things he enjoyed in his own household. ...

[Once] at home in Dublin the Lord was becoming more and more concerned about my future and, after a minor motor accident, went so far as to give me a formal lecture, becoming a conventionally stern parent for the very first and the very last time.

I was going out to play tennis when he intercepted me in the hall. 'Come in here a minute', he said. 'I want to talk to you.'

I said I couldn't, that friends were waiting for me down the road.

'It won't take long', he said. I'd never seen him looking so stern, or so sad.

It was not a memorable address. He was too unhappy to be angry, and I think he was sorry that he'd chosen this particular moment. It was a Sunday afternoon and he was wearing his tattered gardening clothes, while I sat opposite him in white flannels and a red, white and blue Old Rossallian blazer.

Neither of us looked like people ready to buckle-to to the serious business of earning a living, but that was the main theme of the Lord's address.

'I'm not criticising you', he began. 'You must understand that. And I'm not asking you to give up any of your pleasures. I love playing games myself. But you must really begin to think about what you are going to do for a living. I've only got what I earn and if anything happened to me I don't know what you'd all do for money.'

I felt frozen, and bored. I'd heard all this business about approaching bankruptcy so often before.

I closed my ears and my heart and my mind, a process of combating criticism, however helpful and affectionate, that was going to become increasingly familiar later on.

It was the same thing as my regarding anger as a waste of time. It was a lovely afternoon. A moment before I'd been rushing off to play tennis, and now everything had stopped.

I sat there, aggressively silent, looking my father straight in the eye. I could think of nothing whatever to say.

'It's getting to be a very competitive world', my father went on. 'You've got to have some kind of background of knowledge, some sort of diploma, if you're going to get a job that'll give you enough to live on.'

It seemed to be so self-evident I could only imagine that it gave him pleasure to trot out all this old stuff. I couldn't think of any reply to it except to mutter from time to time, 'Yes, of course. Yes, I can well see that.'

'I'm honestly not criticising you', my father went on, 'but you don't really seem to be trying to do anything yourself. One of the bank directors said he'd seen you with the car in the ditch and he said, "I see your young hopeful's been at it again."'

The poor Lord grinned, trying to ease his own hurt.

So that was where he'd heard about the accident. 'It was nothing', I said. 'This madman came shooting out of a side road and pushed me into the ditch. The car's perfectly all right. I'll touch up the paintwork myself. You don't have to bother about that.'

This stung the Lord almost to anger. 'It's your whole attitude', he said. 'You don't really seem to care about anything. If only you'd tell me what you want to do I'm sure I can help you. I know a lot of people in Dublin. They'd be only too glad to do something for — '

He paused. I thought he wanted to say — 'for Lord Glenavy's son' — emphasising, without immodesty, the respect in which he was held.

He changed it to — 'for you'.

I relented, became a little more generous. 'That's very kind of you', I said. 'But it's very difficult', I went on, 'to know what sort of thing I ought to do'.

I shifted the blame. 'I never really seem to have been trained for anything,' I said. 'At least, you were a lawyer, to begin with.'

He let me get away with it. 'I know how hard it is for you', he said. 'But if you had an inclination towards doing any kind of job I'm sure I could get you started.' He grinned again. 'Have you ever thought about it at all?' he said.

I couldn't let him think I had no ambition of any kind. 'Well,' I said, I've been thinking for some time I'd like to be a writer'.

I was frightened to go on. At long last I'd produced a suggestion for my own future, but it was underhand. I told my father I'd like to be a writer because he had known Shaw and Lawrence, Middleton Murry and Robert Lynd, and because he'd written a play himself. It would surely please him, and relieve me of his concern. But it seemed to be a fearful commitment. I felt I'd have to begin to learn how to be a writer the very next day.

The Lord wasn't as pleased as I thought he'd be. 'Writing's a precarious profession', he said. 'It would be years before you were earning a decent screw.'

I thought he sounded like his own father, using an old-fashioned expression like 'a decent screw'. I thought it proved he was out of touch with the modern world of newspapers, books and magazines.

'I've met some very interesting people at Oxford', I said, telling him a lie he couldn't disprove. 'One of them's already written a novel and two more are going to join the *Daily Express* as soon as they go down.' I had a sudden inspiration. 'Wasn't the Old Lord a great friend of Beaverbrook's?' I said. 'There might be an opening there.'

'I don't think you'd be cut out for that sort of world', my father said, trying urgently to damp down the idea before it took too firm a hold on me. 'You'd never be able to do any reporting. I mean, you couldn't use the telephone with your stammer.'

'It wouldn't have to be a reporting job', I said. 'There are all kinds of other things, like articles and so on.'

I had a moment of conviction that I knew was completely fictitious. 'I just know', I said, 'that some kind of writing is the only thing I want to do'.

The Lord looked deeply troubled, almost as though he felt he was worse off than ever.

'It might be a useful sideline', he said. 'But in the meantime you really ought to think seriously about the Foreign Office idea.'

I couldn't believe we'd got back to the Foreign Office again, when I'd gone out of my way, for the first time, to make a definite proposal for my future.

'I'll do that, of course', I said. But in the meantime, when I get back to Oxford I'll check up on the Beaverbrook thing with these two chaps who are going to join him.'

At that moment, though I'd invented them, I could see them and hear them talking to me. 'They tell me', I said to my father, 'that the Beaver's always looking for — for likely lads'.

I found for the first time that I was able to grin myself. Nearly all the earlier clouds had been thrust away.

'I'd better get along now', I said, getting to my feet and picking up my racquet. 'I want to try out my new spinning service with loop and kick-back.'...

But this wasn't the kind of thing I wanted to remember, standing on the rocks at the Forty Foot, looking out at Dublin Bay where we'd sailed every Saturday afternoon before the war, racing in an old 21-foot cutter called the *Garavogue*. The Lord would never give up, even long after the evening breeze had died away into a flat calm and the ebb had begun to carry us south past Dalkey Island, getting farther and farther away every minute from the finishing line in Dun Laoghaire Harbour. 'We'll just hang on a bit longer', he'd always say. 'There'll be a puff of wind sooner or later.'

My sister and I, with a party to go to in Dublin, would beg him to let us get the sweeps out and row ourselves back into the harbour, and the Lord would put on his grim and injured look. Once again we were being irresponsible and feebleminded.

He loved sailing and was for ever inventing methods of marking the sheets with coloured thread so that, after we'd won a race, almost entirely by luck, we'd be able to reproduce the same winning trim again.

He had a passion for games of every kind and, failing the proper equipment, he would improvise a completely new one out of an old biscuit tin, a piece of wood and a tennis ball and play it with a fanatical regard for the rules which we invented as we went along.

He could read three detective stories in an evening with such complete absorption that he might have been under a general anaesthetic and when he'd finished them he could give you neither a glimmering of the plots nor the name of a single character. He relied on the girls in Switzers Library to give him one he hadn't read before and when they slipped up he'd read as many as twenty pages before realising what had happened. ...

Once, he astonished me by saying, 'When it comes to kissing the Campbells run away'. In his case it was almost certainly true.

Or perhaps it wasn't.

I never really knew him at all.

I never knew whether he was disappointed to find that neither my brother Michael nor I had any capacity for business or banking. Michael did make an attempt at a professional career by being called to the Irish Bar, after studying law in Trinity, but he never practised. Like myself, he was eased into a job on the *Irish Times* by the Lord, who was an old friend of the editor, Robert Smyllie. Indeed, if it hadn't been for the *Irish Times*, it's difficult to tell what would have become of either of his sons.

Yet the Lord's disappointment — if disappointed he was — never took the conventional, demanding form. He did say to me once that he should perhaps have been fiercer with me, making me train for a profession, and with Michael, compelling him to go on with the law. But being fierce with people was never his way. I think he laid out in his mind an ideal course of behaviour for everyone he knew and cared about and felt personally injured when they failed to live up to it. And to get them back on the rails he used persuasion so oblique and delicate, and with such concern for their *amour propre*, that it was often difficult to perceive that the process was going on at all. ...

It seems to be extraordinary, looking back upon it now, but on the night of my father's death my mother and I, and Marjorie, went to a party — a wedding reception for Willy Ganly's daughter, Clodagh.

There wasn't any discussion about it. We just went.

The party took place in a hotel about a mile away. There must have been a hundred or more people, nearly all of whom I'd known for years, and yet I can't remember one of them speaking to me about my father, who'd died that afternoon at three-thirty. Willy must have told some of them about it, yet no one mentioned his name.

Or perhaps I wasn't aware of it. I was still totally preoccupied with the business of trying to file away, permanently, everything I could remember about him, in the hope that by doing so I could fill in the enormous gaps in my knowledge of what he had been, and of what he had done. ...

I found my mother and Marjorie standing beside me. They looked strained and exhausted. It had been a long day. I said, 'We'll have a quick dinner downstairs in the restaurant and then we'll go home'.

It was better than sitting down to eat in our own dining-room, with whatever the nurse had left behind in the bed upstairs. ...

The restaurant was full, but the head waiter said he would have a table for us in a few minutes, if we'd like to have a drink at the bar.

'What name is it, sir?' he said to me.

Neither my mother nor Marjorie looked at me, but the three of us knew that this was the time — the very first time — to try it out.

'Lord —' I said, and then my stammer came against me. It was an appreciable second or two before I could say, 'Glenavy'.

'Thank you, my lord', said the head waiter, and went away.

My mother gave a little laugh that might have been the product as much of pride as of embarrassment.

'You'd better get used to being it,' she said. ...

But I knew I never would. I knew now with certainty that my father had been the last, real Lord Glenavy, as his father before him had been a real Lord. They had been great men, with soberly distinguished careers, who by large and public services had merited, in full, the honours and dignities that had come to them.

The disagreeable glow of self-importance had altogether gone.

To keep up my own end as Patrick Campbell would be the best I could manage from now on, and however good it turned out to be I knew I could never take over from the second Baron Glenavy, even if I lived, like him, to be almost eighty years of age.

Nor did I, any longer, feel like the head of the family. The sense of being the busy, efficient organiser and arranger had gone. From now on the most that I was there to do was to try to help my mother.

Gerry McDonnell

PIETA

Bored, I waited for you,
kicking the car tyres
one empty Sunday,
lonelier by the roar from Croke Park.
In the waking state
we missed each other by a mile.
When you were finally
in your hospital bed
I tried to wait around a while
and opportunely fled.

Dreams compensate for life,
we can't distinguish between the two,
one flows into the other.
Years later I am stronger
in the dream —
you'd fallen down unconscious
on a street where we'd never meet.
I held you in my arms
son holding the father.

David Hanly

THE SWEET SORROW
OF RECONCILED PARTINGS
from The Sunday Tribune, July 1991

A friend of mine spent two years in a seminary before deciding that the life and work of a Christian Brother were not for him. It was not uncommon for young men to make decisions which proved hasty and ill judged: our own society has been greatly enriched by those who found themselves unsuited to the priesthood and left without taking orders. And nowadays, no doubt, there is no disgrace in deciding that one is unworthy of or unsuited to the priesthood or brotherhood.

But there was a time when the young man who had 'failed' found himself a pariah on his return home. In many cases, his life was made a misery; in many other cases, in the knowledge that this would be so, there was no going home at all, and haste was made for the bitter boat to England. At the time when my friend realised that he did not have a vocation, there was still disgrace attached, and when he returned to his home his father stood in the doorway, looked at him coldly, and told him to go away: 'There is no welcome for you here.' And my friend left, for a life that took many turns and included a later meeting with his father which constituted a kind of reconciliation. But the fact was that there never was true reconciliation: my friend knew it needed to be done, but somehow never managed to summon what was necessary to do it; by the time he did, it was too late, and his father went to his grave still a stranger to his son.

I relate this story not to cast judgment on the kind of father who would shut the door in the face of his own son just because he had changed his mind: God knows it strikes me as a most cruel thing, but he was a man of his time. No. What pained me, and still pains me, is the thought of a father dying unreconciled with his son, and the thought of the dreadful burden that the son must bear through the rest of his life.

On the night that he told me his story, I had just received news of the death of my own father. I was happy for his release from increasing wretchedness and loss of dignity, and I will handle the inevitable sadness in my own way and as best I can. I might say at once that, unlike my friend, I never had the door shut in my face. Although I made many decisions in my life that must surely have perplexed and maybe even angered my father, I was never made aware of it; the door remained open, giving hand and heart never faltered, judgment was never once pronounced. To be sure, I knew his faults with a terrible intimacy, because he passed them on to me, a legacy I could have done without, and against whose manifestations I battle every day.

But I also knew and appreciated his virtues, his strength, his sense of privacy, his utter probity, his loyalty to his friends. His sense of what was right and wrong must, I suppose, have been grounded at least to some extent in his religion, which was a solid capstan throughout his life, but I always felt it to be something innate; it may be foolish of me to think it, but it always seemed to me that he was born knowing what was right and what was wrong, and did not need to invoke any doctrine to bolster his convictions.

He didn't speak to us much. It was that typical Irish thing, a father and son not really speaking to each other, not really knowing each other. He worked as a commercial traveller with Matterson's. It was a famous old bacon and canning factory in Limerick. They used to send ham to the Tsar of Russia; I remember coming across the invoices one summer when I was a fourteen-year-old working there. But was I close to him? No. I loved him and I admired him, but I didn't really know him. He didn't have that much to say. People used to remark on his honesty, he was the treasurer of everything he ever joined . . . Johnny Hanly was very honest.

Well, he's gone now, and the sense of loss is as natural as death itself. But it is greatly eased by this knowledge: that long before he died, I was able to summon what was necessary to tell him, in public and in private, how much I loved and admired him, and how grateful I was for everything he had done for me and given me. Irish family life has many virtues, but emotional openness is not among them. It is, I believe, a curse of our culture that we find ourselves unable to tell those closest to us how much we care; expressions of love, gratitude and admiration, which should flow naturally between us, rather make us squirm. My father was as much a victim of this syndrome as any other of his generation: he was content to show rather than to express. But expression is important too, as I know too well, having failed miserably and repeatedly to put it into practice down through the years. In the case of my father, though, I did find that kind of maturity which overcame my foolish fears. He did not die in doubt. I am glad of that.

Aside from favoured writers, the two men who continually feature in David Hanly's conversation, are his late father and his brother, the songwriter Mick Hanly, formerly of Moving Hearts: 'I'm very happy to be now known as

Mick Hanly's brother. Medicine Man is a wonderful allegory about our father.'

Mick Hanly

MEDICINE MAN

I have a small time Medicine Show
I dress in hat, waistcoat and bow
Don't have the cure, no just the placebo
I come to town with my mare and steed.
Take off my coat, roll-up my sleeve,
Get down to making Doubting Toms believe.

My Daddy was in medicine too.
He gained the trust of all he knew,
Because you felt that what he said was true.
He did his job and never lied:
What was promised was supplied.
We talk about him with a deal of pride.

And as a life I'd say it wasn't much
He didn't impact upon the world as such
He wasn't even knocked down by the 16 bus.
No bridge or road will ever bear his name.
He isn't listed in some hall of fame.
But he really did impress the six of us.

So naturally I turned away
We didn't have that much to say —
Denied him, day by day by day by day
Now he comes through every pore
He's in my closets, and what's more
In every mirror that's him there for sure.

I have these bottles, large and small
Blue ones, green ones, short ones, tall,
And it's the same old medicine that's in them all
Despite myself I wear his shoes
I'd other plans but you don't choose
From time to time I blow the self same fuse.

And as a life you might say it wasn't much
He didn't impact upon the world as such
He wasn't even knocked down by the 16 bus.
No bridge or road will ever bear his name.
He isn't listed in some hall of fame.
But he really did impress the six of us.

I take my show from town to town
And Moma says when I come down
'Son, he's never dead while you're around
Son, he's never dead while you're around'.

Kieran McKeown

A LETTER

I think of two pieces of writing which refer to fathers and sons. The first is the parable of the prodigal son from Saint Luke's Gospel and the second is a poem by Seamus Heaney called *Digging*.

I have always liked the story of the prodigal son because, in my own tame way, I have had that role in my family. I left home at the age of twelve to follow a vocation with a religious order. I was the only one of the family who ever really left home; I can relate particularly to the prodigal son's desire to leave and go to a 'distant country'. I subsequently left the religious order at the age of twenty but never returned home except for visits. For a while, my leaving the order was seen by my mother as prodigal; my father never expressed his opinion. I still don't know what he thought of his son leaving home at the age of twelve.

My father was a decent, quiet, physically present/emotionally absent Irish father. From all this, you will gather that my relationship with the story of the prodigal son is rather oblique; I would like the story to have been my story and to have received the welcome which the prodigal received. In fairness, I suppose I should say that my father was never unwelcoming; his welcome tended to be passive, non-committal and detached.

The poem by Seamus Heaney, *Digging*, is about his father. My father was a farmer like Seamus Heaney's. The poem ends by drawing a parallel between digging with a spade and digging with a pen and suggests a continuity between the work of Seamus Heaney and that of his father. I too feel this sense of continuity with my father through work, although I 'dig' with a computer. I also see digging as a good image of what I try to do in life in the sense of trying to dig to the bottom of things in order to stand on firmer ground.

I discussed your request with Grace, my wife. She suggested that I write about a recent conversation I had with my own son, Colm, who is eleven. I play a lot of football with Colm and have discussions about players, teams and matches. Recently he asked me if any of my three brothers ever played football. I told him I was the only one who ever played football in our family. He said: 'I got the lucky one, so'. That compliment really pleased me.

St. Luke 15:11-15:32

THE LOST SON (THE 'PRODIGAL')
AND THE DUTIFUL SON

A man had two sons. The younger said to his father, 'Father, let me have the share of the estate that would come to me'. So the father divided the property between them. A few days later, the younger son got together everything he had and left for a distant country where he squandered his money on a life of debauchery.

When he had spent it all, that country experienced a severe famine, and now he began to feel the pinch, so he hired himself out to one of the local inhabitants who put him on his farm to feed the pigs. And he would willingly have filled his belly with the husks the pigs were eating but no one offered him anything. Then he came to his senses and said, 'how many of my father's paid servants have more food than they want, and here am I dying of hunger! I will leave this place and go to my father and say: Father, I have sinned against heaven and against you; I no longer deserve to be called your son; treat me as one of your paid servants.' So he left the place and went back to his father.

While he was still a long way off, his father saw him and was moved with pity. He ran to the boy, clasped him in his arms and kissed him tenderly. Then his son said, 'Father, I have sinned against heaven and against you. I no longer deserve to be called your son. ' But the father said to his servants, 'Quick! Bring out the best robe and put it on him; put a ring on his finger and sandals on his feet. Bring the calf we have been fattening, and kill it; we are going to have a feast, a celebration, because this son of mine was dead and has come back to life; he was lost and is found. ' And they began to celebrate.

Now the elder son was out in the fields, and on his way back, as he drew near the house, he could hear music and dancing. Calling one of the servants he asked what it was all about. 'Your brother has come', replied the servant, 'and your father has killed the calf we had fattened because he has got him back safe and sound!' He was angry then and refused to go in, and his father came out to plead with him; but he answered his father, 'Look, all these years I have slaved for you and never once disobeyed your orders, yet you never offered me so much as a kid for me to celebrate with my friends. But, for this son of yours, when he comes back after swallowing up your property — he and his women — you kill the calf we had been fattening. '

The father said, 'My son, you are with me always and all I have is yours. But it was only right we should celebrate and rejoice, because your brother here was dead and has come to life; he was lost and is found.

Seamus Heaney

DIGGING

Between my finger and my thumb
The squat pen rests; snug as a gun.

Under my window, a clean rasping sound
When the spade sinks into gravelly ground:
My father, digging. I look down.

Till his straining rump among the flowerbeds
Bends low, comes up twenty years away
Stooping in rhythm through potato drills
Where he was digging.

The coarse boot nestled on the lug, the shaft
Against the inside knee was levered firmly.
He rooted out tall tops, buried the bridge edge deep
To scatter new potatoes that we picked
Loving their cool hardness in our hands.

By God, the old man could handle a spade.
Just like his old man.

My grandfather cut more turf in a day
Than any other man on Toner's bog.
Once I carried him milk in a bottle
Corked sloppily with paper. He straightened up
To drink it, then fell to right away
Nicking and slicing neatly, heaving sods
Over his shoulder, going down and down
For the good turf. Digging.

The cold smell of potato mould, the squelch and slap
of soggy peat, the curt cuts of an edge
Through living roots awaken in my head.
But I've no spade to follow men like them.

Between my finger and my thumb
The squat pen rests.
I'll dig with it.

Seán O'Faolain

from VIVE MOI

I feel downcast that I can only remember my father like this as a figure, almost as a type, rather than as a person. His own inner, private life is hidden from me completely. He is to me more of a myth than a man, a figure out of that time, out of that place, a symbol of childhood. Does it always happen when we live closely and long with a person or a place that we come to know them less and less, whether wife, husband, child, or town? With him this happens when I seize even on the one or two privacies of his life, such as his little brown locked box, always on the shelf in the kitchen. To my mother this was Bluebeard's chamber about which she used to tease him, to his great annoyance, saying: 'I wonder what you have at all, at all, in that little brown box? Maybe a little roll of pound notes? Ha?'

I think it contained his razors, possibly a few family letters, possibly a couple of pound notes. I associate it with his one relaxation, a bet on a horse now and again. After all, he had been born in the Queen's County, which borders on County Kildare, both famous racing counties. Down there he had a friend who was supposed to be 'in the know', one Philly Behan, a starter or starter's assistant on the Curragh. To Philly, now and again, he would send a present of a ham, and from Philly there would come, now and again, a letter which my father might, though rarely, leave on the shelf and which my mother would guiltily read. 'There is some talk about a promising three-year-old, Flyaway, trained by Hartigan, for the June meeting, and if Gus Hogan is up I would say he would be worth a bet both ways. 'But when I would hear those words I would not think of his tremors or expectations so much as of the green wonder of the Curragh plain, about which he often talked to us, or of the Great Heath of Maryborough, near his boyhood home, and of all that far-off country from which he, and therefore I, had come. For me that little brown box held green fields, yellow heather, and galloping horses. In this way he really was a bit of the Irish myth and a bit also of the imperial myth, and through their blended ambitions and pieties he achieved wholeness.

He would not have understood one word of this, and if he had he might not have agreed, because he had one other precious dream.

Every so often there would come in the post a copy of a local paper from Kildare or the Queen's with advertisements of forthcoming auctions of farms marked in red ink: 'Four miles from *Emo*. Thirty acres of useful grazing land. Farmhouse and outhouses ... *Kildangan*. Twenty-seven acres, three roods of fine arable land ... Near *Kiladoon* ...'

It was the pipedream of a man who had not enough money to farm a window-box, the uprooted peasant longing for his Mother Earth — incomplete, unwhole, mortally vulnerable away from it. There must have been thousands like him in the Force. He reminds me that we had a semipermanent lodger one year named Ross, a retired sergeant of the Force. He was a finely built man, now grey, though you could see by his eyelashes that he had once been redheaded, with flowing moustaches still russet, partly from his pipe but also from rude persistent health. He was a figure of fun to us children because he was always talking aloud to himself, so loudly that even through the ceiling we could sometimes hear him in his room mixing up his memories of barrack yard and farm haggard:

'Yessir! Nosir! At once! Attention! Dismiss! Halt! Whoa, back, whee! Gee up! That's the gurl! G'wan! Pike it up there, Jim. Fine hay! Dismiss! Yessir! Nosir! At once, sir!'

He had never married. He lived and died on his two memories.

Last night I read with deep emotion this little entry in Cesare Pavese's *Il Mestiere di Vivere*, written at the height of his success as an author in Turin:

> Isn't it curious that at the moment when you first left your home in the country ... it never occurred to you that you were starting out on a long journey through cities, names, adventures, pleasures, unforeseeable worlds which would make you realise in the course of time that that one moment had been one of the richest parts of your Future, wherein the everlasting mystery would prove to be that childish You whom at that time you made no effort to possess.

I wonder what my father dreamed on his happy nights? When we talk about squares how we simplify! In every square is there a buried myth. I think I am trying to persuade myself that there is. I want desperately to believe that my father was larger than I must otherwise think. He was, so evidently, so accusingly, a good man, a loyal servant, an upright citizen, a pious Christian, a good father, that I cannot believe in him as a man at all unless he had, also, some purely personal dream outside those social virtues. I do not want to think of my father as a Father. By being my father he is lost to me, as, for all I know, I am lost to my children. Perhaps I must accept the truth, miserably: that he, happily, lost himself in his children. It makes me feel so ungiving, so helpless, now that it is too late to explain to him that if he had been less good I might now admire him less and might then have loved him more.

Theo Dorgan

SPEAKING TO MY FATHER

How should I now call up that man my father,
Who year after weary year went off to work,
Buried his heart beneath a weight of duty,
Buried himself early so that we might live?

How should I sit here and explain to his shade
That, yes, this is the work I do you died for,
This is the use I make of all that sacrifice,
I move the words as you moved heavy tyres.

True, there is no sickening stench of rubber,
No heat from the curing pans, no rage
At management, choked back by need as much as pride —
But father, the range of uselessness is wide.

Often, as I grew slowly, you'd let slip
A word, a helpless gesture or a look
That shook me to the roots, I'd sense the void
You stubbornly, heroically sweated back.

Now I have everything you lacked, above all
Freedom to shape the workload for the day —
It sounds like freedom, doesn't it? The truth is,
I hate the shiftwork just as much as you did.

There are days lately, as I thicken in years,
When I feel your sinews shift inside my frame,
I catch a look at yours in the mirror, shaving:
Mild, ironical, weary, a bit resigned —

But something else, too: your athlete's way
of planting the feet carefully when troubled
Shoulder square to the blow that may come,
Hands tense to defend what you hold dear.

What troubled you most? The question shies away
When I stab with my pen, clumsy as ever
— I don't even rightly know what troubles me,
Ignorant as when I rode upon your knee.

What would you make of me, I wonder, sitting here
Long after midnight, searching for the words to
Bring you back, soliciting the comfort of your shade
For the odd, useless creature that you made?

Here is the end of all that education,
The void is as close to me as it ever was to you,
I make poems of love as you and Rose made children,
Blindly, because I must.

Father, comrade, the same anger with the world
But not your patience moves me; I make you this,
A toy in words to re-introduce myself
And to ask, what must I do to be your child again?

John Boyd

OUT OF MY CLASS

Mother told me that I was born on the nineteenth of July in the early hours of the morning when everyone was asleep. When I asked her if she was asleep too she only laughed and shook her head. I didn't learn the answer to that question for a long time; it was something that mother didn't like to talk about. She once gave me a strange reply; 'Curiosity killed the cat', she said in a serious tone of voice. I wondered why, because I was curious about everything myself and couldn't understand why a poor cat should be killed for doing no harm.

It was no good asking questions about how you came into the world because nobody seemed to know the right answer. Only one thing was sure: a lady called Mrs Glenfield was there at the time. She lived in Glenallen street and brought me into the world, but how she did it nobody ever said. She was called a midwife and she found babies wherever she went. She found me. Mother said Mrs Glenfield was 'always on the go' after babies. Mrs Glenfield would pat my head when she saw me playing in the street and tell me I was growing up 'as straight as a rush'. But I didn't know what a rush was and a long time passed before I found out that rushes grew in fields, and there were no fields near our house. We lived in a city. It was called Belfast.

I was born in the heart of Ballymacarett, in number nine Baskin street, off Templemore Avenue, between the Albert Bridge Road and the Newtownards Road. It was a small street of red-brick kitchen houses, and was the first home father and mother had after they were married. I was their first child. On my birth certificate father is described as 'Robert Boyd, Labourer' and mother as 'Jane Boyd, formerly Leeman'. There are also the words 'Agnes Glenfield present at birth'. My birth was registered on the fifth of August 1912.

Mother always said that father told a lie when he registered my birth: 'Your father had no right to call himself a labourer. When you were born he was a fireman on the railway. I'd never have married a common labourer, I can tell you that much!' But father argued that he used a shovel all day firing a locomotive on the Belfast and County Down Railway, and so had every right to call himself a labourer; even when he became an engine driver he still called himself a labourer;

'Luk at them hands o' mine,' he'd say. 'I've to use the scrubbin' brush t' git the dirt an' the grease aff them, haven't I?'

I don't remember living in the kitchen house where I was born, for after a couple of years we moved to another kitchen house in Bangor near the railway station. We lived there for only a couple of years as well, and father always said that these were the happiest years of his life, and that he wished he'd never been persuaded to leave Bangor. But mother was discontented there and wanted to go back to the dirt of Belfast; back to grandma Leeman and granda Leeman and all of her relations, such as the Herdmans, who lived on the Newtownards Road, opposite the big chapel whose name I don't know because it was Roman Catholic and we were Protestants.

I've no memories of our Bangor house except that there was a small field at the back where I used to wander because I liked to feel the long grass on my legs and arms. But one day my aunt Ethel, father's sister, warned me, 'Don't go into that big field else you'll get lost. Or the gypsies'll come and take you away. You're like a wee gypsy, Topsy, aren't you?' Aunt Ethel always called me Topsy — a name I liked better than my real name, and wished everybody would call me Topsy, but nobody else did. I think that was why aunt Ethel remained my favourite aunt. I should have liked to have been a gypsy boy living in a caravan and allowed to sit on the roundabouts all day, riding the horses that went up and down, and patting their wooden heads as if they were real horses, which they were, to me. But I was afraid of gypsies because they might snatch you away from the field one day and not let you home at night to lie in your bed.

I also remember walking along the sea wall holding tight my father's hand. Sometimes he'd let my hand go and say 'Careful now, walk by yourself'. But I was frightened that I might fall, for the wall was very high. Father would only laugh and tell me not to fear; that he wouldn't let me go, and anyway he was holding me at the back. Mother never played tricks like that. Whenever mother took hold of my hand she held it very tight and would never let it go, and then I could look at the sand and the sea without being afraid. I could trust mother not to let me go because she was my mother.

One morning a cart and a horse came to our door and took the furniture away. We returned to Ballymacarett and the rest of my childhood was spent there. Our house was number forty-six Chatsworth Street, a parlour house with a kitchen and scullery at the back, a back yard with a water closet, and two bedrooms upstairs. It was known as a 'respectable' street, and the musty parlour, which was seldom used except on Sundays, was a symbol of that respectability. Unfortunately number forty-six was at the Lord Street end. If our house had been at the Templemore Avenue end we would have been more comfortable, especially father who hardly ever got an unbroken day's sleep when he was on the nightshift; and when father was short of his sleep he was shorter still of temper, and even at the best of times his temper was short. The trouble was that father was a light sleeper, and the noises from the street would penetrate our front bedroom, wakening him up and sending him downstairs in his shirt and trousers and bare feet, his braces dangling down behind him.

'Jenny, for God's sake, tell them women across the street to shut up!'

'What's the matter, Bob?'

'I can't get my sleep!'

'Shut the window and you won't hear them.'

This suggestion always incensed father. 'Shut the winda! If I shut the winda how'll I get air? I've toul' ye before but ye won't niver listen t'me: if I shut the winda I feel suffocated! I'm used to fresh air, amn't I?'

'But if you're asleep...'

'I tell ye I can't get over asleep. An' I won't shut m'eyes if them'uns across the way won't shut their traps!'

'They're only at their front doors talking ...'

'Haven't they all housework t'do? Haven't they all houses to clean? God, but women have it easy!'

'They're only having a gossip. I can hardly go out and stop them, can I ?'

'You were out gossipin' along wi' them!'

'I wasn't.'

'I heard ye, I heard ye, I know your voice, don't I?'

If we'd lived at the Templemore Avenue end father would have got a good day's sleep and, what was just as important, I'd have got peace to read and do my homework. But at the Lord Street end there was never any peace and quiet. Always neighbours gossiping, shouting and laughing; coal carts, milk carts, bread carts, carts of all kinds passing up and down; then, all day long, the out-of-work corner boys in Lord Street playing football with a hanky ball, or playing a noisy game of marbles, or getting drunk of a Friday or Saturday night. Father said they were good for nothing, would neither work nor want and were always causing trouble. He told me not to go near them.

Now although our end of the street was the rowdy end I didn't mind the rowdiness all that much. At the kitchen table, where I did my homework, the noise disturbed me only because I was anxious to know what was going on outside. I was all for excitement — if a fight broke out in Lord Street I'd shut my exercise book and run out doors without even bothering to let the ink dry or use my blotter. When this happened and my exercise was left unfinished or badly blotted it would be returned to me the next day with the word 'REJECTED' written across the page, and I'd be kept in after school to write the exercise all over again. Occasionally mother or father leafed through an old exercise book, when it was finished and I needed a penny for a new one, and if the word 'REJECTED' shamed a page I'd be asked questions I couldn't answer. But usually I took care over my home-work and always asked mother to back the exercise book with brown paper to keep it from harm. Five was the top mark and when father leafed through the book he'd say in a loud voice, 'Five, five, five, five! If you once can get five you can always get five!'

'That's asking too much, Bob!' mother said.

'Why?'

'Nobody can always be at their best.'

Father disagreed, but he knew all right what mother meant: she wasn't thinking of me but of herself when she made remarks like that.

Life at home in some ways resembled life at school. At school the teachers who threatened and used the cane were my enemies; at home I regarded father as my enemy, though he pretended to be my friend. When mother and I were alone in the kitchen I was happy; I was always glad when, after throwing my schoolbag in the hall, I discov-ered that father hadn't yet returned from work. Until he returned, the two of us could sit in peace, reading. Mother was a great reader of women's magazines such as *My Weekly* and the *Red Star*; and often when she collected them at the newsagent shop on the Albert Bridge Road she would also collect my *Rover* or *Adventure*. That was the kind of thing that made me love her: buying my magazines for me and leaving them on the table so that I could at once immerse myself in the stories and obliterate from my mind the horrors of school. She had the knack of anticipating my desires. To make my happiness complete she would often produce a bag of sweets for us to share while we settled down to our silent reading.

Then father would appear through the back door and our happi-ness would be broken.

'You're back early, Bob, aren't you?'

Father would look round the kitchen without replying. Mother would leave down her magazine on the sofa and go into the scullery to prepare his meal.

'Nothin' ready for me', father would begin, taking off his dirty boots and throwing them against the fender.

'It'll be ready, Bob, when you're ready. You've to wash yourself, haven't you?'

'I'm hungry', father would growl. 'Have ye potatoes on for me?'

'No. You'd potatoes yesterday, hadn't you?'

'You've nothin' hot then, have you?'

'No. But what do you want? I can run to the corner shop and get you whatever you want.'

With every word I would know that a row was inevitable, and that I would be somehow dragged into it; and I also recognised that mother was in the wrong for *not* having his meal ready. I would want to flee from the house and seek refuge in the street; but, afraid of what might happen to mother in my absence, I would stay on, pretending to read, but in fact waiting for the moment when father's surliness would flare into one of his uncontrollable tempers and he'd strike her, and I'd intervene with cries of rage and anguish, *'Don't father! Don't! Don't!'*, attacking him with my own puny fists until he'd shout, 'Stop you! Git out a the way!'; and he'd take me by the arm and lead me into the hall, where I'd sit at the foot of the stairs sobbing.

After a row quietness would follow, and father would sit down to a makeshift meal of tea, bread and jam; or he might prepare potatoes for himself, disdaining any help from mother, and all the while casting up her faults. Often the kitchen door would open and father would give me a sad look, his face pale and drawn.

'The day'll come, son, when you'll understand.'

And I'd feel his hand touch my hair as he passed me on his way upstairs. ...

More and more I contrived to keep out of our house in Chatsworth Street. Father seemed to be increasingly irritable and was always complaining of mother's neglect of him and her daily trips to Carlton Street, where my young sister was now installed [in grandma Leeman's house]. According to father, this had become mother's real home; he accused her of spending more time there than she did with him; and as for me, he bitterly complained that he hardly ever saw me and that I seldom put my foot in the house except at meal-times and at night. Yet mother, it seemed to me, gave nearly all her time and attention to my younger sister and brother; and father, after his railway work was over, had nothing whatsoever to interest him but would mope about the house before taking himself off to Portallo Street to visit his own parents, brothers and sisters.

Father frequently hinted to me that now I was almost grown up — I was fifteen — it was time I undertook some responsibility in the running of the house. Things couldn't go on like this much longer. Did I know what was wrong? No, I didn't. Didn't I suspect anything? No, I didn't. What did he mean I wondered. All he'd say was that something was 'radically wrong', a phrase he'd picked up in the *Belfast Telegraph*, and he couldn't understand how I could live in the house and not notice anything amiss.

Then one day I came home from school to find father threatening to throw mother out, his voice hoarse with anger. 'Here, take yer coat an' get out! Get out! Get out of my sight!'

Father, still wearing his dirty dungarees, held mother's shabby overcoat in his hand and threw it at her as I appeared in the kitchen. Mother, a defiant expression on her face, sat as if sightless, her hair dishevelled.

'What's wrong?' I asked.

'Can't you guess?' father shouted. 'You're a fool if you can't!'

I turned to mother on the sofa. She was examining her old faded blue coat with its torn lining as if it didn't belong to her. She looked ill and tired.

'It's time you an' me had a talk together', he said to me.

'What's up, father? I don't know what's wrong.'

'If you don't, then it's time you did.'

'Mother's not well. I know that!'

'An' you know what's the mater wi' her, don't you? Luk at the cut of her. . . Is she sober or is she drunk?'

Father suddenly lunged forward, grabbed mother by the shoulders and dragged her upstairs, threatening to kill her as he did so.

'Don't. . . touch. . . me!' mother screamed, trying to grasp the bannister.

I ran into the hall to close the front door, then went into the parlour and sat holding my hands over my ears. Father came downstairs, took out his cigarettes and began smoking. At first he didn't speak, his breath coming in nervous pants. Then at last he said, 'You'll have to know the truth'.

He told me the story of his marriage and how happy he had been until mother began drinking a year or so after their wedding; and he blamed her mother for encouraging her. He called grandma Leeman a bad old bitch, and said he wished she was in hell, for if anybody deserved to be burning in hell the old woman I called my grandma deserved that fate. He talked for a long time, smoking cigarettes all the while, repeating himself and becoming so incoherent that I could hardly make out what he was saying. At last he broke down and wept. I'd never seen father in tears before, and I could hardly keep back my own tears. We sat quiet for a long time and father at last became calm.

Later I went upstairs. Mother was huddled up in bed, a thin blanket covering her. She was asleep and breathing so quietly that at first I feared she might be dead. Then I tiptoed from the room.

After his confession that day father made me his confessor, so much so that mother accused him of poisoning my mind. At times I hated father for his weakness, and at other times I hated mother for hers. Weeks and months passed. Then father told me we were leaving Chatsworth Street. He'd found a house away from Ballymacarett, in a street not far from his own parents, and he said that mother had seemed pleased when he told her, and had promised to behave better. He had decided to give her another chance. A new house in a new district might bring us some happiness, for we couldn't go on living in the same way.

Father believed that our new house would help mother to reform her habits. The sooner we were out of Chatsworth Street and the temptations of the Lord Street public houses, the better. He told me that for years mother had been drinking steadily, bringing bottles of cheap wine home and hiding them in places where she imagined they would never be found. But he had discovered them, and in the most unlikely places: beneath floor boards in the back room where I slept; on top of the wardrobe in the front room; behind the gas meter in the little cupboard off the kitchen; at the back of the coal-shed in the yard. The wonder was that I'd never found a bottle myself, he said. Did I never search for one? Did I never smell mother's breath? Did I never notice her walking a bit unsteadily? Did I never see her sneak into one of the pubs? Did I never notice how things would suddenly disappear — things like shoes, coats, dresses, blankets, tablecloths? He hardly believed me when I told him that I'd noticed nothing; that I'd never come across a bottle or a pawn-ticket; that I'd never been suspicious of mother's behaviour. Why should I be? I couldn't explain to father that, no matter what he might tell me, I'd go on loving mother. Nothing he said made any difference to me. When they quarrelled I could never take father's part, though I knew he was often in the right.

That day, within the space of a few hours, time accelerated and I was deprived of part of my boyhood.

~

The new house was number nine Ranelagh street. It looked raw and damp when we moved in, the back and front garden full of bricks, the pebble-dashed walls not yet dried out. The end of a terrace of four, it struck me as jerry-built and ugly, but as it had a third bedroom as well as an indoor bathroom and lavatory, it suited us well enough. And the small street, lying between a residential avenue and an estate of semi-detached villas built for ex-servicemen of the first world war, certainly appeared to be quieter than Chatsworth Street.

But Ranelagh Street wasn't as quiet as we had hoped it might be. As soon as we moved in we discovered that a mineral-water factory behind the corrugated paling at the back caused a lot of noise; the girls and youths were always yelling and larking as they moved the heavy crates about the yard. Luckily father was on the dayshift at this time so the noise didn't upset him. It upset me more, and I usually put off doing my homework until I saw the young workers streaming out of the front gate. In a way I envied them their carefree spirits as they worked, hauling the crates of empty bottles across the cemented yard and shouting abuse at one another. At lunch-time the youths played football and the girls in their red rubber aprons applauded or booed until the factory whistle ended the game. At six o'clock, the factory finally fell silent and I could begin my homework in peace.

For a while the flit to Ranelagh Street appeared to be a success. Mother would even accompany father to Portallo Street to prove to the Boyd family how well she was behaving. I loved to see her dressed neatly and full of chat, talking to father's parents as if she hadn't a care in the world. As for father, he radiated happiness and did all he could to make her happy. He had a generous nature; and although he'd over a hundred pounds deposited in the savings bank 'for fear of a rainy day', he'd no great desire to have more. He bought new furniture for the new house so that mother could proudly display it, and he could invite his railway mates home for supper and a game of whist. He bought himself a good second-hand bicycle, because when working the early shift he had to be at the railway before the morning trams began. A bicycle was a necessity now that he lived so far away from the BCDR shunting sheds where he collected his engine. He bought me a bicycle too, because my journey to school was even further than his to work; and my bicycle had to be brand-new so that I wouldn't feel inferior to the other boys. And the very first week we moved into Ranelagh Street he bought mother a new rig-out by way of celebration. Father liked a bit of display, whether it was his own railway jacket with its brass buttons, mother in a good coat and expensive Sunday hat, or myself in my black school blazer and yellow and black cap. Clothes, to him, were the outward sign of a family who had self-respect and desired the respect of their neighbours.

In the past he'd been deeply ashamed of mother — ashamed of her drinking, of her getting into debt, of her running about shabbily dressed — but now he hoped that those days were all over. As uncle Willie and aunt Ida had prophesied more than once to him: 'A new environment will make Jenny into a new woman', and father, though he'd only the vaguest of notions what 'environment' meant, had great faith in their judgment. For about six months mother was as good as gold — proud of her appearance, careful with money, and content to work about the house all day and stay in at night to keep him company.

But our idyllic life wasn't to last: our new environment proved to have disadvantages. Mother, who loved neighbourliness found that the neighbours didn't run in and out of one another's houses, as in Chatsworth Street, for cups of tea and gossip. Indeed there wasn't any friendliness beyond a 'good morning' or 'lovely day', followed by a front door being firmly closed. And there were no grocery shops handy where she could make new friends. She had to go as far as the shops on the Woodstock Road; and once free of the house, she was tempted to take a tram to Mountpottinger and call in at Carlton Street. In any case she considered it was only right that she should call — my young sister still lived there, as it was so near to her school.

One day a letter arrived for father from McDowell's shop in Lord Street saying that mother had left owing them twenty-seven pounds.

'What does this mean, Jenny?' father shouted, waving the bit of paper.

Mother, who had given her word that she'd left Chatsworth Street with all of her debts paid, burst into tears and admitted that she'd told an untruth, that she was sorry for what she'd done, and that she'd pay off every penny as soon as she could.

To my surprise, father controlled his temper and handed over the bill in silence. He turned to me, and said sadly, 'What can I do? What can I do?'

But I'd no comfort to offer him and he went to his bedroom, his face very pale, as if stunned by mother's betrayal.

'There's nothing to worry about', mother told me, putting the bill in her little purse. 'Mrs McDowell trusts me. She knows I'll pay back every penny I owe her.'

She had deceived father, and I was certain she was now deceiving herself.

'You can't deceive me', I said as bitterly as I could. 'You can't deceive me any more.' From now on I'd no choice but to be father's ally; and that brought me little comfort.

Mother took to going to bed early, sometimes as early as eight o'clock or a quarter past, pleading a headache and not feeling well. On these occasions father and I would sit in front of the fire, whispering about her together and hoping that she would be asleep. But she surprised us once by coming downstairs for a glass of water and saying as she stood on the stairs on her way up again: 'You two want me out of the way. So I'm keeping out of your way. And I know what you're saying about me.'

It was true: we discussed her endlessly, wondering what could be done. Father was in despair. He thought mother was drinking again, and if she was he could no longer prevent her. He was beaten, and no one could give him any help. All the efforts he'd made had been in vain, and he confessed that without my support he couldn't go on. We discussed what could be done even though he had by now accepted that little *could* be done. All he could do was give mother less money on a Friday night and pay McDowells' bill himself — else it would never be paid. Mother was incapable of keeping her promises. There was no question of that.

So in trying not to fail father, I failed mother. Mother, who needed my help all the more, was denied it. The guilt is with me still. ...

I know nothing of grandma Leeman except her birthplace. I don't know what school she attended, where she worked, what she thought of her husband, what she drank and how much, and why she drank; and, most important of all, I don't know what her real relationship with my mother was. Was grandma Leeman a weak-minded characterless creature? The photograph I have doesn't suggest that. Was she just a harmless ignorant woman who took an odd drink, was friendly with her only daughter, and bullied her easy-come, easy-go husband? Maybe so. Or was she an evil-minded harridan; a 'bitch out of hell', as father bitterly called her? I prefer not to think of her as that, even though father went to his grave believing that to be the truth.

But whatever the truth of this relationship, it was too complicated for father and too complicated for me as well. Absorbed in school activities which were taking more and more of my time and energy, I tried to avoid having to discuss with father the problem of how mother might be 'cured' of her alcoholism. The trouble was that mother would do well for months and father would be happy; then one day she would appear to be ill and father would at once — rightly or wrongly — accuse her of being drunk, and a row would follow. Because I couldn't understand the reasons for mother's drinking, I tried to shift part of the blame onto father, accusing him of being too short-tempered and too suspicious; while he in turn accused me of giving him no help or sympathy and of being concerned only with myself. Then, after an acrimonious argument, both of us would become sullen and resentful, refusing to speak. At meal-times the three of us would sit in silence. Finally, father would be unable to endure the atmosphere any longer, and he would thump the table and shout: 'What can be done, tell me? I can do no more! It's hopeless, hopeless!'

Driven to despair, he would threaten to leave mother if she didn't keep sober or to throw her out of the house. She had pawned his Sunday suit, her own clothes, even her wedding ring. That she'd pawned her ring and deceived him by replacing it with a valueless one from Woolworths had broken his spirit. And this deception symbolised for him that their marriage had finally collapsed.

One evening when I was alone in the house, reading as usual, I heard a noise at the back door. It was mother. She stood on the step, one hand on the wall to prevent herself from falling. I caught hold of her by the arm and struck her. Then I let her go and she fell on the cement path. I picked her up and carried her into the kitchen and laid her on the sofa. For a moment I thought I'd killed her, but she opened her eyes and put her hands to her head. When she withdrew them she stared at me, her eyes glazed and her face smudged with dirt.

'What happened, son?' she said, staring at the blood. And I burst into tears, terrified and ashamed.

Your acts of shame live the longest and your worst live until your death. That act I've lived with till now, and not confessed till now, but confession won't wash it away; for it cannot be expiated.

Alcoholism is a disease and is now treated as a disease — or not treated at all but neglected. Father may have heard that alcoholism was a disease. He must have, for I remember we had long discussions in which he tried to persuade mother to go into hospital; but always in vain. She shook her head and refused to go. Father pleaded with her, and asked me to plead with her, all to no avail. Mother denied that she needed treatment in a hospital, denied father's accusation that she was a drunkard, and maintained that she was the victim of untruths. Mother, for some reason, avoided using the word 'lies', probably because she had to tell so many.

Father was a generous and uncomplicated man who, if he hadn't married mother, would have been high-spirited and full of laughter. He'd a taste for elementary mathematics, got pleasure from trying to solve puzzles or from playing whist or draughts, and most of all from mending clocks. When things were going well at home and he saw me putting away my books he used to say: 'How about a game of draughts? D'you think you cud beat me?' I never could get the better of him, and when he lifted two or three of my 'men' and was able to declare in triumph, 'Now crown that one!' his dark brown eyes would twinkle with pleasure and he'd announce to mother, 'Hi, did ye watch me wipin' the board wi' this boyo? Who's got the real brains in this house, me or him? Answer me that!'

Mother gave him years of misery and he spent most of his married life worrying about her; yet he managed to retain affection for her. In a buoyant mood he would confess: 'She's her own worst enemy, boy. . . No doubt about it. . . Her own worst enemy. More's the pity.' Then, seeking guidance, or more likely, consolation from me, he'd ask: 'What wud ye do if ye were in my place? Tell me that now'. But as I couldn't give him a good answer, he'd offer me his own advice: 'Never you git married! But if you iver do, have a good luk at the girl's mother because that's what she'll turn into at the end.'

All I know with absolute certainty is that mother recklessly threw away her life, and died prematurely because of her recklessness. Like myself, she was easily bored and found the life she was born into almost intolerably boring. Restless, volatile, gregarious, she loved gaiety and gossip and was entirely without malice. Her neighbours in Chatsworth Street, whenever they met father on his own, would shake their heads in sorrow. 'Ach Bob dear, now don't be too hard on her. Everybody has their own weaknesses, haven't they? Your Jenny'd go miles out of her way to do anybody a good turn — even a stranger. The sorry thing is she'd niver do a good turn till herself.' ...

So what father had predicted was turning out to be true: I was jobless and looked like being jobless for a long time. All my efforts had produced what looked like being a useless degree.

'What *are* you fit for, son?' father asked me time and time again.

'Teaching, I suppose. Or journalism.'

'But there's dozens o' teachers running the streets.'

'That's so.'

'Then what chance have you?'

'No chance.'

'Then what'll you do wi' yourself?'

I could give him no answer to that question. Ever since I'd won a scholarship at the age of eleven until now in my early twenties, I'd been a source of bewilderment, annoyance and perhaps secret pride to father; but now I felt that if I hadn't betrayed him I had certainly failed him. Mother had also failed him, had wilfully failed and betrayed him, or so he believed, no matter how I might argue to the contrary. For now, at last, I was convinced that mother was bereft of all will-power and required all our help. But father refused to accept my pleading and accused me of deserting him. Talk was cheap. I was betraying him. I hadn't to contend with mother and I wasn't responsible for her behaviour day after day and week after week. In father's company I took mother's part; in mother's company I was unable to rise above a mood of sullen hopelessness. The only way out was to leave home and I applied for teaching jobs in England and in Berlitz schools on the continent — without success. After a while I gave up sending out applications.

It was father who put me on the track of a job, and quite by chance. One morning , having driven a mainline train into the Belfast terminus, he was standing on the foot-plate idly watching the passengers come up the platform when one of them, a businessman he knew by sight, handed him the *News-Letter*, a newspaper father never read unless given a present of it. While waiting to take the next train out he glanced at the jobs vacant column and saw an advertisement for a temporary tutor. When he came home he handed me the carefully folded paper.

'Would that job suit you? It's only temporary but it might be worth trying for. Nothing venture, nothing win. An' it'll only cost you the price of a postage-stamp, wouldn't it? Why not write an application? You're a dab hand at that.'

So, at father's insistence, I applied for the tutorship and was interviewed at an address in Waring Street. A tall, thin, well-dressed man shook hands with me, introduced himself and gravely waved me to a chair opposite his desk. He sat down facing me, my letter in his hand, and explained that his son, aged nine, was convalescing from an operation and would be unable to return to his English preparatory school for a couple of months.

'If you accept this post I'd like to make it clear that the boy must not be subjected to any strain. No homework, for instance. No cramming. Nothing like that. These are the terms of employment.'

He handed me a sheet of paper; I agreed to the terms; he thanked me; we shook hands; and I was back in the street. The transaction was over in a few minutes. Father's omen that I would get the job had come true.

As soon as father returned from work he wanted to hear my news even before he'd eased off his boots and taken off his dungarees. I told him what had happened in Waring Street.

'So you got it, boy!' he exclaimed, rubbing his hands with pleasure.

'Yes. But it's only temporary and part time. Mondays, Wednesdays and Fridays, from half past two to half past four.'

'That'll hardly kill ye, will it?'

Father laughed at the shortness of the working hours, a total of six in the week. He found it extraordinary that a six-hour job should even exist, not to mention be advertised in the *News-Letter*; and when I told him that the pupil was convalescing and wasn't to be allowed to study hard, father's amazement was unbounded.

'Does that mean you've to take it aisy wi' the young fella?'

'Yes, that's so.'

'Just sit on yer behind an' talk till him?'

'More or less.'

'That won't take the sweat out a ye, will it?'

Father could hardly believe our luck.

'God, I forgot to ask ye how much they'll pay you?'

'Two pounds ten.'

'Two pounds ten! For six hours a week! Sure you haven't made a mistake? You must a got it wrong, boy!'

Mother took the news calmly; she never doubted that I'd find a teaching job, sooner or later.

'But you don't understand, Jenny! They're payin' him two pounds ten for six hours! Imagine, two pounds ten! I can't believe it!'

'That must be the rate for the position', mother explained. 'Teaching is a profession, you know.'

'Oh, I know that! I'm ignorant but not as ignorant as you make me out!'

Father was overjoyed; for I think he'd almost despaired of my ever getting anything, even a temporary part-time job; so I'd to retrace the entire interview as if to reassure him that it actually took place.

'You tell me, the father's a stock-broker?'

'I think he is, but I'm not certain. He has something to do with the stock exchange.'

'Oh, that's where the money's made. In the stock exchange. Willie and Ida say it's just a big gamblin' place where the rich get richer. Your boss won't be short of the ready cash, that's for sure!'

It was as if I'd come into a fortune, though the remuneration for the ten weeks' tuition amounted to twenty-five pounds, and from that I'd have to deduct the rail fares — thirty in all — to and from Cultra on the Bangor line. It amused father that he might be driving the train in which I was a passenger dressed up in my best clothes, and we'd an argument over whether I should travel first, second or third class. He was strongly of the opinion that I should travel first; mother's opinion was that second would be suitable, while I could see no reason why I shouldn't travel third. Father wouldn't agree to my travelling third, especially as he could get me second-class privilege tickets which he insisted he would pay for himself. So we settled that I was to travel second. That evening father slipped me a fiver to buy a new overcoat, shirt, and pair of shoes. 'You've got to be well rigged out, son, for a job like that.' And I was.

Harry Ferguson

IN THE HANDS OF MY FATHER

For Tom Ferguson: Born 18 February, 1931; died 11 June, 1993

For many years — perhaps ten — I have had a recurring dream that my father is dead and laid out at home on the bed. I am by the bedside and suddenly see him move. I run from the room and tell everyone. There is joy in the house: he's *alive*. That's it. I wake up. It's one of those dreams where very little happens; where the detail is much less significant than the powerful feelings it evokes. There is life after death, so far as my father and mother are concerned. It was always immensely reassuring.

But now it's for real. I *am* by the bedside looking at my father's dead body. I stare and stare at him, but no matter how hard I look or for how long I watch him, he does not move. I can't wake up because I'm not asleep. He can't wake up because he is dead. Now there is no relief. There is only helplessness and sadness, sadness: For fuck sake Da, wake-up, wake-up, PLEASE. But he won't; he can't. And nothing will make the feelings of reassurance come.

He is laid out in the coffin which is placed on the middle of the bed with the lid removed. He is wearing his best white shirt, a black tie and his best black suit. He looks so like himself. It's him. So handsome. My mind goes back to the wake of a relation of my wife's father, Bernie, that I attended in Co. Longford in the late-1980s. The deceased was laid out on the bed dressed in a shroud surrounded by people, some of whom were praying and saying the Rosary. His wife greeted us immediately with the question: 'How do you think he's looking Bernie?'. I thought the question absurd and irrational: 'The man is dead, for God's sake. What a ridiculous thing to say!', I told myself.

But now, as I stare at my own father's body, it makes *perfect* sense to me. Offering opinions on the appearance of the dead seems not only entirely appropriate, but natural and even essential. I want to talk about little else. I feel relieved, proud even, about his appearance. He always did look well when dressed up and this was no exception. My mother, as she has done for over forty years, has helped him to be turned out perfectly.

I feel his face and it so cold. And yet there is warmth in his face. His eyes are closed. I see his eyelashes in a way that I have never seen them before. They're longer than I imagined and quite lovely. His hair, which has been silvery grey for some time now, is lovely and soft and light to the touch. His mouth is closed and his lips are together. There is a slight smile on his face.

I come to see the importance of getting this right because the expression never changes. He was always such a restless man, and the unrelenting stillness of him really unsettles me. No matter how often I leave the room, when I go back he is in the same position on the bed and nothing has changed. This is the most shocking thing about the dead body. It remains the same, while everything is so different in its presence.

I begin to wonder if I ever really studied him properly when he was alive. Yet I can look at him, kiss him and touch him now in a way that I couldn't or wouldn't, even a matter of hours ago when he was alive.

His hands seem so clean now and much softer than I have ever seen them before. They have turned white and are ice cold, crossed across his chest. Just a few months ago before he took sick, they still bore the marks of the years of wear and tear from working the land: healed cuts, chap marks — and were much thicker and bulkier. I once told myself that I should photograph them, but never did. Too late now. I wanted to preserve them for posterity, for their sheer cragginess and toughness and because, somehow, they epitomised his life. These were hands that rarely cleaned or fed me. My mother did all the domestic work involved in rearing my brothers and sisters and I. But they are hands which embodied his strength; his relentless capacity for work and how he fullfilled his duty to us by providing.

I used to silently compare my own hands with his and feel so soft; a right wimp. I couldn't hack the hard manual work on the land that made hands like his. But I wanted the sheer masculine glory of those hands: a form of strong manhood without cuts and bruises, without weathering the cold and the wet; without tears.

But there are other ways. At the age of nine he took me to see the farming soap opera *The Riordans* being filmed near where we lived in Co. Meath. Batty and Benjy, two of the main characters, dirtied their hands on the soil of the earth just before going on set to start filming. But all the cosmetic dirt in the world couldn't turn me into looking like a farmer, never mind *being* one. The longer I was away from the land the softer, more useless I became. In his presence I felt like an almost totally impractical, even at times a weak man.

Although proud, he never seemed to begin to understand my work as a university lecturer. We joked about it, but it irked me that I could never convince him that I did *not* get four months holidays every summer. Somehow what I did never counted as *real* work. My will to work the land went, and it was that will that drove my father on. Was it that too which lay behind his irritating inability to listen, and extraordinary impatience? 'C' MON!' he would roar, if things weren't going his way. As if it was *always* our fault. I always envied his amazing sociability and generosity. Within minutes of walking into a strange pub he could be in a round with the key players in it and have discovered all sorts of mutual connections and interests. There was a great, almost organic, strength in his ability to connect with people. From the time, as a late teenager, when he began to buy me pints and let me smoke in front of him, I'd try, awkwardly, to join in with the mens' jokes and conversation. I found real security in his shadow.

As people arrive at the house in droves to pay their respects (just how does news travel so fast in rural Ireland?. . .), they invariably go straight to see my father. I take strength from the curiosity and dignity that is shown for death; and the life: a neighbour farmer tells of how every year my father cut his silage and always started the job so early that he would have it finished before he had even got up: a man who went to school with him spoke of how Da, at the age of twelve, ploughed a local field which experienced farmers had great difficulty even getting into, and Da was known as a genius with machinery, at getting the most out of the land and rearing animals.

A fuller perspective on his life emerges as he lies there in death. Even before he died, during his final hours, when the doctor visited he reflected on the fact that 'Tom has been a lovely patient. He never complained and has always been so good humoured'. He emphasised though just how difficult it always was to get Dad to take sickness seriously and have anything to do with him. He recalled the time Dad went to him with a very serious cut that he got when working at silage. The doctor told him that it was serious and that he would have to go to the hospital — 10 miles away — to have it stitched. Dad refused and insisted that the doctor himself: 'STITCH IT NOW! I haven't time, there's more silage to be cut!' The doctor duly patched it up and my father went staight back to work. Lesser men (like myself) would have been off work and living on the physical and emotional trauma of it for days. Not Tommy Ferguson.

Such an outlook was part of his great strength and inscrutability, but it was also his great weakness as it led him to deny his physical vulnerability. It was just this which rendered this entire situation so unbelievable. That he could be dying of lung cancer before our eyes and not insist: 'Ach, doctor, give me the new lung and throw a few stitches in it, it'll do rightly — I've hiefers to feed!'. I couldn't help telling myself if he was different, took care of his body more; if he *had* only gone to the doctor sooner with that bad cough, we wouldn't be sitting around with him on his death bed at the mere age of sixty-two. If only ... if, if. ... His body had simply given up. No stitch in time. Too late now.

It was his will to work the land and to provide that made those hands what they were; and his illness which made them shadows of their former selves. The nicotine stain is there upon them; the stain of that which killed him. Perhaps it is the hands and not the eyes that are the true window to the soul of fathers. We kind of recognise this in our respect for a 'good strong handshake'. It was rare for my father and I to shake hands. And when we did, we didn't really shake them at all: we *touched* hands. Perhaps that is how it should be; how fathers and sons can be affectionate. All men can shake hands, but only men who are special, one to another, can touch hands.

Did we touch enough? Could work-worn hands like these have been more tender? How did I use *my* hands with him? Did *I* caress enough? Did I initiate enough contact with him? Who is to say whether enough was enough?

The oddest thing of all is that my father isn't here to respond to these questions. I expect him to burst into the room at any minute, smiling, and say, 'Well . . . what'll 'is have to drink?' and have the entire place engrossed in conversation. Yet he is here. But he won't answer. He can't answer.

But being with him in this way has brought some answers and reassurance. These are healing hands. Never again will those hands be set to work, lift a glass . . . or will I be able to touch them or they me. Yet I shall always remain proudly and lovingly in the hands of my father.

Keith O'Flaherty

I BELIEVE IN THE FATHER

I believed in the father . ...
But did he believe in the son?

He was quick to tell me when
I took up a tool wrong, or a wrong tool,
In a manner he perhaps did not intend
But even so would make me feel a fool.

Did he believe that I had let him down?
He had a fiercesome frown
And sometimes he would show
Irritation or sarcasm, and I'd know
He thought something I tried to do
Just would not do.

Yet never did I feel him disapprove
When in my adult life I'd make a wrong move.
Though he must have had misgivings
When he saw that I had stopped living
By his creed; a creed he must have hoped
Would have meant I could have coped
In a world of backward change or
Moral danger.

Of those life-rules, in which he so believed,
Often he heard me tell how I perceived
Them: as self-righteous strictures
Plundered from the Holy Scriptures
By those dictatorial saints of plaster:
The rural parish priest and country school-master.

Did he see, in rebellious me
The way he used to be
With his own father?
Or was he rather
A dutiful, respectful son?
Though he did obey the need to run
And find a place to be himself,
All by himself.

From rustic, rural Kerry to urbane, urban Kilburn:
It shows a man of strength he did not turn
Away from his beliefs,
But kept the Faith and the Pioneer Pledge
When he might gain a social edge
By leaving his Catholic past behind,
Letting the wrappings of his upbringing unwind.

Much later, in the face of my apostasy
Was he ever tempted to riposte to me
That a faith like his, deep held,
Would be the only way to keep Hell
From winning
In a world of sinning?

He seemed instead to choose the pragmatic
Over the dogmatic,
And to avoid argument would agree with me
That his certain truths
Were an uncertain shield
With which to keep aloof
The immoral grime
And nastiness of our Time.

As I grew wiser, though, I came to see
That he believed and had great faith in me,
And this belief was never laissez-faire,
But full of care, and very fair, and ever there,
And he did not need to be asked twice
When I might need his strength or his advice.

Did he know that I believed him immortal?
That I never thought nor
Dreamt he'd die
Before the self-indulgence of my
Telling him how I loved him, respected him,
And more important still, believed in him
Despite his difficult ways, and mine.

And at the end,
From the hopeful, hopeless care I was able to offer
Could he tell I never would have scoffed or
Belittled his views or his life-time beliefs
If I had known how he would wither, like an Autumn leaf,
Before the Sun, or son, could give him warmth again.

Joseph O'Connor

from DESPERADOES

After his wife had left him, Frank's life began to change very quickly. He could not sleep any more. He grew afraid of the dark. He could not sleep with the light off in the bedroom that he had once shared with her. He would wake up shaking from nightmares.

His son was thirteen then. Very quickly, he seemed to change too. He grew sullen and stopped talking to his father, sometimes saying nothing at all for a whole night. He began to wear black clothes; he would wear nothing unless it was black. It would infuriate his father more than almost anything else. 'Black bloody clothes', he'd say. 'Here comes Father Johnny Little again.' He would tell his son that he looked like a bloody corpse or a Christian Brother, but his son wouldn't even laugh. He would sit with his eyes fixed on the television, flicking from channel to channel with the remote control, refusing to say a word.

He tried to encourage his son to bring his friends home from school, but Johnny never would. He couldn't bring his friends home here, he told his father. He would laugh, bitterly, when Frank asked him why. He would laugh as though the answer was obvious, and soon he could not say the word *here*, meaning home, without a sneer appearing on his lips.

One day Frank got a telephone call at work from the head priest at Johnny's school. The priest wanted to know where Johnny was. He had not been attending classes. Was he ill? Was there something wrong at home?

That night Frank asked Johnny what he had been doing with himself for the last month. He just wanted the truth, he said. There would be no punishment: he simply wanted to know. Johnny told him he had been walking the streets, getting the bus into town to play the gaming machines in the amusement arcades on the quays, hanging around in the Dandelion Market, the Botanical Gardens in Glasnevin, or the bowling alley in Stillorgan. He'd had a row with one of the teachers.

His father laughed. There was nothing wrong with the occasional mitch from school, but there were exams coming up and Johnny would have to think about them. He made his son go back to school.

He made him promise to say if he was ever in any trouble. There was no problem that couldn't be sorted out, he said, if they were friends, and if they were honest with each other.

'I could never talk to my old man', Frank would say. 'I don't want that for you and me, son. Do you understand?'

Johnny would nod but never say anything.

For a while, he did go back to school and he seemed to do quite well. The art teacher said he was very good with his hands. He liked History and English too. He got a good report at Easter and won second place in an essay competition. He was picked for the debating team. And then one May morning Johnny came down to breakfast and told his father he just didn't want to go to school any more. Frank laughed.

'Son, you're fourteen. Why do you think I'm out on the streets day and night? It's so you don't have to do the fucking same.'

'I'm fifteen', Johnny said. 'I want a job. I want to go to London and get a job in a recording studio. You're always going on about how you left school when you were bloody three or something.'

'I was thirteen, and anyway that's different, son. It was a different time in those days.'

'Funny how it was alright for you and it isn't for me.'

'Don't say that to me, Johnny. Now your mother's gone, we have to be buddies.'

His son rolled his eyes. 'Funny how everything was so great in bloody Francis Street.'

'God, what's up with you these days, Johnny? Do you miss your mother, son? Is that it?'

Johnny shook his head. 'No', he said. 'I don't. And nothing's fucking well up with me.'

'Now, don't you speak to me like that, Johnny. Don't use that language with me.'

'Oh, right. Funny how it's alright for you to use it. I heard you use it often enough.'

'Yes, well', Frank said. 'You do as I say, son, not as I do.'

Johnny and Frank began to have terrible arguments. Johnny would curse at his father just to annoy him. He would steal money from the pockets of his father's jacket and then lie about it. He would go the whole week-end without saying a single word. The head priest rang up again. Johnny would have to be expelled, he said, if he didn't start coming to school every day.

Frank stopped working nights so that he could be at home with his son. They began to learn to cook together. They made simple things, lasagna, casseroles, spaghetti carbonara. He began to drive him to school again, the way he had done when Johnny was a child. He would wait outside the school gates to make sure he had gone in. He would wait for a quarter of an hour and then drive to work.

For his sixteenth birthday, Johnny asked for an electric guitar. Frank took him into McCullough Piggot's in Suffolk Street and they got the most expensive guitar in the shop, a Gibson Les Paul. His son's friends began to come around to the house every night then. They had guitars too. Some of them were older than Johnny, and they seemed a little rough. They also wore black clothes and one of them wore a dog collar. But they were only middle-class kids going through a phase, Frank thought, and, anyway, there was never any harm in music. They would sit in the front room playing loud raucous guitar for hours, the same three chords over and over again, but Johnny seemed to be happy. Frank bought him a Marshall amplifier for Christmas. 'Fuck', Johnny said when he saw it. 'Happy Christmas, Da.' He hugged his father for the first time in two years.

But Frank was not happy. He was not sleeping well and he was tired all the time now. He felt depressed and anxious, permanently in the grip of some kind of vague terror that he could not understand. At work, he began to lose business. Worse, he began not to care. He would get up in the middle of the night and worry about dying. He tried to hide all this from his son, but sometimes he couldn't. And even though Johnny was more communicative, he found himself snapping at him, for the smallest things. He went to see the doctor and started to take anti-depressants.

And then he began to work nights again. He would start at seven or eight, when people were going out for the evening. The other drivers couldn't figure it out. There wasn't another boss in the city who worked nights. But Frank Little would work until two or three in the morning, when the nightclubs closed down on the Leeson Street strip. Then he would go for coffee in the Manhattan in Rathmines, or the Gigs Place, or some all-night joint of the Northside full of drunks and prostitutes and off-duty special branch man. When the sun began to come up Frank would drive home. It was the only time he felt content, driving alone through the empty streets of the city. He would go home and make himself tea, sometimes watch a video. He would go to bed at five or six, exhausted. He could sleep then, because there was no darkness to be afraid of any more. At eight thirty or nine the sound of traffic outside would wake him, and he would stagger out of bed, wash, get his son up and ready for the day. Then he would drive him to school and go to work again.

One morning he drove a human heart all the way from Dublin airport to Saint Vincent's hospital in Elm Park, where a dying young man was waiting for a transplant. He sped through the streets of Dublin, a police motorbike up ahead of him on the road, and he thought about the heart on the back seat of his taxi. He wondered what would happen if he just stopped his car and cut that heart open with a knife. He wondered if it would tell him something he didn't know about people and what they were really like.

At ten in the morning he would go home and back to bed. He would sleep until two or three in the afternoon, wake up then numb and stupid with tiredness, lungs rattling with nicotine. He would shave and take a long shower, and at four o'clock he would drive down to the school, collect his son, bring him home, then make his dinner, watch a few hours of television, check that Johnny was studying, and go back out to work.

One day in 1979, one of the drivers knocked on the door of Frank's office. He said he didn't want to interfere, but some of the men had been talking, and he thought there was something that Frank should know. A week before, one of the other men had been called to McGonagles nightclub in Anne Street at three o'clock in the morning. There had been a punk rock concert at the club. Johnny had been there and he'd been very drunk. The driver had seen him, he was sure. There had been a fight and the police had been involved. He didn't want to interfere, the driver said, but he just thought that Frank should be told. He had sons himself, he said. It was very late at night for a sixteen-year-old to be out on the street.

Frank confronted his son and they fought. Johnny admitted that he had been going into town late at night, sneaking back home before Frank got in. Frank warned him that he would forbid him to go out at all if he had to. He took away Johnny's guitar and locked it in Eleanor's old room.

They began to fight almost every day then. And there were times when Frank lost his temper completely with his son. One morning they argued viciously about the best way to boil an egg and Frank slapped him hard in the face. Johnny left the house that morning and didn't come back for three nights. Frank was wild with worry. When Johnny came back, he held him in his arms and they agreed to make a new start.

One afternoon shortly after that, Frank got a phone call from the police. His son had been arrested in Switzer's for stealing a Christmas candle. He drove down to Pearse Street station to find Johnny locked up in a cell. He said he had wanted the candle as a present for his mother.

When Frank got his son home from the station he dragged him into the kitchen and hit him. Johnny exploded with rage. He stood up and punched his father in the chest and threatened to break his jaw. They held on to each other as they pushed around the kitchen. They argued and shouted late into the night.

The next morning they went to the juvenile court together. The magistrate said Frank would have to give an undertaking to be a responsible parent; otherwise his son could be taken away from him and put into care. There was a very dangerous road ahead for Johnny Little, the magistrate said. In another year he would not be a minor any more. In another year he could be sent to prison.

Once again, they tried to make up. They promised that they would try to be friends. Frank gave the guitar back. He said he'd allow Johnny to play in a band, even if it meant staying out late during the week, if only Johnny would just tell him the truth. Johnny agreed. Frank bought him a new stereo.

Frank tried to meet another woman. He thought it would be good for Johnny to have a woman's influence in his life. On a Saturday night he would shave early and put on aftershave and go to one of the hotel bars where he knew middle-aged people went to meet each other. He was a taxi driver. A taxi driver got to know secret things about a city — where you could drink after hours, where you could pay men to get someone shot, where middle-aged people went to try to meet each other.

But he had no way with women. They made him nervous. He didn't like disco music. He felt stupid, a man of his age, dancing around to disco music. Once or twice, he met women he liked, but after about ten minutes he could not think of anything to say to them. One night he danced with a woman called Rita and she invited him back to her flat in Raheny. He left her waiting while he went to the toilets to pour cold water over his face. He stood in one of the stalls for almost ten minutes, staring at a graffiti scrawl that said FUCKING UP THE IRA, before deciding that he could'nt do it. He slipped out into the car park without even saying goodbye and drove home.

Johnny got into trouble at school again and was suspended for a month. One night, shortly after he went back, Frank caught him smoking a joint and threw him out of the house. When he returned next morning, Frank didn't ask where he had been. His son started going out with and older girl whom Frank didn't like at all. He began to slope around the house with the same old sullen expression on his face. He went out every night with his guitar under his arm, refusing to say where he was going.

Frank would try to sleep, with his light on and his radio playing quietly, waiting for Johnny to come home. All night long he would listen to the sports channel or the BBC World Service, to news of wars and disasters and earthquakes in strange faraway places with exotic names that he knew he would never see. He wondered if he would be lonely for the rest of his life.

Then he bean to go out at night again, because he could not bear to be alone any more. He knew it was wrong. He knew he should have been at home every night, waiting for his son, but he couldn't stand the loneliness. He would do anything not to be alone in this house full of memories. He telephoned friends he had not seen in years. He contacted people he did not even like and went out with them for long nights in smokey pubs. They would always want to know what had happened between him and Eleanor. He would come home drunk, close his front door and straight away feel crushingly lonely again, as though he had not spoken to anyone in days.

He stopped swimming. He began to put on weight. He began to let his appearance go and to drink too much whisky. He began to take valium and mandrax. He was prescribed stronger anti-depressants. One night he was so lonely he drove to the lanes behind Mount Street where he knew the prostitutes lived. He sat there for two hours, trembling with nerves, trying to summon up the courage to ring one of their doorbells.

He stopped washing every day. He wore his dirty clothes until they stank. The drivers at work would joke about it; they would pinch their noses when he left the room. There were nights when Frank drove his taxi down onto Sandymount Strand and looked out at the sea, wishing to Christ that he had the courage to drive his car in and drown himself. Things Frank Little would never have thought about he began to contemplate now, as a matter of course.

One afternoon in 1980 his son came home drunk from town with a Mohican haircut and a tattoo of a broken heart on his wrist. When Frank saw the haircut he nearly lost his mind. He and his son fought terribly. He hit his son in the mouth and Johnny threatened to kill him. He said it was all Frank's fault that his mother had gone away. He screamed and raged. He picked up a glass and smashed it against the wall. Frank found himself crying.

'You little fucking bastard', he wept.'How can you hurt me like that?'

His son tried to apologise, but Frank slapped him away.

'Go to your mother, you little fuck, if you fucking love her so much. You're like her anyway. Why don't you just fucking go with her and let me be?'

Later that night Johnny knocked on the door of his bedroom. He came in and hugged his father and told him he was sorry. Frank put his arms around his son and the two of them sobbed with desperation.

Johnny began to stay at home then. He began to cook for his father. And whenever his band was playing he would insist that his father came along. Frank went to see them — the Bitter Pills — playing in the Project Arts Centre, the Baggot Inn, the Magnet Bar in Pearse Street. They always played support, to the Bogey Boys, the New Versions, the Brush Shiels Band and the Radiators from Space. Once they even supported U2. Frank loved to watch his son dancing around on the stage, although he couldn't understand this music at all and the volume made his ears throb. He liked being around his son's friends. He liked talking to them, liked the way they were enthusiastic about everything and never asked any questions. He began to feel a little better and to take care of himself once more. He began to go swimming again, every day, in the heated pool in Fitzpatrick's Castle Hotel in Killiney.

One night that summer he was driving down Dawson Street in a freak hailstorm when a middle-aged woman flagged him down outside the Mansion House. They got talking. She was a widow with a grown-up daughter who was married to a vet and living in Australia. She worked in Kenny's Shoe Shop on Grafton Street. Frank liked this laughing Dublin Woman. He liked her voice, its kindness and its warmth. He drove her out to Churchtown and just before she got out of the taxi he asked if she wanted to have a drink with him sometime. She said yes, why not, that would be nice.

That night he told his son about Veronica Grady. He said he hoped Johnny didn't mind, and Johnny laughed and said of course he didn't. The next Saturday they went into town together and Johnny helped his father pick out a new suit and a couple of ties in a trendy shop called Alias Tom. The ties were a little more colourful than Frank would have liked, but his son insisted. 'Go crazy, Da', he said, laughing. He would want to be looking his best, Johnny said. He would want to be looking well for his date.

They went to dinner in the Grey Door in Pembroke Street and talked for so long they were the last to leave. The week after that they went to the opera. They got tickets for 'Evita' and went to that. They went to see Bitter Pills playing at an outdoor concert in Blackrock Park. On Stephen's Day that year they went to the races in Leopardstown. Frank loved being with this woman. She made him feel human again. She made him feel like a man.

After three months, Frank and Veronica decided that they wanted to live together. It happened very simply. She said she was looking for a commitment. She was having a lovely time, she said, but she had come to care very deeply for Frank, and she wasn't a girl any more. Frank said that was fine. He was looking for commitment too. They talked about him selling up and moving in with her and they wondered what was the right thing to do. Sometimes when he thought about Eleanor he would have an attack of guilt. He would discuss it with Veronica and she always seemed to understand. She was never unpleasant about it. Once they were truthful with each other, she could put up with a lot, she told him. In time he came to feel that he could tell this woman anything. It was something to do with age, he knew. Young people talked about honesty, but older people could actually *be* honest. He told her this and she laughed. He thought about Eleanor again, but she had never even telephoned after all. She was probably with somebody else herself, for all he knew. Frank began to think about the future. It was exciting. The prospect of not having to live life from one week to the next filled him with joy. It was not as exciting as being young again, but it was certainly the next best thing. And in the end they agreed that it was more simple for her to move in with him.

Johnny never got on with Veronica. She was relaxed with him. She said she didn't mind where he went or what he did. She said he was old enough to make his own decisions, and as time passed he seemed to resent this. It was odd, but Frank noticed that Johnny seemed actually to want to her to be angry if he came home late or cursed. His son began to pick arguments with Veronica. He would leave the room if she argued back. Soon, if she criticised him at all, he would go upstairs and pack a bag and leave the house. There were many nights when Frank and Veronica drove around the streets of Dublin trying to find him. Veronica tried to be patient, but sometimes she would tell Frank that she thought it would be better for her to move out again. She was not Johnny's mother, she said. She could never be his mother, that was too much to ask of her. There were nights when he had to plead with her not to leave him. She told him she didn't want to go, but that something would have to be done about Johnny.

Frank quarrelled bitterly with his son. He said he loved Veronica and wouldn't have her life made difficult. He asked Johnny if he wanted to live with them, or go and find his mother in England. Johnny was seventeen then. He didn't want to live with anyone, he said. He hated his father and his mother.

'You fucked me up', he yelled.'The two of you fucked me up. You never gave a damn about me.'

Frank threw him out of the house that night and told him never to come back.

A few nights after Johnny left, the telephone rang. It was Eleanor. She had come back to Ireland and was staying with her sister in Chapelizod. She knew about Veronica, she said, and she didn't want to come back to Frank anyway. He asked if she wanted to meet and she said no. He said he wanted to explain about Veronica. She told him she wished him the best, but that she wasn't interested in explanations. They talked on the telephone for nearly an hour, the two of them numb with loss. They wondered where they had gone wrong. They said all the things that people say when they lose their love. They had worked hard. They had done all the things that people are supposed to do. But Frank and Eleanor had simply lost their love, in the way that happens sometimes, almost imperceptibly, when luck runs out and the dream of love melts away into nothing more than a set of arrangements.

Johnny came back to his father's house for a week. He and Veronica fought again and he said he wanted to go and live with his mother. He said he was sorry for hurting Frank's feelings, but he thought that if he could get to know his mother things would calm down in his life. Frank said he understood. He and his son agreed that they would meet each other every Saturday morning.

Some Saturday mornings Johnny would turn up at the car park of the Victor Hotel. Other mornings he wouldn't. Frank would sit by himself, waiting for hours, before going back home to Veronica. And some Saturdays he was so hurt that he would not go home. He would go to a film for the afternoon. He would sit in the cinema and watch the same film twice over to fill in the time. Sometimes he would drive out into the countryside by himself. He would drive to Glendalough and walk around the lakes. He would drive out to Poulaphouca, Greystones, Delgany, Avondale, the places he had gone to with

Eleanor before they were married. When he got home he would lie to Veronica about all the things he and Johnny had done. He would tell her how well they had got on with each other. He would lie because he was so hurt and because he could not bear her sympathy any more.

And then things seemed somehow to improve again. His son began to see him a little more often. They went for drives and walks together. Sometimes they went to the matinée of a play. Johnny was in his final year at school now. He seemed to be getting on well with his teachers and to have some good friends. He was enjoying living with his mother, he said. It was nice to have a chance to catch up. He began to talk about university. He thought he would like to study law.

His son was having difficulty with his studies, so Frank paid for him to have extra tuition in a private school in Leeson Street. He made him promise to try for the place in university. He told him that he would pay for him to take a trip to America, if only he got a place in university.

Johnny sat the Leaving Certificate and scraped a place doing arts at UCD. The night he got his results, Frank suggested dinner with Veronica in the Guinea Pig, an upmarket restaurant in Dalkey. Johnny turned up late and very drunk, with a sullen girl who was wearing black lipstick and a low-cut dress. He refused to speak to Veronica. He refused even to acknowledge that she was there. When his father asked him not to smoke in between courses, he stood up cursing and walked straight out of the restaurant with the girl. They didn't see each other again for three months.

And the, one night at the end of the summer of 1982, Johnny rang his father's house to say that he had run away from his mother. They had not been getting along, he said. They had been fighting every day for months, and his mother didn't understand him at all. Nobody understood him, he said.

They met that night, in Bowes pub off D'Olier Street. Johnny had been crying and was very upset. He went back to Frank's house after closing time and stayed for a week. Frank arranged to get him a flat in a modern block near the university and told him he would pay for it.

In October that year Johnny started attending UCD. He liked it, he told his father, but he couldn't decide what he wanted to do. He started with English and history and then moved to philosophy and politics. After Christmas, he moved again, to sociology. He got involved with the students' union. He was arrested one day for occupying the office of the Minister for Education. He failed his first-year exams and repeated them in the autumn. He failed again.

The night he told his father about this they had a furious argument. Frank asked his son where his life was going. He told him he was a spoilt little brat. That he was selfish. That he was a coward and wanted to cling to all the pain of his past, because it was easy to do that.

None of this mattered any more, Johnny said. He was going away to Nicaragua to pick coffee. Everyone else was talking about it, but he was going to do it. He would be back in three months and he would get his life together then. But he would do it without his father, he said. He would live his life without his parents now. It was September 1983. He never wanted to see his parents again.

Niall Kelly

FATHER'S LEGACY

This poem came into being some thirty-three years after my father died (dropped dead 8.30 am aged forty-eight) when I was thirteen. I came from a family that never dealt with death and so, while still a child, my grandmother, two aunts, an uncle and I'm sure others died without my realising so. In keeping with the practice, on the morning my father died I and my sisters and brothers were packed off to friends and kept out of the way. I never attended his removal or funeral!

Grief unshed.

In February of 1991 I was driving from Clonmel to Shannon for a flight to London and then on to Brussels. Going through Limerick Junction at around 2.30 pm, snow started to fall and I realised there were going to be delays on the way. Arriving in Shannon I was told there was a delay of one hour. I repaired to the bar and, uncharacteristically had two drinks. Followed by some wine on the flight, I was in fine form for the Muse at 35,000 feet flying out of London.

This poem formed after many attempts. I realised it had been going around in my head for quite some time, in fact, months. I never did title it.

> In a voice of one betrayed I said, You died.
> With such speed and shock I never really cried
> to mourn your going.
>
> My deepest feelings since are deep denied
> as close relationships mistrust belied
> any real chance of knowing.
>
> I didn't have your love
> to teach me how to love
> and came to love my children through letting them love me.

I'm not sure what it says about my relationship with him. It certainly says a lot about the lost relationship and the effect it had on me.

Derek Shiel

MY FATHER

My father was, I thought, christened Alexander O'Donovan Shiel. He was born on 26 June 1903, in Dublin where he lies buried to the south of the city, in Deansgrange.

When a boy, he lived in various parts of the country as his family moved about due to his father's employment; certainly, they resided for quite a time in Belfast, and there he knew what it was to be ridiculed as a Catholic. How many schools he attended he never divulged, but he did mention an incident at one of them: he never forgot seeing a large boy, brutally taunted in class by the master, eventually rise up against him in rage. Such a retaliation still astonished my father but he thought it had, in the circumstances, seemed justifiable. Abruptly, at fourteen, it proved necessary for him to leave school, in order to support his mother and younger brother by getting a job; what he did at first I never discovered but the important factor, a part of family history, was that my father found that he hated being an employee and so, in his early twenties, with another man he set himself up in business; from being repairers of wirelesses in one room they gradually expanded into a company as electrical wholesale distributors, many years later starting a separate company in Belfast. And, despite failing health, my father was still the managing director, by then the owner too, of Kelly and Shiel, when he died in 1966 at the age of sixty-three.

My parents met each other in Dublin, at a small dancing club, unromantically named *Leggett Burns*. He was the first man to whom my mother found herself really attracted: she has often remarked on how late they were permitted to stay out dancing, my father walking her home in the early hours of the morning. Their acquaintance developed into an innocent courtship, but one that was to be actively opposed. Quite unlike her own father, she admired his appearance and charm, his drive towards fulfilling his ambition; other men had taken a liking to her but it was with my father that she discovered what it was to fall in love, and he with her. Her parents' disapproval of an engagement centred on his being a Catholic, for they were Presbyterian; my father countered their reservations by deciding to change his religion so that he could marry her. This was a daring action to take in 1931, for he ran the risk of being ostracised either as an individual or in business but, in fact, as far as I know he never was. Conversions were more likely to be from Protestant to Catholic since that was the prevailing religion, with strict tenets about the upbringing of children. However, my father's decision was not quite as surprising as it may seem. His grandparents on his mother's side had, inexplicably, brought up their children in alternate religions: he had an aunt who was a nun and another, a Protestant, married her Church of Ireland suitor; thus, he was exercising an option already found feasible within his family, and such choices have continued in my generation, though not without domestic hush . . . or hue and cry.

By the time of my birth my father was already an up-and-coming businessman, the firm having moved from one room to two, and then across the street to an entire premises. In the late thirties, he had travelled to Leipzig for a Trade Fair, seeing for himself the intensification of patriotic fervour in Germany, and in the summer of 1939 sailed to New York, in order to secure an agency for windchargers, (before rural electrification these were often purchased by Irish farmers wishing to generate their own power). I was born during the morning of 18 April in the year the War began, a second child, coming almost mid-way between an older brother and a younger sister. My mother was advised to give birth to her children under sedation and so my father would have come to see the new baby sometime later in the day, as was customary. Our background is complicated: our father was Irish but with some Huguenot blood, whereas our mother, although born in Dublin, is the child of an Irish mother and an American father, who was born and brought up in Kentucky. His family most probably originated in Germany, or the German part of Switzerland, and his wife's forebears had, in the previous generation, been settlers from Scotland.

Ireland chose neutrality in the Second World War and my father was not a man who felt any obligation to fight for the British; he retained mixed feelings about them, the English in particular, until much later, having lived through a period of foreign rule, the Troubles and the gradual coming into being of a Republic. He became an air-raid warden, provided with a helmet and gas-mask I would in time discover and play with, discarded in the attic. I can recall blackout curtains drawn tightly across my window and ration books, also Armistice Day when, curiously, small paper Union Jacks, glued to sticks, were for sale in Dublin streets. Otherwise, I am not sure that the War played a great part in my life until, long afterwards, we as a family discussed German concentration camps.

While still small I met my father's mother briefly. He and his brothers and sisters adored her. By them she was seen as good and, at the time I was born, their father was seen as bad. She had apparently gathered her children around her but this maternal stratagem my father would, when older, come to reconsider. She was an austere grandmother, in her manner quite distant; what I remember about her are two incidents. While staying with us she slept in my room and one day, as the door was open, I went in to find her kneeling by the bed, saying her rosary; I had not previously seen anyone do this and left the room before I could be noticed. In the drawing-room the pattern of the carpet included a vividly designed border, on one occasion, down on my knees with crayon or coloured pencil I was scribbling across the tufts when, from her chair, she severely reprimanded me: I was horror-struck.

She is the O'Donovan of my father's name; each member of his family was extremely proud of their O'Donovan blood. Both her parents had died in her adolescence and she was sent to live with relatives, who arranged a match with Isaac Shiel. He proved to be quite the 'boyo', a drinker and a womaniser, whose money disappeared — he went bankrupt — more than once, an aunt suggested. She came to believe she had married beneath her. However, the clan of O'Donovans were no strangers to misadventure. At one time a well-to-do family owning a castle, they were numbered amongst those ordered by the British to convert to Protestantism or forfeit their property; in refusing to adopt another religion they lost home and lands. This was, I am told, but the start of many varied failures of fortune, through successive generations. My grandfather parted from his wife, whether because his family disowned him or because he simply abandoned them remains unclear; this was the reason for my father's quitting school when he did. My grandmother had turned all of the children against their father but it would seem he, himself, had played an animated part in this debacle.

One of his sisters related to my mother how my father had as a young child hero-worshipped their father — something I was not at liberty to do — but that as he grew older his devotion crumbled . . . to a degree I am aware of only as I write this. At some later date my father altered his own second name, substituting his mother's surname, O'Donovan, for his father's christian name Isaac. When the business was running successfully, Isaac Shiel, finally reduced to living in an old people's home or perhaps one for ex-alcoholics, would turn up at the office to ask his son for money. At first given occasional sums, he was eventually turned away and, when he died, my father refused to attend his funeral. He was never alluded to or his name mentioned. Yet without hesitation my father went to England for the burial of his mother and afterwards wore her gold wedding-ring on his marriage finger.

At the age of four I fell ill with pleurisy and primary tuberculosis, needing to remain in bed for several months. My great grandmother on my mother's side, about the same age as my father's mother, died shortly before Mrs Shiel, so each of my parents had to leave home to attend funerals. One afternoon I remember crying alone in my bed-room about what was called 'death', about my grannies being dead: I could sense, obscurely, that I did not understand those tears.

My father was of average height, about five feet nine, slightly long in the back in proportion to his legs. At first he was slender, dark haired, and, when I was small, frequently wore glasses, although later he used them only for reading. Good-looking in an unusual way, having a long face, emphatic, downturned nose and long ears, he possessed remarkably pale eyes of a watery greyish green and, as with many men of his period, he wore a moustache. He didn't show his teeth unless he happened to laugh, neither were his lips revealing; it was the distinctive gaze or the whole form of the head which caught your attention. Nervous, wary or aloof in expression he frequently exuded an energy, tremendously pent up, so that, in recalling his body, even if solid it felt taut . . . and restless. . . it craved space. He could not bear to be hemmed in or linger amongst crowds, needed to leave the door of a room open, in case he should suddenly wish to leave it.

His clothing was conventional: a range of brown, grey, navy blue, casual wear being of no consequence other than his indispensable shorts, worn even in winter indoors, part of his body's urgent delight in freedom. But he was not devoid of interest in his appearance. A long row of ties hung in his wardrobe, he enjoyed wearing evening dress, on more formal occasions white tie, winged collar and tails. We were allowed to help him prepare, polishing his patent-leather shoes, inserting cuff-links and studs, brushing his shoulders before helping him on with his overcoat. He would progress in his last years — somewhat to my astonishment — to morning-suit and grey topper.

His happening to laugh surprised, even disconcerted me. He did laugh, in company could suddenly break into a guffaw or would enjoy telling an anecdote, possibly exaggerating details here and there. Rather than being humorous he enjoyed fun, was responsive to wit but not at all at ease with hilarity. For the seventieth birthday of my American grandfather he made up an amusing long poem of rhyming couplets, and it is two Limericks he taught me which first come to mind, each I can now see indicating an aspect of his upbringing.

> Willy, in the best of sashes,
> Fell in the fire and burned to ashes,
> And, though the room grew cold and chilly,
> We hadn't the heart to stoke poor Willy.

When my father was born little boys still wore dresses with sashes until about the age of four. A photograph exists of him, wan-faced and blankly staring in such a dress, to the knees, and small buttoned boots.

> Jimma, Jamma, Jimma Jelly,
> Went to bed with a pain in her
> — don't get alarmed, don't get red —
> Jimma went to bed
> With a pain in her head.

As a young man, a polite use of language was considered essential when speaking of girls! Where humour was concerned the epitome of my father's delight was in the opera of Gilbert and Sullivan, which he would quote and to which he sometimes invited me. He possessed a book of the complete librettos and often consulted it; particular songs and the antics of celebrated actors were a source of constant pleasure, of his own 'innocent merri-ment'!

We lived in only two houses and the first was where my brother and I were little children, where my sister was born, and which we left as I was recovering from pleurisy. Momentous for me though these events were, there were others no less so. My most intimate memory of my father is of him taking me on his knees to play ride-a-cock-horse, being bounced up and down and then suddenly, as he parted them, falling between his legs. Or I would play around his shoes, emptying out his trouser cuffs of the grit and fluff inside. I can too, only just, remember his occasionally getting down on all fours to carry me on his back around the dining-room. But it was wartime, my father's business was beginning to grow, he would bring paper-work home in the evening ... this was the period when he wore his glasses almost constantly; somehow, I learned to restrain myself, not to go near him, that I needed permission before I could reach out and touch him. I stopped clambering onto his knee.

When I started going to kindergarten, my father would take me there on the back of his bicycle and my mother pick me up at lunchtime. Occasionally, we would go by tram. One day I refused to say good morning to him, so he would not bring me to school: I was in disgrace. After that, such a confrontation was not to be usual between us. My brother, however, suffered a much harsher punishment and more than once. My room stood at one end of the landing and my mother would read to me after I was put to bed; I recollect her trying to persist while, outside the closed door, my brother was being beaten with a hair brush. So distressing were his screams that I asked her why she did not go out and intervene. This was the only physical violence I ever knew of but sufficient to convince me that I must try to be good ... it was imperative. Little did I realise what would accrue from that decision.

Another ominous event occurred not many months before I grew sick. My brother asked our father a pivotal question: 'If God is our Father, how can we have a real one as well?' After listening to this conversation, without consciously realising it, I hatched a plan of escape: could I switch my allegiance, I wondered?

I slept in a bed with vertical bars behind and either side of the pillow. In the night I woke up and, taking hold of them, found they were hot. Next morning, as my mother was away, it was my father who came in to get me up. When he heard of my perplexing discovery he was surprisingly kind, and, even if the bars were cold now, seemed to understand. He told me to stay in my bed and called the doctor.

In the growing complexity of the household, before falling ill, I had felt myself disapproved of: I was not conforming to my father's requirements of a son. Of the various consequences of my sickness the most crucial was that we fell out of love, one with the other. A chasm opened up in my life that God the Father could not fill but where would I find another father? I recognise the pattern father had passed down to son, my grief no greater probably than my father's at the loss of *his* father, but I must have vowed not to allow myself to participate in such pattern-making: I remain childless.

My father, in the forties, assumed greater responsibilities, not only as husband and parent, but also as a managing director; even before the War ended we had moved to a larger house and some years afterwards a disused distillery was purchased for the company and an increased workforce employed. As managing director he chose a role in which he could fulfil himself, behind his desk he was confident of his position, demonstrating that he was shrewd, determined, tough and authoritative, could intimidate, did not make conditions attractive for his staff, but underneath his severe exterior he was constant and could reveal himself to be kind: I think particularly of his comforting a man with a hare-lip, who broke down in his office after just producing a son with a similar imperfection, or his great pride in a carpenter, whose work he considered first-rate, or his unremitting loyalty to two employees with drinking problems.

Without his being aware of what had happened between us, I can see my father as spasmodically attempting to forge links. There were times when, to our utmost surprise, he would decide to put my sister and me to bed: he would count, count so much for a jersey, so much for a shirt, for a vest, we becoming wildly excited as we hurriedly threw off our clothes. Then he would make up a story — he never read any — one especially intrigued us, of earwigs, Peter and Paul, who had audaciously, mischievously, crawled over the wall and down into our garden. If I needed his help with mathematics, which I often did, after his supper was over he gave it unstintingly. Then began, before I went away to school at thirteen, the first of our rituals: on alternate Thursdays he would take me to the cinema; once on an impulse we dashed from one theatre to another to squeeze two films into one evening. If he called at the library on his way home, he might unexpectedly borrow a book for me to read. When I was adolescent he often invited me to lunch at his Club; Christmas Eve, in particular, became another such ritual. It began each year with family errands, followed by a generous lunch and, before returning home, a bouquet of flowers would be bought for my mother, as decoration for the Christmas table.

He was, without question, the paterfamilias, governing and dispensing. As young children we often felt no more than appendages to the marriage, our mother his real concern, the one to be turned to and fondled. In the evenings we had to respect his weariness, were schooled to become sensitive to his moods, gauging when to ask a favour of him. Secretly he wished, I am certain, to be seen as a patriarch — that was his ideal — an unwavering provider. Our extra-curricular activities were legion, music, tennis, riding lessons; before a school entrance examination I studied Latin, mathematics and French privately. I even took rare art lessons with the painter Anne Yeats. This dedication to our upbringing becomes all the more poignantly abundant when set against the background of his childhood impoverishment and ensuing unease about money.

To call my father a snob would not be correct and yet elements of the definition are apt. He was bigoted and could be haughty but I never saw him pursue people because of their ancestry or status, in spite of his admiration for achievement; nevertheless privacy and apartness were essential to him, but so were moral standards, manners, refined social behaviour, even if, under pressure from his own seething emotions, he could break the rules of courtesy he strove so rigorously to uphold.

I do not see my father as warlike, he never suggested that warfare was inevitable or necessary; instead he was at war within himself, all his aggression mustered against the possibility of attack by or upon his own mutinous or disarrayed emotions. He could become overwhelmed by them and give vent, startlingly, to unpredictable outbursts of fury. As a rule, he fought to keep himself under control by maintaining distance, either with a hostile glare or by actually moving away, or by tactical withdrawal behind a smoke screen of silence. While, in his acute receptivity to perceived insult, it would be his own body which would take the chief impact of his imploded ferocity, to those nearest him would be transmitted shockwaves they must attempt, necessarily, to absorb. If a situation were to become unendurable, rather than being able to defuse its intensity, there would be confrontation, through flare-up or outright explosion. In the aftermath of such eruptions, a heavier silence settled over the room, then penetrated slowly through the house, bearing the sour odour of shame, the leaden weight of wrong-doing. But whose? What the cause of his hurt? Who the offender of his person? What the depth of his wounding? The message his presence conveyed was 'leave me alone', whereas what he, silently and essentially, was crying out for was the utmost consolation. Implicit, behind the extravagant display of his turbulence, was the plea for understanding, for acceptance by us, for forgiveness. That plea could not be uttered. And we, usually too baffled, or bruised, or horrified, could not respond in the ways he desperately, though covertly, longed for: we resented this scarcely comprehensible man. Did he, I now wonder, ever make out what, seemingly from nowhere, pursued him? 'Perish the thought!' was a favourite phrase but the tormenting phantoms of his earliest life never did.

Definitely my father was religious, but whether spiritual I cannot know — did he pray? — that is an example of what would not get shared. To become a member of the vestry, an elder in his local church, made him proud. For the family, being to church was an important ritual: we must wear gloves, his sons their suits, have money for the collection plate, speak to other members of the congregation after the service; people were occasionally invited back for drinks, the minister might call in the evening. Moral values were firmly inculcated, marital fidelity mattered, not getting drunk, 'Neither a borrower or a lender be' was a frequent quotation, but forgiveness was *not* an item included on the list. It took my father twenty years to forgive a man at church he felt had behaved badly towards him; however, he did manage to speak to him some years before he died, and openly shared his relief in doing so. Younger men went to him for advice and I am told he gave certain close friends money, sent his elder brother parcels when he was a prisoner-of-war. He was the proposer of the first Jewish member to be elected to his club.

From his moral values stemmed his strong sense of civic obligation. During the War he joined the board of an institute, the Mount Street Club, set up to help men in difficulty or out-of-work. Subsequently, he joined the Dublin Chamber of Commerce, became its chairman and then chairman of the Chambers of Commerce of Ireland. In the first of these roles he was instrumental in setting up the Junior Chamber for men at the outset of their business careers. He became Chairman of the Board for the Employment of the Blind and after it came an unusual request: would he serve as Honorary Consul for Austria in Dublin? This post gave him the greatest pleasure for, eventually, his standing in the city was being recognised . . . as it would be one more time. As his funeral processed from the church, sets of traffic lights were extinguished along the route and two police outriders escorted his hearse to the burial-ground.

'If you can't be left-wing when you're young, when can you be?' I said to him once. 'Oh, I quite agree', came his affirmative reply. He was, I suppose, a sort of liberal, without particular political affiliation, but, having grown to maturity in what became a Republic, he was himself republican, albeit in discreet ways. Either by paradoxical example or by words, he instilled in me a terror of fanaticism. The role de Valera played in the development of the country was one my father could respect and endorse; he voted for him, but not exclusively. The leader he most unreservedly admired, however, was President Roosevelt. My father must have set up in business not long before the Wall Street Crash and he spoke to me in fulsome detail about what Roosevelt had initiated and what feats the New Deal had managed to accomplish. Just before the outbreak of war, when in New York, he could witness the outcome of these innovative measures.

Despite his being prone to anxiety I became aware, as I grew up, of my father's optimism, although, surely, the heartiness of his appetite had amply demonstrated this to me already. 'Let it not be said that Mother ever reared a jibber!' he would comment, laying a hand flat on the table. He told me how exciting he thought it would be to live to the year two thousand. Fascinated by the advances in technology, he adored watching the flight of aeroplanes, would stand gazing down into the washing-machine, lost in wonderment; he could recall vividly the day when in a hotel and still only a boy, he had first switched on an electric light.

That my father's business in the early sixties was being faced by quite new challenges was not evident to us as a family, nor was the extent of the changes to come even clearly apparent to him. His company was, in fact, only made secure by two calamities — a fire and a flood. 'All you need now is an earthquake!' my mother quipped. A decade later she would, most regrettably, be proved right. He began to suffer from palpitations, gradually becoming housebound; he could always walk but more and more lay in bed or sat dozing in a chair. 'Your father slept his life away,' was how my mother saw it whereas to the doctors his fatal illness was caused by hypertension.

Taken eventually to hospital for about a week or ten days, in his gradual decline, like some rare and contradictory plant, he flowered: he was, at last, completely the quiet, courteous, gentleman he had for so long striven to become. His composure was touchingly evident. He never mentioned the fact that he was dying but, when told of the award the Austrian government wanted to present him with, he nodded towards my mother, merely saying, 'You take it'. Nevertheless, while having obtained the whole dignity a dying person is capable of rising to, against his will, he must suffer the physical indignity of having a catheter inserted. As horrible was another decision made by the doctors; when my mother asked if she could spend the night by his bedside, her request was refused. I believe we failed him, that by not fighting strenuously against that decision we deserted him, but I am forced to admit, perhaps typically, he, himself did not ask anyone to remain with him. In retrospect, it would have been out of character if he had chosen to die surrounded by the members of his family.

In the early hours of the next morning my mother and I were summoned to the hospital and, on arrival, informed of his death. His body was still warm. As I leant over and kissed his forehead, what surfaced in my mind were the words 'Bone of my bone, flesh of my flesh'. Out of me had been drawn, involuntarily, the acknowledgment of our kinship.

My father found a way of dying impeccably: in so doing he revealed himself to have become, in my eyes, a warrior. He chose his moment to leave when two of his children were married themselves and I just about to mount my first exhibition. I discovered that I did not have cause to mourn our parting; across the divide which separated us we had made in his last six years much headway. Even if I did not fulfil his dream for both his sons, of obtaining a university degree, I did receive a diploma from an art college. Seeing me in gown and mortar-board gratified him and when, following a year's post-graduate painting, I was awarded a scholarship to visit America, he offered to pay my return fare so that my money might last longer . . . it did, I travelled widely across the States for over a year.

After my return, I went to live in London and there it gave him pleasure to see my name in an art college prospectus as one of the tutors. On his business visits he and I would meet; in the evenings I would be his companion at dinner and, by ourselves now, we began to converse, I, I must admit, often sharing my woes without being fully aware of doing so. During the first evening of one visit, after complementing me on how I looked and listening to my extended news, in the gentlest way possible he ventured to ask how I thought he looked. His vulnerability shamed me. On another occasion he suggested we go to see a film, a film he warned me I might find slightly off colour, but would I mind joining him? I have no memory of its being in any way indecent and I was, after all, over twenty-one and myself a sexual being. Again it was his courteous attentiveness — 'don't get alarmed, don't get red' — which took me by surprise and humbled me.

During his increasing bouts of unwellness, including a short time spent in hospital, I would write to him and he would reply, usually briefly but with concern. I still keep one of these letters. Our correspondence mattered to him, I heard from my mother, and quite likely set the scene for a poignant and macabre event. Having picked me up at the airport he suggested a drive and took me to the Forty-foot, where, over many years, in many weathers, he had swum either in togs or naked, depending on the time of day. We then followed the narrow strip of coast road beyond the Martello Tower and stopped the car by a slope of grass, as I thought, to admire the sea view. My father recounted that among the rocks had been found a few days before a young woman's body. That we should be quietly contemplating the whereabouts of a murder was beyond belief, for if there was a subject my father had always shied away from it was death. After a pause he remarked, 'It's strange but while I've been in hospital I never once thought of dying'. I listened without comment. This covert admission of what he was thinking was, I can now see, the moment of our closest intimacy as two adults, father and son.

Had my father been able to choose his own career he thought he would have liked to become the conductor of an orchestra. He, of course, demonstrated his authority, his ability to control a large group of people was obvious, but he would have needed to make plainer quite concealed aspects of his character: music could, for instance, have allowed his sensuality more ample expression. Perhaps the nearest I saw him come to such a role was when, as host, he stood at the door and would throw wide his arms in welcoming approaching guests. His mother played the piano, a brother and sister studied painting and sculpture for a few terms, the same brother then finding himself as an actor. It is feasible that this wistful dream of my father's, in no way based on musical talent, has affected me more profoundly than I ever realised: is it not another aspect of that yearning within each member of his family to be more than they were, in terms of social position, of career, of vocation even? My father imagined he would have liked me to work in his business but it is obvious that I could not have fulfilled his dream for me and fulfilled myself. My own career, however, bears an intricate relationship to that of his family: I have found myself from my beginnings as a painter branching into the arts they attempted or pursued. I make sculpture, some of it percussive sound sculpture, I have written and directed for theatre, and, adapting a talent of my American grandfather, who was a dedicated plantsman, have practised as a landscape gardener. These means of expression, I tell myself, I attempt to manage and direct; maybe I should say orchestrate.

Dimension — that one word — sums up what I inherited from my father. In order to survive, I was compelled to develop dimension, rather than direction, within myself — height, breadth and depth of perception. Where others are constrained by limitation I was constrained by the reverse: to strive towards comprehension of many different facets in the make-up of living. Through moral and filial obligation, adherence to religious principles, through being trained to be polite, at whatever cost to myself, I needs must become considerate towards others. Since in the household my father's position was paramount, so were his moods of the utmost importance. Above all else it was his silence which unnerved me. He might withdraw into a daze — seated at the end of the table — staring into space; it was, I suppose, for him a means of contemplation, whereas for me it meant severe loss. Attempting to understand that silence incapacitated me: gradually I grew more aware that I was not capable of loving him as he wanted to be loved, and worse, that in discovering myself I was *not* becoming what he wished me to be. His discomfort became mine, his silence, behind my talkativeness, mine in that more and more of myself was withdrawn, frustrated and jarring within me. Because of his, or my, unease I preferred distance to closeness between us and yet, when meeting or parting away from home, we always kissed, right to the end of his life.

After my education was completed and my career just begun I became divided, undermined by a slowly released depth-change. Without knowing how or why, under the intensity of such pressure I split in two, in my heart half of me exploring my creativity, the other half impeded by having to conform to others' patterns. Addictive habits were formed of trying to understand the silence of men, of putting others' needs before my own and, as a result, periodically blowing up or collapsing under a stress I could not fathom.

Having, as I came to believe, lost all sense of my own will, I was driven deeper and deeper inside myself in an effort to locate and rescue it. Beneath a flurry of activities I often became static: confused by the profusion of the world about me, and its values, and by the complex of emotional and creative desires or inhibitions within. Since there was no one distinct objective ahead I did not seem to advance — and so I got nudged, little by little, into seeking a synthesis of dimensions — by degrees wholeness began to present itself as my essential goal. Had I lived in another period, it is possible that my dilemma could have been categorised into the role of a monk. Instead it now feels appropriate to choose a more atavistic role, where work and sexuality define and enhance one another, where as an artist I am at once creator, celebrant and mediator.

John Creedon

THE STORY-TELLER

Recently I was in Cork and spent a few nights with my father. He is in great form. Flying. Seventy-six and just back from the World Cup. He brought me back a copy of *The Irish Post* in which he was 'quoted n-all, man'. His 'Match Analysis'. He's in great ould spirits. It's no bother to him to take off on a journey like that, or to Morocco the year before — out with my sister. He's a great man for the road — he spent his whole life on it anyway: when he was fifteen he drove his first truck, his father's. Before that one they had a Model T, because he remembers having his first ice-cream and told me about having it. It was in Macari's of Washington Street. He had come into Cork with his father and his father had pulled in on the right hand side of the street — it was long before the highway code, obviously — and went across to Macaris. His father brought him back his first ice-cream and my father took one huge gulp of it and he said he thought he was scalded, burnt you know. Apparently his father got great crack out of that afterwards.

He was saying to me one day that his father was a bit of a disciplinarian. That he was a good guy really, but he took his responsibilities very seriously. Once ever he remembers getting a right thumping from him: he was a small lad, and there was a woman (like a bag-lady today I suppose) in the village and my father and the kids used to tease her. Seemingly my Dad joined the posse, hounding her around the place. My grandfather spotted him through the window of the hotel and called him in and took off his belt and leathered him. He told him, words to the effect, there would always be greater and lesser than you and basically taught him to have respect for people.

My father went from working with his father, who had the hotel, and the mill and post office and that kind of stuff in Inchigeela, to working for a forerunner of CIE, I suppose, because he spent years with CIE anyway. He was originally on the trucks and spent the Emergency drawing turf, among other things, including cattle. Once the Board of Works, or the equivalent, had a handful of men building a pier in Crookhaven I think it was. So this woman had opened her front parlour as a dining room and, as he said, it was bacon and cabbage on Monday, bacon and cabbage on Tuesday, bacon and cabbage every day even including Friday. He was singing the praises of mustard which was all the rage in Cork at the time and the woman had never heard of it, wouldn't hear of it. Would have nothing to do with it. So he obviously brought down some mustard one day, mixed it up and had a scoop of it on the side of the plate when she came in. Seeing the mustard she grabbed the plate, swiped the mustard off with her apron and said 'Christ, them damn chickens! They get everywhere.' He loves that, the 'Tailor and Anstey' kind of story, and being away quite a bit he has loads of them.

During my teenage years he was doing the long-distance buses and staying overnight in Ballybunion or Glengariff or Killarney to do the first bus to Cork from there in the mornings. I suppose that was rough in its own way on my mother who had to stay at home, look after the shop and bring up twelve kids at the time. So in those years I didn't see huge amounts of him, though at the time I didn't realise it. But I suppose that's true of any childhood experience: you think it is the way it is, you think what's going on is a fairly normal day, but looking back on it in, say fifteen years on, the whole period might seem a strange period in my life and I say 'God, that was a strange period in my life!' So in the same way, his being away didn't seem strange — I'll see him this evening, or Thursday, or whatever. No panic, he'll be there.

For some reason I'd often see him in the mornings. He used to make breakfast for us, the three boys at the end of the twelve. He was always in great form in the morning. I suppose the house was quiet and there was no hassle going on in the shop. We used to have to start early to get to school in Carrignagower, so we used to be up at half six and it was mountains of bread and butter and tea. Sometimes he'd boil an egg or something. Jez, he was mad about us, always — one of his lines was: 'Christ, I feed my men well.' We were his little army going off to work.

I remember another time bringing Nonie, who worked for us, home to Inniskean and we ended up in this bog somewhere. I remember my father distinctly coming to the rescue: he carried me under one arm, like a package, and my other two brothers under the other arm and paraded across the bog on the clumps of grass. He was a huge man when we were growing up — twenty stone. But he's shrivelled down a bit now, though he's still 'a match for anyone'. He has a stick now and he says 'Your Mam was always worried about me, but sure as long as I have the stick and the dog then I'm all right, boy'.

He grew up in Inchigeela and Mam in Adrigole. I don't know how they met, but I know they had their honeymoon in Dublin, and it's like everything in his life, he has a story about that too. As he said once 'Your poor mother! The first day of her honeymoon and where did I bring her? The Central Mental Hospital in Dundrum!' Apparently he went to see some fellow he knew from around the area that 'no gaols would hold'. He was a boxer or something and, according to my father, was always in trouble and had escaped out of Brixton and other places, ending up in Dundrum to be visited during their honeymoon!

They were great ould pals really, my parents. I suppose a bit like the Tailor and Anstey in their own way, though my mother had a hard gig really with the twelve of us and the shop. But even in their old age they were in London, about a year before my mother died. The old fella was very bad on the legs — it was before the hip transplant — and my mother wanted to do the shops. So they made some arrangement about where specifically to meet up again after they parted company for a time. My father wandered off looking around some antique shop or something and by the time he got back he was flaked with the heat and the legs were giving out on him. He found an old orange box or something and sat down on it outside Harrods or somewhere. But being a big man, it collapsed under him, and with the bad hip he couldn't get up. So he said he spent the whole afternoon sprawled out there, no one came to his aid. By the time my mother found him, she was in hysterics, but he was after collecting a few bob in his cap on the ground beside him! She thought this was gas.

Ah he was a bit of a romantic all right, because I can remember even as a kid seeing he had ways of getting around her, if he needed to. If she was giving out that was okay. 'She's in a storm now, so leave her get on with it' kind of thing. But as a teenager I used to see that as a weakness in him: 'A bit of a wimp — putting up with it. I'd give her a mouthful'. And then I think later I realised that the Buddhist Way, the Gentle Path, is not only the wiser, but the braver. So I've learned to say that much for him, that what I often thought of as cowardice in him, was very often the tougher and braver road, really.

When you're one of twelve, you've very few occasions with one or other parent alone with you, or better again both your parents alone together with you. I don't remember ever actually looking for it, but if it happened, this was great. I have one distinct memory. I remember once going to Dungarvan in the car with the two of them, they were asking me to sing, and then the ould fellow threw his arm about my mother and began to sing 'Darling I am growing old' and I thought she'd say 'Yerra, go on, shut up'. But no. His arm stayed around her shoulder the whole journey. I'm sure they were oblivious to me and it wasn't for my benefit. So I could see that when they were on their own — or with only one — there were moments of tenderness there.

I'd say that in his youth, my father was definitely a party animal, because he wasn't stuck for a few bob and he was a gregarious kind of man and probably had a few beers with a sing song. Maybe he still was like that when the older ones were young, but by my stage he was quiet, attentive, did his job and what was asked from him. But one Christmas Eve, when I was a young fellow, he came in late — half-seven, instead of his regular half-five — because he'd got his Christmas package, or something, and gone for a few beers with the boys. I have a very vivid picture of it and he was just a bit bleary eyed, but not legless and it wasn't late at night. When I came in I knew there was a commotion going on. He was sitting alone in the middle of the kitchen on a chair and when he saw me he said 'How'a you boy? And how's my boyeen an' all?' And I thought this was a bit gushy and that he was even more like Santa Clause. But my mother had taken to another room in the house and everyone was giving out to one another — Don, my older brother was 'packing the knotted handker-chief' and leaving. And I wondered what was going on and how could they all be doing this to me and spoiling my Christmas on me. Anyway the room my mother had taken was adjoining mine and after I'd gone to bed I heard my father come upstairs and standing outside the door whispering 'Siobhan! Ah come on Siobhan, for Christ's sake, sure 'tis Christmas Girl. Come on' as I fell asleep. When I woke up in the morning I felt: 'Yeah, it's Christmas' and then I remembered last night's commotion, and my parents fighting and thinking something terrible is going to happen. So I looked into my parents' room, not the one she'd gone into, and there they were the two of them, snoring. And I went 'Yeawh' — it was the best Christmas ever! He never did it again, and as long as I can remember him he'd only ever have a few beers and now in recent years he's got diabetes.

Another Christmas story I shared with him had to do with the shop, just a few years back. Earlier on Christmas Eve one of the drunks he used enjoy scarpered with a stolen armful of apples and oranges while my father was serving a customer. When the shop was closed there was a knock on the shop window and I said to him not to bother with it, and he made his usual reply 'Yerra it might be someone stuck for a packet of fags or a pint of milk'. So out he goes, opens up his security system, bolts, chains, the lot and there was the man returned to the scene of the crime. Swaying on the path with the armful of fruit he said to my father: 'Connie, you wouldn't have a couple of bags for this lot here, would ya, to get this stuff home?' And my father looked at me and said: 'John, two brown bags please for the gentleman'. Then he helped him pack them and sent him off with a 'Stay off the beer now over Christmas'. Is it any wonder my father always announced his bedtime with 'I'll retire now with heavy losses!' They talk about turning the other cheek ... that was the best example of it I'd ever seen before or since.

But to avoid deifying him, it was the drama, the story that he loved, and especially with all the drunks or street people he befriended. And he loved me telling him stories as well. Mimicking people and coming in telling him. He'd be sitting there nodding, trying to draw more out of me.

He loved the prayers. I used to say the Rosary for him and he loved it. I don't think the guy saw any darkness in his life at all, even the sorrowful mysteries for him were grand. Once the rhythm got going he'd be grand. 'John is a great man for the figaries' he used to say because I used to have loads of embellishments at the end of it. But there was no guilt in their religion and they didn't put any pressure on us and certainly not after a particular age. But the way he practised religion was about miraculous medals in a 'Padre Pio is the only man for that,' kind of a way. Not a philosophy really, but a set of rules to keep you out of harm and the pageantry that went with it. But in his own way a reverent man. 'There's no need for dirty talk.'

I didn't have many rows with my father really, because it would be very hard to argue with him — with my mother, yes, but not with him. And he didn't like it if I got into heated debates with my mother. I remember one day, a typical thing, I was in first year in university and going on about something to her that I was into at the time. My father first gave me the odd wink trying to cool me down when it got heated until I turned on him saying 'What's it got to do with you anyway?' And he was hurt and said 'Oh yes, Mister High-n-Mighty, just because you're above in university now I suppose none of us knows anything'. And he was right too, really. He was never violent either, even though he used to round us up in Pine Street with a stick. Herding us home. But you wouldn't back answer him anyway because he was always so big.

Now we're more like pals and he is very fond of slagging, though not in a personally hurtful way. Last month we went to Gouganebarra and he got into the car with my three boys in the back and they're a bit in awe of him really because they see so little of him. So he turned and said: 'Now there's three rules in the car: no farting, no fighting and no singing — definitely no singing, right?' 'Right', said the three of them quietly and before I had the car into third gear he launched off into 'Oh we do like to be beside the seaside' and they were corpsed out of it because he kept it up the whole way singing old vaudeville songs I had never even heard before. They loved it. But then all over the place he meets people who love him — going over on the plane to the World Cup, in New York, everywhere he meets people who enjoy meeting him.

I now realise how alike we are in ways, even though he has done a lot more living than I have. Like at times when I'd be calling the children, or trying to make a point to them, I hear him, like a ghost I'm carrying around with me. The more I look back at it I suppose, when growing-up you see, you reject, and then, you become, after all.

James Galway

AN AUTOBIOGRAPHY

My father was a little guy — I'm not all that tall myself — with tremendous shoulders and arms; the kind of physique, in short, needed to be a riveter in Harland & Wolff's. Not that I can recall him doing an awful lot of riveting. I hasten to add that this hardly placed him in any special category; the decline in shipyard jobs in Belfast has been going on for a long time. I have an idea that my dad really only bestirred himself when the family badly needed something. He never complained much. Whatever his problems, and he must have had his share of them, he generally made the best of things and on the whole created a happy home for his wife and two sons. I certainly cannot remember any of us going short of anything important. There was always enough to eat; we had clothes on our back; there was always a fire blazing in the old-fashioned, black, iron range. If I wanted a gramophone, radio or flute, it always turned up eventually even if I had to wait a few years to get it.

I often meet people who want to sympathise with me because I come from what they like to call an 'underprivileged' home. It would be easy to be defensive about this and certainly for years, particularly after I first went to London, I suffered from a mild inferiority complex. But I also have to say that much of this talk of underprivilege seems nonsense to me. It never occurred to me, or anybody else living in Carnalea Street, that we were underprivileged. We were too busy getting what fun we could out of life to worry about that sort of thing. Perhaps I am an innocent. Did I not feel envy or resentment when I walked up the Malone Road (which is where the Belfast nobs live)? When anybody asks me a question like this, I feel they must have a slate loose. To me it would seem that they have little idea of what life is really about or what gives it substance and meaning. I am very much an apolitical person and perhaps if I had gone to university and met the kind of crowd who studied at Nanterre or the Sorbonne in 1968, I might be able to produce a right tale of woe. But the idea that a large house or a couple of extra bathrooms have anything more than a marginal effect on one's life, strikes me as a minor lunacy. I am far from advocating poverty, bad housing, deprivation or anything else as a method of self-improvement and certainly over the past couple of decades I have gone out of my way, perhaps, to obtain my share of material things. But it seems to me that in the end material accessories add up to little more than the trivia of life. I suppose it is largely a case of what you never had you never miss. As for this inferiority complex; it is not until you find yourself invited to dine in houses that look like small palaces or to meet and talk to people who seem to know so much more than you do and who are part of this very nice background, that you begin to feel inadequate in some way. Nevertheless, I have never at any stage felt envious of these people, although I admit I was impressed. I have tried to explain working-class feelings to people who regard me as a visitor from another planet. I tell them that everybody in Carnalea Street thought Winston Churchill was a mar-vellous fellow even though none of them had any real idea why he was so great. All they were aware of was that he smoked enormous cigars and rode around in big cars and lived in a big house. His head could have been a water melon for all they knew. But so far as they were concerned, a man who could afford big cigars and big cars had to be good. When I first met people from superior backgrounds, I suppose I more or less reacted naively. To some I must have seemed stroppy, vague, even unpredictable.

At any rate, none of us in Carnalea Street ever worried much about those who were better off, or ever felt any resentment. We accepted ourselves for what we were, which we thought was pretty great. None of us dreamed of moving into bigger or better houses. Even now, that is the kind of problem that comes right at the bottom of my list and I can honestly say that given the choice I would still wish to be born in Carnalea Street and be reared by the same mum and dad and to be, for better or worse, exactly the same James Galway that I am today.

Both my parents were musicians. My mother, Ethel Stewart Clarke, played the piano, although she never learned — or even tried — to read music.

She worked as a winder in a spinning mill in West Belfast, but most people still remember her as a popular pianist. She played everything with a very curious harmony, but she produced sounds that most people considered very attractive. Certainly she was in great demand for meetings of the local women's guilds and that sort of thing and many of her old friends have told me that, once she stopped playing, attendances fell off markedly, that it was no longer the same scene at all.

Apart from the wonderful way she brought up both me and my brother George (who, incidentally, has earned himself a considerable reputation in Ireland as a jazz clarinettist and teacher), one of her bequests to me was a really large family. I have cousins all over Belfast, almost all of them from her side. They mainly run supermarkets and that sort of thing, but one of them once almost made it big as a pop star. Whenever I make one of my flying visits to Belfast, it warms me immensely to realise that I am part of such a large tribe. Kids I have never seen before come up to me on the street and demand to know, 'Are you Jimmy Galway?' When I admit it, they say, 'Well, I'm your fourth cousin.' I have yet to bump into any fifth cousins but no doubt there are a few hanging around.

My father, who was also called James, was more talented than my mother. He played the piano-accordion with several small dance-combos and enjoyed his fair whack of profitable engagements. His abiding love, though, was the flute. He was a member of the Apprentice Boys' Flute Band, and was, in my judgement, a really good player. He understood harmony and knew a surprising amount of theory although he was never a 'taught' musician. Like everybody else in the Belfast flute bands, he picked up the skill and techniques — and even learned the music itself — from fellow bandsmen. You learned from the fellow next to you, or the one a bit older than you, in the flute-bands. My father was lucky, too, in that he learned a lot from my grandfather, yet another James Galway, who came to live with us during the last years of his life. In his day my grandfather had been a famous flute player — as had his father before him. I remember as a small child, when George and I were sent upstairs to bed, lying listening to my grandfather downstairs playing away softly on his flute. He had a few little special tunes of his own that he was particularly fond of and he would play them over and over again. Clearly he was a talented player because he taught many of the learners in the Apprentice Boys. Incidentally, the Apprentice Boys was one of the most famous of the flute-bands and won many competitions. It went out of existence suddenly one day when the Luftwaffe dropped a bomb on its band-hall — which is one you can chalk up to Goering.

I would have liked to have known my grandfather much better — my memories of him now are mainly of the many times he caught me stealing the sugar ration during the war. When he died, we had a wake, I remember. The essence of an Irish wake is that the dead fellow lies in his box in a corner while the neighbours troop in to express their condolences and then sit around the fire and consume a fair amount of alcohol. By the time everybody has had his share, the entire event becomes a great deal more endurable. You could even say that most people *enjoy* wakes, although in Belfast we never get up to the antics people get up to in the country parts of Ireland, where wakes used to be hilarious affairs. There are historically-vouched-for instances where a parish has *borrowed* a corpse from a neighbouring parish in order to have an excuse to hold a party. Not that my grandfather's wake was a solemn affair. Some of the amusement was apparently caused by me.

I was about as tall as a sixpence at the time — now I'm twice as big. It apparently upset me to see my poor grandfather lying there in the box (the lid of the coffin was still off, of course) and not being given anything to eat. Particularly when everybody else in the room was busy stuffing his face. So as a dutiful grandson I got a cheese sandwich and began feeding it to my grandfather. By the time my mother discovered what was going on the poor man had half a cheese sandwich stuck between his teeth. My father was heard to declare that as 'long as the chile [Belfast pronunciation] didn't waste half a bottle of whiskey, what does it matter?' This little episode and the fact that my grandfather wore a moustache and lived to a ripe old age and that he used to play the flute softly in the twilight is all that I remember of him now. ...

In later years even my own father used to come home roaring drunk every Friday evening. He was never violent or anything like that; just way off in that world only drunks inhabit. Although he was clearly spending money that would be far better spent some other way, my mother never protested. That was the way the world was then and particularly among us working-class. The wife never dared to argue with her husband; he was the boss. It sounds now like a good case for the women's libbers but my mother was essentially a happy woman and she and my old dad used to have many a good laugh together. We tried to make, and get, fun out of everything. Some people would be miserable in Buckingham Palace, others can live in Carnalea Street and still have a good time. Much depends upon your outlook.

There came a stage, however, when my father's drinking had started to be more than a joke. George and I decided it was all getting too much and that he was getting a bit out of hand, so we had a long serious talk with him (both George and I were into our teens by this time) and to be absolutely fair to my dad, it proved very effective; we had no more trouble. ...

I heard plenty of good music — as well as the other sort — and I don't suppose many kids brought up in better homes enjoyed equal advantages. Not many, I suppose, learn to recognise the Mozart G Minor or the Jupiter Symphony before they are ten; I knew them both by the age of eight, just listening to my father play them. He was devoted to Mozart, as I am myself.

My father never made the mistake of trying to force me to *like* Mozart. If I had preferred to go into jazz as George did, he would not have objected. So long as you wanted to play music, that was all that mattered. Not that there was ever much chance of avoiding it really. I quickly graduated from 'Baa-baa Black Sheep', which I sang at my mother's knee, to Bing Crosby's 'White Christmas' and 'Rudolph the Red-nosed Reindeer' and then into the big cowboy tunes of the day such as 'Old Smokey' which we heard sung by our heroes, such as Gene Autry or Roy Rogers, when we went to the Saturday morning matinees, at the local cinemas. It was much later before we could afford a gramophone, but someone gave me a record of Al Jolson singing 'Mammy' which I treasured for years. One neighbour did have a gramophone and I used to run up the street to hear my record on this old wind-up affair. I would never have been satisfied merely to *listen* to music, of course. From toddler days I was fascinated by Dad's flute and, as I grew older, he found it impossible to leave it lying about the house. As soon as he turned his back, I would be playing it. He tried hiding it and then, when George and I kept finding it, he took it apart and hid the separate pieces. It made no difference: indeed, it only made the game a kind of musical hunt-the-thimble. It really maddened Dad that there was no place to hide it. Why he never simply belted the living daylights out of us, I can't imagine, except that from the beginning he set out to encourage our musical inclinations as much as possible.

He first bought me a mouth-organ, but if by any chance he had hoped through this ruse to get me to lay off the flute, he was mistaken. Nevertheless, I was as proud as punch of my new possession. The only trouble was that I could not play it properly. Everything sounded wrong. I soon discovered that it had only diatonic scales instead of chromatic. To play properly, you need semitones. With a mouth-organ which can only play in C, for instance, you cannot play anything in B flat. So I had to get one with a button on the side which, when pressed, allowed me to play half-tones. Dad paid £2 for it in the local music shop and I repaid the money over a period, although I now realise that he surreptitiously added an extra bob or two himself every week. So suddenly there I was, belting out 'White Christmas' and other favourites and having what I can only describe as a whale of a time. From the first, I discovered that playing music made me *happy*. When I am asked why I chose music as a profession, I can only answer that I had no choice in the matter. Music made me happy; it still makes me happy. As a kid I could sit down at two o'clock and still be bashing away at five, unaware of the passage of time. Mind you, I am not talking about scales and theory and so on; I hated that sort of thing as much as any youngster.

Even while still fiddling about the month-organ, I got into the penny-whistle — which, incidentally, I recommend as a first-class way for any kid to learn music. I was seven or eight when Mr. Shearer, a neighbour, gave me a violin and I owe him nothing but gratitude; it was a most generous gesture particularly as he had two clever sons of his own, but the trouble was that the old violin was rotten with woodworm. Dad took it along to a shop and got them to treat it, but the best way I can describe the resulting ensemble is to say that when I stood there trying to play, it was like something out of an old Charlie Chaplin film. Then one day the bow came apart in my hands — and that was that.

By this time, my dad, realising that I had potential, had decided to turn me into a real musician and so he gave me some lessons in the rudiments of theory himself. But once I got the violin, he arranged that I should take lessons from 'Wee Dickie', a fellow-member of his band. Wee Dickie came round to the house on his motor-bike, had a cup of tea and then put me through my paces. It was all agony, of course. Scales bored me out of my mind and I couldn't stand the rigmarole and ceremony of getting the fiddle ready to play; tuning it up and so on. I preferred the tin-whistle; you just blew it and there you were, you had a nice time. ...

My father, who was known either as 'Wee Jimmy' or 'Porky', was quite a character in his way — a real working-class hypochondriac. He complained constantly of headaches and was round to the doctors at least once a week for something or other. I don't think the doctor ever discovered anything really wrong with him, but he would give him a bottle of coloured water or a rub or something like that and pack him off home. Dad was always taking headache powders or pills which, in the end, did for his kidneys. It was like baiting a bear half the time in our house. Between lack of money, frustration and head-aches, he had a rough enough old time and occasionally we got some of the backlash.

We became slightly antagonistic to each other later on because of his ideas on bringing up children and my lack of appreciation of what he was trying to do for me. He had a real leather belt and if he caught me up to mischief, there was always trouble. His way of showing you who was boss was to leather you one. He didn't didn't bother to talk too much logic, but just laid it on right away. I remember once, when I was about eleven, going through his pockets to see if he had left any cigarette ends and coming across a cigar he had forgotten to smoke at some Orange Lodge 'do' the night before. It was the first time I had ever smoked a cigar — which I did while chewing an aniseed ball. At the time I told myself, 'This is the high point of your life, boy — sucking an aniseed ball and smoking a half-cigar!' For a moment I felt like Cornelius Vanderbilt or Diamond Joe Brady. Then I got sick. When dad came home, he gave the air one sniff and demanded, 'Who's been smoking around here?'

'Nobody', I answered, looking the colour of death.

He went immediately to his best-suit jacket, which hung on a nail beside the door, fumbled in the pockets and, not finding the cigar, came back with the belt and laid one on. 'Now, get upstairs and practise!' he ordered. But I was much too sick to do so.

One thing I must say about him, though; however stroppy it might have been between us during the day, it would always end up with me kissing him good night and him kissing me back so that we could all go off to bed happy. He was really a very simple guy and always wanted to end the day well; he liked to think when he went to sleep at night that he didn't have an enemy in the world. When George and I were young kids, he came up every night and sang a little song to us before we fell asleep. He had this little rhyme about a flea — 'If they bite, squeeze them tight, they won't come back another night'.

I think he could have been a very good musician, if leaning more towards the entertainment side than the classical. After the Apprentice Boys' Band finished, he more or less dropped the flute in favour of the accordion which he played in dance-bands. He certainly taught himself to a fair degree of competence on both instruments. He learned harmony to such an extent that he could tell which chords were going on in a piece and could analyse a symphony. I remember him teaching me the Jupiter Symphony because he had to play it in some competition. He had pasted this piece of music on to a bit of brown paper so that it wouldn't get dirty or torn and he would play the theme from the symphony for me, at the same time humming away, 'bomp de bomp', trying to teach me. Afterwards he would sit in front of the fire and say, 'Mozart's the greatest composer, you know.'

He was a good leader. Put him among a crowd and out would come the accordion and soon there would be a sing-song under way. He and my ma would lead the singing, him on the old accordion, Ma on the piano. Dad bellowing away in a very forthright manner above the din. By his very enthusiasm he would encourage everybody present to join in.

There were, however, also some very sad things that I remember about him now. Once when he came back from Londonderry, he tried to get work as a dock labourer. In those days they had a green, yellow and red button system — green meant you were guaranteed work, yellow that you got some if there was plenty going, and red meant you stood no chance. He had got as far as his green button when one of the trade unions objected and the opportunity was lost. This got him dead peeved, naturally, and this was when he went through one of his bad patches. You saw his temper then; he was ready for a fight every five minutes. But there was this terrific other side to him — his tremendous love of music.

One of the things that made him supremely happy was that just before he died I took a Sunday off and went over to Belfast. At the hospital he was on so many drugs that he was really as high as a kite but he managed to recognise me. A couple of kids came in with a guitar and sang some hymns. Afterwards, I got out the flute and played. When the ward sister came along and I played the 'Carnival of Venice' and some other unaccompanied variations, he was fit to bust with pride. I had been making quite a few TV appearances just previous to this, so he died feeling that he had achieved something after all.

When I said good-bye to him, he thought he was going to be well again. They had only removed one of his kidneys, part of his liver and roughly a quarter of his bladder by then, but he was still convinced he would get better. When I said good-bye I knew I wouldn't see him again. Next day I was back in London. Then I was due to play in Dublin. After that, it was a big concert in Belfast with the Zagreb Soloists. He died the day before I got to Belfast. His doctor turned up at the concert and explained how he had had everything arranged to take my father to the concert in an ambulance. I don't suppose I ever played the Four Seasons quite the same way before or since.

He had this idea that a man should be strong, should be a tough street-fighting man. And he revelled in the fact that he was strong himself. During the later part of his life, he gave up smoking and took to reading the Bible every day. I used to think, what a funny guy, reading the Bible all the time. Mind you, he also read cowboy stories and James Bond and that sort of thing. And since I found my new way of life, I now read the Bible every day myself.

Dad was obsessed with the flute when I was a kid. He thought paying the flute was the next best thing to believing in God. He would talk about it for hours on end. 'You should have heard your grandad do this', he would say, as we listened to the radio. He was constantly saying things like, 'Did you hear the BBC Symphony Orchestra today — that flute was great?'

We went through this phase when I was trying to assert my independence and then his sense of humour would come through. Every time I came in at night, he would ask me where I had been. I wouldn't tell him.'Who've you been playing with?' I wouldn't say. If he was in a mood, I'd just about give him the minimum answer.

One morning, when I had to go off somewhere, we were having our usual passage-of-arms after breakfast.'Right, have you got everything?'

'Yes, I've got everything!'

'Have you got your music and everything?'

'Yes, I've got my music and everything!'

'Did you polish your shoes?'

'Yes, I polished my . . . shoes!'

'Don't swear at me — do you know where to go all right?'

'Yes, of course I know where to go!'

He waited until I was half-way down the street that morning, me still hopping mad, then he leaned out the doorway and called after me, 'Hey, Mozart!' He had taken to calling me Mozart or 'big fellow'.

'What is it?' I yelled back.

'You've forgotten your flute!'

It absolutely doubled him up.

Fred Johnston

ULYSSES, MY FATHER

They lean on the same wall, these men
playing Homer, making each voyage
to the lobster-pots a running legend
sculpting their lives out of hearsay
and myth, with no poet to write it
all down, keeping it conversational,
passing it on as if not intending to,
a clumsy dog round their feet
and the world still wide enough.

My father didn't voyage that far, didn't
find a wall, believed in something else,
and had a story for me once
that broke my heart —
my mother dead, he was making everything
count, so deeply burrowed in sorrow
only myth let in any light —
he found, in some old pubs, mythic men
like himself, waiting for something final
to happen,
and meanwhile they talked and invented
the world, as men do in a war.

My father's story, then, concerned
a train trip to North
and he had met a girl, a student, who'd
talked to him, they'd bought each other
drinks, she could have been his daughter;
they'd said goodbyes at Victoria station,
nothing more to it — and he made so much
of it, told me how wonderful and full
of life she was
and I listened, bought him whiskey, went
home as fast as I could, not able
to listen to much more.

So these old men play Homer at the
harbour's edge and talk about going to
jail for snatching salmon,
whipping the fish with a gaff and line
out of the river —
their stories amuse me but my father's
made me weep
for I knew it came from a different place,
and as I get older I sometimes share
that place with him,
but mostly I'm there alone.

OUR APPRENTICESHIP

Jim and Peter Sheridan Interview

Peter: On the way in here we were talking about the Credit Union Movement, which was Ireland's answer to the money-lenders in the 1950s. The Movement was established by the Church to get people out of the poverty trap of resorting to moneylenders. And they were the kind of issues that my father was really interested in. That and looking after the old folks — fairly humanitarian things.

He was a very humanitarian man. And in order to fund some of the activities he was interested in he decided to start a Drama Group and charge people in at the door and make some money. So I found myself at sixteen playing Joxer in *Juno and the Paycock* to my father's Captain — which was a really strange experience — and also playing Vladimir in *Waiting for Godot* to his Pozzo. We used to tour around the Amateur Drama Festivals in Ireland and occasionally win prizes. Jim won a prize once for being Johnny in *Juno and the Paycock*.

So the drama group came as a response to that kind of stuff, but it was really a unique experience. It was a group of about thirty people my father had assembled and the area we lived in was right on the river, which is a really important part of the fabric of the City of Dublin. It divides the city between the wealthier Southside and the poorer Northside.

The river has played a central part in the literature of the city. And also, economic change is probably first manifested on the river, because as Dublin developed as a city the whole mechanisation process, which began in the '50s and '60s and began to take over the city, meant that that neighbourhood which was established as a kind of a place where dockers would live and work suddenly began to disintegrate socially. So my father in what he was trying to do in establishing a drama group was responding in his way to those kinds of issues.

We were based in that area in a little hall called the Oriel Hall, which had been an arms dump for the IRA in 1919-20. Sean O'Casey who was actually in love with a local school teacher did his first four or five plays there, which he wrote as plays for the school kids to perform in this local hall.

So my father had the first meeting of the drama group in that hall in 1966. I remember we were all sitting around reading Lady

Gregory's *Spreading the News* and I had this huge urge to read and I was probably the youngest in the room. I remember the feeling when working through that play that this was by miles the most logical way to tell a story — because obviously everyone in that culture can tell a story. Everybody in Ireland can tell a story, tell one joke or sing one song or whatever it is. But this seemed to me to actually be the most logical way to actually tell a story.

My father always believed that if you live in an area you fully partake of the processes that are going on there. Like, we went to the local school, though he could have sent us to a school out of the area. He made us play with a lot of the local tough kids. He's the kind of man who's always trying to address where he is and what he's trying to do at a particular point in time. So his response was to start a drama group which drew in some of the people from the tough end of the neighbourhood and some of those people were extraordinary actors — they were utterly amazing, and just incredibly real. So it was just grounding in the reality of all that and not just a nice way of spending your evenings: it was a kind of addressing something fundamental.

Can you imagine how I felt as Joxer, who's this leech character who hangs onto the Captain — the central male character in this play who does no good. He does nothing. Every time someone mentions work he says 'Oh God, I've a terrible pain in me legs' and Joxer, the leech is worse. Jim was playing Johnny, the Captain's son. So I've got this real relationship going on on stage between my real father and his imaginary son in the play which is also real. Because you're also his son really outside of the play — and I'm the leech looking at all this tension going backwards and forward across the stage! I used to get of flashes of 'Who am I? What's my real role here?'

Interviewer: Jim, what do you remember — because I know that with my siblings we remember different things?

Jim: It's very odd to hear Peter talking, I haven't got a memory like that. I just erase the past, because some of the times its like listening to someone who has total recall and at the same time, suddenly I'm listening to someone who speaks very like myself, who's got free association — but I remember all the stuff he remembers about the start of the theatre . . . and my father was really an extraordinary character I suppose. He is, because he's still alive, but we, I, tend to talk about him in the past tense. I don't know why.

Me Da loved dressing up, like you know, he'd dress up at Christmas. I think all of it was that the theatre for him was really where his heart was, and he just did the other stuff because he needed diversion or whatever but really his heart was in theatre and he was doing it for pleasure with good intentions behind it.

For me it was competition with him. I don't think it was like that with Peter. Like 'let me direct the play — let me write the play — let me act in the play'. And he'd give the part to Mrs Coffey or Hughie O'Donnell — remember that? Did you not feel the same stuff? Yeh? But you always got the good parts anyway, I got Johnny Boyle with the arm.

I: So did you begin to work outside the family's theatre group, to prove something to your Dad?

J: No — inside — I hacked away at it.

I: How long was it before you decided you should work elsewhere?

J: I don't know . . . We did a few shows in the Oriel Hall which is an amazing place: it had this bar going across, and I remember, after most rehearsals, our time was spent not on who acted well but who could jump off the stage and catch the bar.

But me Da was always in the plays. We were just trying to assert ourselves and we wrote plays together. Peter wrote *Paint it Black* — I don't remember what it was about, and my play — *Karak*.

P: But it was interesting — in the break up of the family drama group, which was my Da's response to where we lived, the group began to change when Shay and myself and one or two others decided the classics were dead. Good and all as the O'Casey plays and the Lady Gregory plays were, they weren't where it was at — and where it was at was new work and doing something new. What's interesting is that my father instinctively defended that position, even though in a kind of a way it meant the end of the group for him, because all he really knew how to do was act. He didn't know how to put it together. And so in a kind of a way he stepped back to see where we would take it, how far we would take it.

J: You know what's really weird? What I find really odd is we are talking now about our Da and I've never considered until it came up here — how weird it is for your father to be part of making something alternative. Like his not saying 'Well you shouldn't do those plays'. But we totally accept that as normal. And I think it just doesn't come from the Oriel Hall and Theatre.

For some reason, my parents decided to move into this big house and have all these lodgers when I was about ten, and suddenly we moved out of the nuclear family — somebody said this to me: 'The lucky thing was yez weren't brought up in the pressure of a family'. You see we always saw that as a problem, because when you have lodgers suddenly you're told 'You're not sleeping in the front room tonight. Go to bed in number whatever'. So that can be seen as a kind of victimisation, or whatever.

Basically that whole Mother-Father thing was gone and there were all these people in the house. They were all there before we started doing the plays. Suddenly we were relating to people as human beings. Say like when we were twelve or thirteen we knew everything — like there were guys, nineteen or twenty, going out trying to get laid, which was very difficult in Dublin — coming back drunk, out of their mind. And we grew up by proxy. That's a good one: we grew up by proxy and so we've done that for the rest of our lives.

I: Most of my students tell me they have to fight their parents to make art — parents play the conservative role.

P: My Dad's view of the world was a kind of a Greek view. That families are about the exchange of thought and the interacting of ideas. My Dad loved a really good argument. When we were at school an argument could begin at eleven o'clock at night — which was when most of them used to begin — and go on until three or four o'clock in the morning, like without blinking an eyelid and we'd all be there. This is not just Jim and I and our other brothers and sisters but including the lodgers. So we're talking about an audience here of maybe fifteen or sixteen people at times. My father had his chair at the table and a six-pack of Guinness. The argument would start when he'd look around at his audience and he'd say 'Jesus had twelve. How many have you?' That was one of his great ones.

J: And if that's the starting line of an argument you're headlong immediately straight into total conflict. And another one of his was: 'There are rules, and there are fools' — 'One and one is two. You can't get away from basic facts'.

P: But he would accept that it was mathematically possible to prove that one and one is not equal to two.

J: Now that drove him mad.

P: He always said — and its funny because I just had an experience of it — that 'the world is going to be ruled by plastic. There'll come a day when you won't feel your week's wages in your hand, and that's a bad day for human society'. I think he's right, because in his work he dealt in goods and services. He would say these things and they were like red rags to a bull to him and me and we would contradict it immediately.

J: 'The Beatles didn't play their own instruments.'

P: 'Mick Jagger had a backing singer, who sang while he mimed to it.'

J: 'Sergeant Peppers is all well-n-good, but they don't play their own instruments.'

P: Even when they went on television and did that world broadcast of 'All you need is love', he goes. 'And everyone thinks they're singing'.

J: It's weird though — I mean, you always have the relationship with your father, like he has to be more complex — there's always something more complex there. You can never get to the bottom of it.

P: But what we were getting around to was that School of Argument which began at eleven o'clock at night and which he thought was the centre piece of every day: sitting around the table and having the discussion. Then remarkable things would come out, like he was very pro-British, which was remarkable for someone from our kind of background which was very Republican. And that would lead to enormous rows. Then when the whole Northern Ireland thing blew-up in 1969 that led to enormous contention, because all sorts of things become immediately real. To give an example, when Bloody Sunday happened in Derry in January '72 it was a time when we used to pretend that we still went to mass but we'd actually be in the pub having a drink. I always remember the night of Bloody Sunday, coming in and saying 'isn't that terrible, what's happened in Derry', and no-one said 'were yez not at mass?'

It was like what was happening in Derry was too real. And from about sixteen or seventeen there was a couple of times when there would be a few fisticuffs in the house between Shay, him and I over stuff because we were at the end of all that. We were in that time where that stage of the family's evolution was over.

J: What's odd about the agenda here — I mean your interest in asking about our Dad — and we haven't even begun to talk about our mother. You know it's a family thing and I find that really great and interesting and actually very easy to relax into. And it's a funny thing that I find that kind of thing in America. So when I went there I settled in without any problem for seven years — I couldn't do that in England.

That's because of something to do with the family, which is a unit that's impacted upon by society — you know you have the family unit which is impacted upon by society and then you have the family unit which has to control the world. I mean, if you want to control the world you have to stop the natural simple authority of the family and displace it by doing Eton, Oxford, etc.

I think something weird happened when Henry VIII — the English — decided that primogeniture was the keystone of society. At the one hand they made family so vitally important and at the other they made it very unimportant except for one inheritor. Because they were suddenly making value out of inheritance. It was not that the best in the family will inherit, like it was in the clan system. It was that the eldest will inherit — even if he is an imbecile, or mentally defective.

That's a more civilised structure on which to base society rather than having a fight every fifty years. And you see it in America with the Kennedy family which is not a monarchist kind of thing — as the English see it — but a total regard for the family of the Kennedys.

You know Yeats said about the Irish:
I carry from my mother's womb
A frantic heart
Great hatred maimed us
At the start.

Now that's an easy quote in a way , isn't it? But what does 'the start' mean in that sentence, where does the start begin? That sentence has intrigued me for a while. A lot of people think it means when you're born. It could be in conception. So the only thing you need for a family is love — before the creation. That's a family. You can have two kids, different parents, and if there's love in the situation, in creation, they're linked much more than if there is anything else in the situation. That's family. So if you're trying to have primogeniture you haven't got the great love.

I: What about your father's effect on your careers?

J: Well when we did plays — from *Juno* to *Dr Faustus,* to writing plays ourselves — the only thing that was worth while was actually writing the plays. He wrote *Paint it Black* and I wrote *Karak Ter Less.* They were the worst plays ever. We actually put them on.

The energy to not feel embarrassed about expression is the whole thing. It's not got to do with, is it good or bad? It's got to do with you've got to express an interior — that's all: express an interior. So you know all the great people I've ever seen writing novels, plays, films or whatever, they've set up the companies to do it. They're business and creative people.

So when our Dad set up (the drama group) to save the old folks or whatever, the big thrill was getting twenty at the door and having done the show and having given it to somebody to actually get the money to actually express it. The reality is the expression and not being afraid to express yourself.

Now in Ireland, to express yourself for centuries meant trouble. Forget plays. Forget anything. Just to express yourself was trouble. So that theatre and the art forms existed in a kind of parallel with the religious divide — the Catholicism and the Protestantism, and we supplied the English with their soul. I mean, after Shakespeare and a few other writers, the Irish writers are creating the moral conscience of England. Now when Joyce came along and said 'I want to express the moral conscience of my race' it's a bit like: 'Hey, give us a break!' But there's also truth in it.

P: But that operates on two planes: on the individual level of self expression yes, but also on the level of a class thing in that the self expression of those who are socially disenfranchised also has to be fearless. And that's in our case the really important corollary of what we're talking about. I mean that I think that from our father we got that whole thing in huge abundance.

We got that theatre was a natural form of story telling and that the fearless thing was a natural part of that package — but also in the articulation of the society from which we came, we got some sort of validation from the area we lived in. Who these people are. What they represent.

I'd go further and say that in fact it is the self expression of the disenfranchised and the dispossessed that's exactly at the heart of the art. And that exactly what the Irish brought to the process was that we were the dispossessed. It's the great heart that something has that makes its art great, not some kind of cerebral academic nonsense that people in ivory towers put around it.

And what I find extraordinary, as I go through my life, is that I keep continuing to meet so called citadels of what art is about and they're the antithesis of what I think art is all about. But you have to continue to work and fight to keep saying what the arts are all about.

J: But Peter, let me take that now. It's just that I like to think that each time you talk that you've nothing to offer except self discovery. So if I'm appearing to be off the wall, it's only because I continually ask myself questions. ...

Michael Conboy

MY FATHER

When I think of my parents, I suppose because of living with my mother for so long, I always think of my mother. I don't really think of my father.

My father died in January 1977, just before my eighteenth birthday.

Within the next year and a half both my brother and sister got married and moved out of the house. Then there was just me and my mother in a big house which she wasn't able to cope with and I wasn't interested in anything at the time, so she sold it and got a lovely apartment around the corner in Castle Avenue. I lived with her there for most of my adult life until she threw me out, when she had enough of my drinking. It was the best thing that happened to me, because I went downhill rapidly after that. Whatever little bit of stable influence living at home had for me was lost and I went completely crazy until I ended up in a bed-sit, doing nothing — except constantly drinking and drugging.

My father was from Mayo, just outside Ballyhaunis — a place called Aughamore, from very peasant stock. Really poor, big family. I don't know anything about his parents. They were both dead, I think, before he got married. But he had a lot of brothers and sisters and it was the usual pattern: they all emigrated — to London and Canada, and there was one who just disappeared off the face of the earth for thirty or forty years. My father was probably lucky compared to the rest of his brothers and sisters because a lot of them — particularly the ones who went to London — didn't fare too well, getting caught up in the isolation of the big city, drinking and all that. They were very limited workwise. My father was a very timid man — ineffectual is the word I was thinking of about him. And I can identify with that; I have that within myself. Obviously through recovery I've made some ground on it, but when I was active (in my addictions) I was a very ineffectual person. Really I was just getting nothing done, fearful of everything . My father was that way — but the big thing for him was meeting my mother. She was the opposite, a very pushy, controlling, domineering woman. I suppose that's why she was attracted to my father. I remember asking her what she found attractive, why she liked my father, and she said 'Ah I didn't think he was all that good looking. He never tried anything. He was timid when I went out with him.' I could see why she would be attracted to that; she wouldn't have any time for a man who was self-possessed or had high self-esteem. She wouldn't be able to cope with that, coming from where she was coming from.

She came from a really dysfunctional background. Her father was a binge drinker and her mother was also a very domineering controlling woman, not a particularly outrageous background but subtle — it was this control and guilt. My father's family — his brothers and sisters — were all active in whatever they were into, whether it was drink or pills or whatever. Very easily led, very easily dominated. So I grew to see how my father and mother were well matched: my father went along with my mother.

He was a carpenter by trade. An uneducated man in terms of school — leaving it at thirteen — but very good with his hands and endowed with a very good work ethic. My mother's background had everything to do with work: you were what your job was. Her people were shop-keepers and they worked all the hours God sent them. So she was constantly getting it from the cradle: 'Work, work, work is everything.' And who you are comes from what you have. Because my father was such a good worker, when they first met he was a foreman with a big outfit which later went bust. Through my mother's pushiness he went out on his own in the late sixties. That was a boom time and it was ripe for him. There was plenty of money coming in and we were living in a lovely house in Clontarf. Very middle class, very snobby. But I think my father always felt inferior — in fact, I know that — being from the country he had a chip on his shoulder about the Jackeens. He always had this strong affiliation with the country although he was living in the middle of Dublin. Because of his make up, he was stressful. He couldn't cope with stress at all. Obviously through being self-employed he was in a stressful business, employing different people on different jobs. He used to do some work down the country. But in Dublin the satellite suburbs were mushrooming and he got a lot of work there — but the vandalism on the sites was widespread and he just couldn't cope with it. He drank on it and he was a chain-smoker.

He was a small man, smaller than me. My brother and I are quite tall, we get that from my mother's side. He was also unhealthy, carrying a lot of weight and being a heavy smoker and drinker. I think he actually drank alcoholically though he was integrated into the whole pub scene and spent a lot of time with his golf cronies. He would do his work and then go to the pub and come home at whatever time to have a steak. That's what he ate, steak, boiled potatoes and friend onions. He was a real Irishman in what he ate.

When I think of my father — and I very rarely think of the man, because my mother looms so large she overshadows my sense of my father — the memories I have are that he always drove a big car and loved it. It was his way of showing the world he had a few bob. I remember sitting in the back, watching him getting stressed out with traffic, cursing his head off and the chain smoking causing him to spit out the window; because he had this smoker's cough he'd be bringing up phlegm and spitting out the window. And the pub, the image of me sitting in the car outside the pub with the bag of crisps and the bottle of lemonade. I have memories of that. They are sad memories, real alcoholic family memories — getting home, coming in from the pub — the picture I always get in my mind is of him coming in wanting his dinner, watching the news and going to bed (or going out to the pub again for an hour) and my mother goading him like someone prodding a bear. He was the sort of man who sat on all his emotions. He'd explode. She'd prod him and prod him and they'd start arguing. I have memories — I suppose they are cliche memories — of lying in bed as a child listening to my parents arguing downstairs in the kitchen.

He wasn't a violent man. He was a very gentle man. I have some of his traits; that gentle side, and I really like that. And he could not stand injustice to anyone in a weaker position, or cruelty to animals. He couldn't cope with injustice and it used to do his head in — the little man getting it in the neck really upset him. Also cruelty to animals, even just giving a dog a kick or something. I remember him giving out to me for killing a fly: 'You shouldn't do that. You should open the window and let it out.' So because of my mother ruling the roost at home, I think he stayed off-side a lot. Work was a good excuse, even though as a successful contractor he wasn't doing any of the physical work anymore. And the golf of course was a great one — disappearing with the lads to play golf and drinking after it.

I left school when I was fifteen and went to Cathal Brugha Street for two years to train as a Chef and then I went to Kerry for nearly a year. I didn't see my father then and during that time he got ill with cancer. Because it was the liver he deteriorated rapidly. I missed all that, which was a good thing really not seeing him go down so fast. But I remember the shock the first day I got back. I walked into the kitchen and Dad came in. I was always fond of my Dad, very fond of him. I went over and gave him a clap on the back with: 'How's it going Dad?' He always wore a hat and I whipped the hat off his head and got the shock of my life. Due to the treatment for the cancer he'd gone bald. He was bald on top, but he always had a rim of black curly hair. Now that was all gone and he was left with a few whispy bits. I remember I dropped the hat, stunned, and just wandered out into the hall and started crying. An auntie, who was staying in the house at the time, came down and copped what had happened and gave me a hug and said: 'You know your Dad is not very well. He hasn't been well.' But even then there was a cover up there: 'He has cancer of the lungs,' which he hadn't. He had cancer of the liver. He had cirrhosis of the liver, which was only hinted at. Again the alcoholic family — secrets, and that kind of thing.

He was dead within a couple of months. I remember I was working in a kitchen and someone came in and said: 'Your sister rang. She wants a lift home with you. She said she'll drop in and you can get a taxi home.' She never did that kind of thing usually and she told me in the taxi: 'You know your Da is dead'. I remember I cried. I just cried. No big deal. He had been in St Lukes and I used to go and visit him during the month or so that he was there. But that's one thing I was very grateful for: that I did grieve for him at the time. After that it was funny how my mother went through the thing of 'her Michael' — because she had this fantasy world she'd built up around 'her Michael' and her reality after he died was far removed from reality reality! But we recovered very well as a family as such. It just showed how he wasn't such an influence in the family. Things went on because the power house was still there in my mother.

But it's amazing: my sister, who's just come into recovery, has always had this huge problem with my father — having him 'up there', again this fantasy of a loving perfect Daddy.

I think I was always a bit ashamed of him, or embarrassed a bit by him. I remember on Parents' Day in school not wanting kids to know this man was my father because he was real culchie looking, the big belly on him, which wasn't a nice thing: feeling ashamed of your father. But when I look at it, the whole bloody family were a complete and utter mess: and there's no one to blame. I went through my period of blaming and trying to change people. Blaming my Ma, particularly, and blaming my brother and my sister and thinking that 'if they would only change .....' At this stage I think that I see things for what they are: that my family of origin was a disaster. Though a lot of them are dead, I've resolved most of it now. I've only my brother and sister left and both of them are in recovery, but we don't make any bones about it that there's any great big connection there. We need to get on with our own lives now and we're not much use to each other as family. The Fellowships we joined are our families

They would come to me when they wanted to deal with their addictions, but once they were up and running we've all come to the same conclusion and decided it's time to break the chain and cope as best we can with our own lives, trying to give our own kids some sort of healthy nurturing.

Another thing. Because my mother pushed him so hard, my father was able to accumulate some wealth — nothing major, just fairly comfortable middle-class, well-off — but because he couldn't cope with it he died young. He was only fifty-four and he left my mother quite well off, very comfortable. But because she was always finan-cially insecure, she found herself with finances that she could not enjoy in any way, shape, size or form. She could not spend money. She was crippled with arthritis and she could have gone off and bought herself a villa out in Spain. She couldn't. She didn't have that capacity, but of course she used it as part of her need to control us, especially the married son and daughter. She was only in her late fifties and she could have had a wonderful life. She actually had a miserable life despite what he left her. Before I came into recovery I hadn't a pot to piss in. But within a couple of years I went from being long-term unemployed, unemployable, no responsibilities — nothing except the trousers I stood up in, my rent being paid by rent allowance — I went from that to being a family man (my wife had a child when we came together). Because my mother couldn't spend her money there was a few bob there for me to inherit. I feel like it was a sort of gift, like: 'Maybe we didn't give you much of a start in life on the emotional side, but at least there's a little present. We weren't able to enjoy it because we were just so all over the place, but you enjoy it.' Which I do. And because they couldn't enjoy it, it taught me that money isn't everything. And so when I do get (and I can) that feeling of financial insecurity I think of them, my mother who couldn't spend it and my father who died before he could enjoy it. If he'd only looked after himself instead of getting stressed out of it.

They didn't have the capacity for enjoying life, and in a way I think it's that whole thing of a child in an adult's body trying to cope with life. It's difficult, very difficult; if you haven't got the tools you're in for a rough ride. My father had a very rough ride.

He was put on this pedestal as soon as he died, which was all fantasy. When he was alive nobody paid much heed to him, but as soon as he was dead, 'Aw, he was marvellous. He was great' and that kind of thing, which wasn't really the case. I can't remember having any conversations with the man, and no physical closeness. Thanks to recovery I've got in touch with that, the sadness of that. There were no hugs or kisses. I don't think he could cope with anything physical, he was so very much of his age and generation. Very awkward around women. I remember asking my mother about that and she said sex was something he fumbled at and only did in the dark when he was drunk, that he never saw her with her clothes off. That would be her way of telling you. She was a strange woman, very outright, and she loved to gab. If you were willing to sit it out you could get some fairly detailed stuff about her life and my father's life — told in her own way. You'd have to decipher a lot of it of course, but because she loved to gab she'd give you quite a flavour of what he was like.

When I look back on him now my main feeling is one of sadness. Sadness that there's nothing there. There's no great emotion of any kind involving him. I mean with my mother there's a lot there. A lot of it was bloody shit, but at least there is something there. He was so emotionally unavailable to his child. It's like a child who is bold, constantly irritating, even being beaten to a child is better than being ignored because it means at least he has his father's attention. And because of that vacuum with my Da, I've had to work hard at it with my wife's child and now with ours and she and I have to work at making sure that the kids feel the safety: that both of the parents are there pulling together. I didn't have that, it wasn't the way my mother and father related to one another — not two equals working towards a common goal, involved in an evolution of a relationship giving and taking equally and trying to nurture their kids.

So what did I get from my father? I suppose the very things he hadn't got himself. Remembering the emptiness when I think of him the most important lesson I learned from him is to be there, physically and emotionally, for my children. Remembering how unequal it was between my parents — my mother ruling the roost — I feel my father was another child in the house and I don't want that. But I have the gentleness he passed onto me. I have that for my wife and for our children. Since I got into recovery one of the really curious things I realise I got from my Da that I really enjoy — me, a Dub born and reared — is a love of the countryside and nature. I really enjoy it now and of course it is a great cure for the kind of stress he couldn't handle. Now I love being in the West of Ireland, especially around the area where my father grew up as a child. He should never have left it. But then where would I be!

Eamonn Grennan

BIRTHDAY WALK WITH FATHER

Eighty-one you'd have been. Given the fine day,
I dawdle the afternoon away in the woods
with binoculars. Sudden shapes of small birds
appear disappearing between leaves, delicately
peck at beech moss, nibble tree ferns. As a boy
you collected eggs from hedges along the Boyne:
only one a nest, prick it, blow the insides out,
save the whole hollow orb as trophy, laying
its speckles or solid colour in a hinged box
on cotton wool. Today I see the beech leaves
have begun to uncurl their little fists, turning
that pale translucent green you once described
as stained glass. Did they shine out at you
from early on, I wonder, speaking that gracious image
to your eyes? Stopping to look, I imagine
you stopping to look and thinking, *just*
like stained glass—maybe a window you'd seen
in a chapel somewhere as a child, or at the seminary
before you gave it up, turned teacher, married.
So much closed off — not even a mystery,
just a blank map. Still those gathered eggs and
beech-leaf lozenges of stained glass took root,
letting the two of us walk out together — almost
companionable along the cusp of spring — to meet
your eighty-second year, me all eyes
for the small birds I spy on from a safe distance, you
with your worried gaze on the ground, in silence
minding every concentrated, precious step.

T. M. R. Jackson

A FATHER'S DEATH

Dad died the first day after the holidays. He died in harness, treating an old lady's varicose leg in the front surgery.

'Something's happened to the doctor!' she said, rushing out with her stockings down and her bandages trailing untidily. 'He can't talk, and he's breathing funny.'

Trevor was called. Stroke was diagnosed. The ambulance was asked to come around the back lane through the noisy tin gates of the yard, to avoid the public scrutiny of the street.

I went to my room at the top of the house. The 'Crow's Nest' we called it, distant from the other two floors. I knelt to pray by the bedside. I looked at the cheerful *Daily Mail* Mercator projection of the world over me — all so familiar and normal, shipping routes dotting the oceans. Donald Duck grinned at me from the white wardrobe.

Yet Dad was taken bad — very ill. Disaster was threatening this quiet haven. Tension gripped me. What ... what ... could I pray for in these circumstances?

'Lord, please look after him, and do what is best for him and us all. Thy will be done.' ... It was all that I could stammer repeatedly until Mum called me down.

The ambulance had come. Dad was on a stretcher, being carried down the long narrow yard. Mum walked beside him. His big ruddy face was suffused with a tinge of purple, and was strangely stiff. As they tilted him in he tried to speak. His mouth worked and dribbled. He grunted, and the left hand flapped. His blue eyes stared with the effort. Mum had tears in her eyes. She held his hand.

'Jackie dear, you'll be all right. We'll follow you to hospital', she murmured unsteadily. Then the doors closed and he was gone.

That was the last that we saw of him alive. We drove the fifty miles to Dublin. It was dark when we arrived at the hospital. Mum parked and went in alone. She came out crying quietly.

'He's dead. He died just after admission. They said nothing could be done. It was a subarachnoid haemorrhage. Just like Maureen. Do you want to come in and see him?'

I shook my head. I felt strangely aloof and devoid of feeling. 'No ... no thanks.'

'He was a kind doctor who spoke to me', she said. 'He said that it might be better for an active man like Dad to go this way, rather than live crippled.'

I nodded, thinking of the walks in the woods, the fishing, the sailing, the sawing of timber, all the energy and bustle of being in his company.

So we drove away from the warm lighted hospital, looking for friends and support. Coffee, and phone calls in the nearby mews. Consolation chats and drinks. Offers of help and accommodation. Numb sense of the old order tilting and sliding into the past.

Eventually we stayed with my uncle in Howth, a delightfully eccentric and artistic man. He too was recently widowed. Six months previously his dark-haired vivacious wife, Maureen, had gone down to the beach to swim. A headache nagged at her. She made light of it, and remarked that her sight seemed fuzzy. But the ache would not leave her. It swelled to agony, and then squeezed her into a coma. Five harrowing days followed of snoring in hospital under lights and drips, family bedside vigils, until death terminated the nightmare.

Dad was buried close to her. It was a vast gathering — endless handshakes and murmurs of regret. There was no clear memory of faces, except for Christy the town loafer and idler, who had whinged and wheedled so often at our door. He had come the sixty miles to say his farewell.

Looking over land gently sloping to the sea, I suddenly felt that this was where Dad was happy to be, and that his spirit was free from the ruins of his body.

'Goodbye, Dad', I whispered, as the earth rattled onto the coffin, and the minister intoned ... 'Earth to earth ... ashes to ashes ... dust to dust ... ' 'Goodbye, Dad. Thanks for everything, and for the company'. The thought that the big clean burly figure was irretrievably gone swept over me, and the tears came for the first time.

Billy McKee

MY FATHER

I have tried to think clearly about my father. It is not easy. Every aspect that comes to mind is always followed by a qualification.'He was this — but also he was that' — 'I felt this about him — but I also felt that'. There is real difficulty for me in sorting out the order of importance of feelings I had for him. An event that happened recently helped to put all this in context. It was to do with my son. I will mention it later.

My main memory of my relationship with my Da (from the period of say, ten years old until I was twenty-seven, when he died) is the fact that I did not regard him as being an important factor in my life. That is, I did not live in fear of him, I did not expect opposition in any large way from him about anything I wanted to do, I did not feel an overweening desire to impress him.

The main negative I remember (and this extends further back than the age of ten) was having this awful, ugly feeling each Saturday and Sunday. You see we were never well off. My father was a factory labourer, and did not earn much. He never drank during the week, but always drank on Saturday and Sunday. Most Saturday and Sunday afternoons he would come home fairly drunk. He would sit at the TV and talk and argue and laugh drunkenly at it. He was really just a total pest and nuisance when he was drunk. He was never violent, never abusive in any way.

But still, I can remember countless times when I would be outside the sitting room, with this awful, awful feeling in my gut — later I discovered the name for it, it was anger, or rage, or hatred. In my childhood years I was not mature enough to realise this. For me, it was just this awful feeling that I had each time I saw him in the house with drink taken. And saw the rows between him and my Ma (again, there was never any violence involved).

I was an only child. All through my early years I was (probably) spoilt. Certainly, as a teenager, I had a lot of baggage about this in my head. What is certain, what I know for sure, is that my Da was emotionally dependent on me. I hesitate to use that word as it smacks of all the psychobabble that I detest so much. But I use it because it is one of the few things I am sure of in my Da. He never, ever hit me. This was always left to my mother.

Always, when he was sober, (which was most of the time — if he had a drink problem it did not intrude right into the fabric of our family in a devastating way) he always wanted to please me. My mother told me a story about how my father, when I was very small, say two or three, liked nothing more than to take me to the park and play. And another about how, when he'd gotten home from the factory one evening and had been told that I'd taken my first step, he'd become upset that my mother and her mother had let this happen without him being there. My mother told me that her mother had said often about him: 'If ever there was a fool of a man over a child it's him.' This is a true summary of his attitudes to me.

So I grew up a well loved child. There is no doubt about that. But what did I see in him that I wanted to define myself around or against?

I can remember nothing that I saw that I wanted to copy (there may be one thing but I'll mention that later). Things that I saw that I wanted to exclude from 'me' were more obvious. He was shy, meek, uncomfortable with nearly everybody. In fact, he did not drink almost at all until my mother said to him — before they were married — 'Why don't you take a drink or two and be at ease with people?' — so he did, but it only made him a bit of a pest. So, *I* would never be shy or meek or uneasy. But I *was*, as a child I was painfully shy, unsure. As a teenager this was the main monkey on my back through the maelstrom of adolescence, and well into my twenties. He drank, as I have explained, so, I would never drink. I ended up, at the age of twenty-seven, not long before he died, in Alcoholics Anonymous. I spent four years in AA until I realised I wasn't an alcoholic — just neurotic, screwed up and immature and all the rest of it, and trying to fill in all the cracks with pints of Guinness

He was dependent on me. So, if *I* had kids, I would never be a father like that. I think I have that trait in me, but there is much more difference there.

An example of all three things together: I was in fifth year in secondary school — I packed it in that year, but not for any reason connected to what follows. There was a parent-teacher meeting one night. My father went to it. He came home later with drink taken. He talked to my mother. Then he talked to me. I didn't really want to know what had happened, I knew that what *was* to have happened *hadn't*, for example that he had not sat there and talked to my teachers when his turn had come. I got thick, and childish, and didn't want to hear his excuses, rather I concentrated on the 'you've let me down'.

What had in fact happened was entirely predictable for my Da. He *had* gone to the meeting, but as most of the parents there were from what he would have seen as a different class and status to him, he had felt totally out of it. He had 'bottled it' as would be said nowadays. He had however, quietly chatted with a Christian Brother — who was not my teacher, or was only one of my teachers — and then meekly, in all probability hating himself, made his exit. From there to the pub, whatever pub was nearby, to have a few pints and face his own failure. That done he had come back to the home, to explain to my mother, and then to face me. My memory is that my mother tried to smooth things with me. This says to me now, twenty years later (and I assure you that I have *never* until now thought about this since that evening) that she had an understanding of him, that she saw things in him, how he was, that let her see his difficulties.

But I needn't tell you, *I* didn't (and how would I, at fifteen). I indulged in what I now know to be emotional bullying. I undoubtedly rubbed his face in it. I don't feel at all guilty about that. It was wrong, I shouldn't have done it, but that was the way I was. The way *we* were. It was as inevitable that I should behave that way as it was that I should do anything, it was the product of how we interacted in our family. I never knew until I sat down to write this that in some ways human families are like plants. One plant drops a seed nearby, and the seed becomes a new plant that as it grows threatens, lives off, and eventually possibly starves that which gave it its existence.

It was always that easy for me to manipulate my father. I thought I was totally different to him. But with time I realised all the things I most hated about myself were those things that I had inherited or copied from him.

I said earlier that maybe there was one positive area where there was something that I had taken from him. That area involves political attitudes. At the age of about sixteen and from then to the age of thirty-two, I was involved in left wing politics. There may be an influence here, because from my earliest days I can remember him (he was a life-long trade unionist) talking about Larkin and Connolly. But even here the influence is hard to validate, because when he was drunk, he'd be arguing with the TV about Hitler. And with the drink in, he was a great admirer of Hitler. When he was drunk the anti semitic stuff would come out. This had, I suspect, something to do with the fact that in the working class areas of Dublin, in the twenties and thirties, a lot of the moneylenders were Jewish.

I think that there must after all be a tie up, because in my early adolescence I had Waffen SS posters up on my bedroom wall. I see this for what it was then, and not what it means nowadays. Then it was a piece of juvenile attitude, the War, Fascism, a thing of the past.

But I suspect my passionate involvement in left-wing politics was more an expression of my need for a geographical escape from the area I had grown up in. I was still in my teenage years. Years that I did not at all enjoy. Years where my opinion of myself, my estimation of my own worth, was absolutely zero. My father in these years was what I imagine almost every father was to his son — a waste of time, space, energy. Someone who you just wanted to avoid.

Some sharp, fleeting memories cross my mind, mostly painful at the time. At the age of eighteen I remember going out with my mates and dropping into a pub and catching him with a prostitute. Some years earlier, when I was thirteen, I saw him going down a back lane near our flats, also with a prostitute, a skid row wino.

I remember my mother reading a thing she'd cut out of the *Sunday Press* doctor's column — 'Do I have V.D.?'

Sitting in the local pub with him — I would have been about thirteen — hearing the craven way he addressed the barman when ordering his drink. And seeing the contempt that the barman had for him.

On holidays in Wicklow (we went there almost each year through the sixties) seeing my father and mother arguing in the street about going into the pub for another. (My memory is that he was already jarred).

His absolute shyness and inadequacy with members of my mother's family. Him wanting to monopolise me for conversation (even when I was small) so as to avoid having to talk to anyone else.

These things are alright now. They are recalled not with resentment, not out of 'poor me' ism. I have no problems at all with them. They are simply the things that come to my mind when I think of my father. Other things also come to mind. These are different, but also bear on 'me' — and my son.

His absolute delight when he heard that the first job I got was in a place in the inner city area of Dublin that he came from. He would have known some of the blokes there from the flats he grew up in. I know, now, that his hope was that I would appear a great statement to them about him — I really think that it's not just that fathers want their kids to do better than they did, but in some circumstances to be proxies to overcome or do the things that they always felt, at the core of their being, they were not able to do — did not have the courage to do.

His always wanting the best for me; the thing I said earlier, about him being intimidated by the parent-teacher meeting. The reason was, as I said, the class of the parents and difficulties with that. But he was as pleased as punch when he and my mother managed to get me to go to that school.

His pleasure when, as an early adolescent, then teenager, he could bring me to events like the Irish internationals (soccer, only. Rugby and GAA he never would have dreamt of going to see). He would sometimes meet an acquaintance there and I can still hear the pride in his voice when he introduced me. Then his quiet disappointment when, say from fourteen onwards, I refused to go. Eventually he stopped asking me.

I was drinking, with my parents approval, from about seventeen. (I had been drinking from a few years before that). But I only ever had one drink with my Da.

I was twenty-four at the time. That was an occasion when we went out for a gargle with my uncle — my Da's brother-in-law — and even then I was invited only because he (my uncle) had cancer, and hadn't long to live. I remember that evening clearly for a couple of things. One, I saw my uncle differently than ever before. I saw him as a man, and not an uncle. I was too close to my father even to see that. He was still 'me Da', this name was redolent of no authority. I do remember one thing he said though, after we'd had our few pints and left my uncle to his bus. He told me that he reckoned that I didn't go to mass. I was about to start the 'Ah Da, for Jaysus sake will yeh stop' routine when he stopped me in my tracks by telling me that he didn't either; instead he went in the boozer most of the time. I felt close to him, then.

In late '82, he got the chance of voluntary redundancy from the factory. He took it. I remember me, him and my Ma all going into the big Bank of Ireland branch in College Green to see an 'investment analyst' or some such person we had absolutely no experience of. My Da had got about fifteen grand — for thirty years. He put in eleven thousand, and kept four, gave it to me. In my own investment deal. Just gave it to me. That was January '83.

In February '83 — he'd been complaining of pains — we were told he had cancer, terminal lung cancer. The poor bastard never even got the chance to enjoy a cent of the redundancy money. The four grand that I got — I had already started drinking it, and generally blowing it.

Of that summer, as he got worse and worse, in and out of hospital, I have some memories. One is of helping him out of the flats and guiding him the six or seven hundred yards to the barbers. I didn't want to take a taxi. I wonder why is it when writing this that my eyes are filling with tears. That the tears are not for the pathetic state he was in then, but tears at the memory of him coming home from work in the late fifties and the early sixties, and me running to him and getting a lift on the child's saddle I now remember — now remember, for the first time in three decades. Of how happy he was to see me, of how he always had sweets, of how I venerated him when I was small. Of how I thought he knew everything. Of how I was always secure then, the security that a child has who knows that he is loved. Of him playing football with me when in those times of long ago everything was as it should be.

Perhaps it is my innocence I am nostalgic for. I do not know. But anyway, we had to stop a few times along the way to the barbers. He was really bolloxed. He looked wretched. He was having the chemotherapy then, and he was losing his hair (up until then, he had a full head of hair).

Of wallpapering the sitting room when he was in the cancer hospital, so as to surprise him when he got home. And working at it through the days, up until eleven in the evening, trying not to drink. And finding myself, each evening, running full tilt up the street to a boozer, and the barman seeing me come in and pulling two or three pints for me.

Of him, lying on the sofa at home where he spent most of the last months of his life, turning to me, when my mother was out of the room (we hadn't told him he was dying, officially he had a 'cyst on the lung') — him turning to me, after he'd tried unsuccessfully to do something and saying, staring me right deep into my eyes, 'game to the last, what?'

Of, at the end, the last few weeks, helping the poor fucker out to the jacks, him naked, incontinent, looking like something out of Auschwitz.

Of being sober for the last three months of his life. Of, for the first time that I know of, saying something deeply felt to him. I had gone into my parents' bedroom, where he was lying (with a ripped open bin liner under the sheet as an incontinence blanket) and saying, after preparing myself: 'Da? ... I love you Da'. He said, and it was hard for him to speak — 'Thanks'.

I cannot tell you how fortunate *I* feel for being able to say that to him.

At the funeral I cried for him. For *him*.

When I grew into what I regard as maturity (in my thirties) I saw things more clearly. Him and prostitutes: my mother and him had a bad sex life. My mother was raised with the normal (for the time) 'It's dirty, it's filthy, it's to be discouraged' stuff.

Many other things about my Da I have been able to understand only because there is a person now, a small human being, who calls me 'Da'.

My whole aim with my son is not so much to 'give him the things I never had' — that's true, but that's the *easy* bit (the easy part of the hard bit). It's to avoid him inheriting any of the faults — characteristics that I have in me that I despise.

I have developed. I am not shy or inadequate with people. I can talk to anybody, and as they say 'bullshit with the best'. I am self confident, at ease with women, regarded as charming, and all the rest of it.

I now face a testing time. I am still in the area where I grew up. I am still poor (although I have reason to believe that I am on the elevator out of poverty into a middle class income, and I'm fighting like hell for that, mainly for my son), but in this area, things and people are a lot 'harder' and more cruel, than they used to be. My son is a lovely intelligent and easy to play with kid. He's soft. He's a little too soft. It has been spotted. He is being bullied. Also there is guilt there for me. When I reached teenage years I couldn't wait to sever the ties with my neighbourhood. When we got married I moved back to the flats of my youth, because that's where we could get a place. So I'm seen as being 'different'. Also, as I don't gargle in the locals, again I'm different in the eyes of the very small amount of small-minded people. Also my wife is from a 'different' area.

So, a few of the older 'children' have picked up on that. Older means fourteen to sixteen-year-olds and they are mouths. I saw one messing with my son yesterday and in a fury at the fact that a fifteen-year-old could be bullying him, I ran down and threatened the fucker. This is a highly dangerous thing to do: it may lead to them picking on my son even more; it may lead me into giving your man a dig or a clatter and pouring fuel on the fire; it may lead me into confrontation with his family and as he is still technically a minor, I could be done for assault (I stayed awake last night thinking about this).

But I will not have my son unable to play because some little shithead wants to mouth. I will not betray him. I will not let him down.

I am at the end of what I have to say. All that I have said about *my* father, and my son, means that I undertake the responsibilities of being a father with the knowledge that at a certain stage my darling little boy, as he still is, will inevitably reach the stage where my presence, the presence of his 'Da', he will find a suffocating encumbrance. I hope he does anyhow, or else there's something wrong.

At this moment, as at other times since my son was born, I have a profound sadness that my Da never got to see my son. Also, I really wish I could see him just for a short time, and let him know that I understand him and that I'm grateful to him for how he brought me up. And tell him that I love him.

John Scally

ONE MAN AND HIS DONKEY

My father died when I was five. After that, my grandfather became possibly the most important person in my life, even more so than my mother. I was called after him. Even his birthday was the same as mine. With his grey hair, weather-beaten face, commanding presence and enormous eyelashes, he was not a man to take lightly. His attraction to frugal living would have made him a kindred spirit for an ascetic. He was a devout man. I wondered if he ever stepped down from this heightened plain of spiritual existence to the world of mere mortals. Once I asked him: 'Will you ever be a saint, Grandpa?' The question amused him. Although he answered with an emphatic 'No!' it failed to prompt the series of singular revelations half-hoped for.

He was the eldest of thirteen children, born to a farmer who owned only five acres of land. It was a life of extreme poverty though he did not know it at the time. It was a world before television and radio. He thought it was great. I remember him telling me: 'If you are reared in your bare feet you will never get pneumonia out of the snow'.

I sat beside him in the chapel for Mass and religious ceremonies, especially the parish mission which we had every second year. The announcement of the mission was greeted with some excitement. It became a distant second to the weather as the most important topic of conversation in our County Roscommon village.

'We'll never feel it 'til the mission' was the standard comment. The priest tried to drum up some enthusiasm and spiritual fervour by describing it as 'an occasion of grace'. Not that grace was ever much in evidence on those days. Public enemy number one was sin. The preparation beforehand was a fastidious enterprise.

The trappings and ceremonial of services were more elaborate and formal than normal and all the component parts were done with enormous care for detail. Even the choir's attention to musical offerings of praise was better than usual, rising from the truly awful to the simply bad. That hardy perennial, *Soul of My Saviour*, was used throughout the week with reckless abandon. It was like using one's best china to feed the visitors, the family of workmen, the children at a birthday party and the dogs and cats.

Nevertheless, for most people, my grandfather included, the mission was one of the parish's great social occasions, serving as a fashion show, a community centre, a place of entertainment and two opportunities per day to meet with the locals. Some of the women wore hats. The hats in turn provoked intense discussion in the clusters of women's gatherings outside the chapel afterwards. Their talk was inevitably fascinating for many reasons, not least of which was that delightful blend of articulate bitchery and polite, well-dressed savagery. The comments represented, in condensed form, the spontaneous venom of the parishioners, charming little darts, wicked little stabs, though sometimes not so little, which were merciless, battering some poor unfortunate, without relief or hesitation, until the conversation was abruptly halted when one of the fold was summoned to the car.

Those gatherings were no place for the meek, whatever degree of sensitivity a person had needed to be complemented by a very tough skin. This sharing of gossip and humour helped to keep the community alive, but also revealed the heartache and quiet desperation which underlined so many lives in the parish.

Our house was the traditional Irish Catholic home. Statues or pictures of the Blessed Virgin adorned every room of the house. An annual family ritual was a visit to Knock on the fifteenth of August. Saying the rosary was part of the furniture of our lives. For all these reasons devotion to Mary, the mother of God, was as important to my childhood as reading comics, playing football and watching *Wanderly Wagon* on the television. The Blessed Virgin Mary was a kind of indirect line to God, a spiritual insurance policy. There were many times I resented this imposed religiosity. My grandfather took this devotion a step further by wearing a scapular around his neck.

There was nothing my grandfather enjoyed more than snoozing in front of an open fire. His personality was a fascinating juxtaposition of a sympathetic saintly man and a curmudgeonly critic. He was never too nice too often, although pleasantly adaptable. The rock solid centre of his well-intentioned soul was beamed through the dignified serenity he communicated among all the kidding. Anyone who fell victim to his instinctive irreverence would not forget the experience. Every so often he felt obliged to employ his caustic wit and the cutting edge of his gift for mimicry to transcend the slight shrug of boy-next-door amiability.

He was a great babysitter because there were always shafts of tenderness in everything he said, even when he was angry. He was not given to theory or to brash statement, a man of no pretension. His motto was: *Say little but say it well*.

His voice could have a saturnine quality when he told stories but he varied his delivery with hushed tones alternating with booming narratives which presented a gripping interpretation of the old stories that got to the dark, demoniac undertow beneath the saccharine exterior, creating an atmosphere of astonishing fertility.

Although he was not a *seanachai* or storyteller in the strict sense of the term he was acutely sensitive to the fact that an area was not built on its buildings or landscape but on the memories and stories of its people. Through these memories and stories the greatest myths, legends, eternal romances and fairy tales were written and re-written. He felt that the past was too precious to let slip into oblivion.

If he had a fault it was that he saw the old days as a golden age, innately superior to the modern world. Although I loved his stories, I was not sure I would have liked to have grown up at the turn of the twentieth century. All the families were large, between eight and sixteen children was normal then. He lived in a house with two bedrooms and a kitchen. The toilet was the back garden. Two pigs were kept at the bottom of the garden. The pigs were the family's nest egg to be sold on occasions like first holy communions, weddings, serious illnesses or whenever money was needed. My grandfather smiled wistfully as he remembered Porky and Betsy: 'Those two pigs were the first bank I ever knew'.

I loved being with him on the rare occasions he was working with the horse. I was enthralled by the magnificence of the animal, noble, imperious, majestic, powerful. Yet my abiding image of him always was in the donkey and cart, which he used to transport himself the mile-and-a-half journey to one section of our land, and the three-quarters-of-a-mile journey in the opposite direction for the second part. The donkey knew the road so well that there was no need to steer. He was a very docile creature who needed hardly any instructions. He would stand still whenever requested. The only flaw in his make-up was that he had a fear of water, arising from the fact that he had fallen into a bog hole in his early years. He would steadfastly refuse to go near any water, which was a major problem in winter when a lot of our land was flooded.

Sitting on top of a load of hay or sticks I got a different perspective on my magical, mysterious and bountiful environment. I began a brief affair with ornithology, as I could see hundreds of birds in the hedge-rows. Some of my friends at school spent their evenings stealing birds eggs and vandalising nests. My grandfather made me solemnly swear that I would not partake of such activity. He saw it as a crime against nature and psychologically and spiritually unhealthy: 'Every time we kill something, something inside us dies too'.

Although he was the most unfussy eater I have ever known, his one great culinary weakness was mushrooms. He would wake me up early in the mornings during August and I would go out mushroom-picking under the warm glow of the rising sun while he started gathering cows for the milking. Under his tutelage I learned quickly that most valuable skill for any practitioner of my new profession — how to tell a field which would yield mushrooms from one which would not. Once in a blue moon I would reach treasure island — a seemingly limitless, just-popped bunch of pure-white mushrooms lovingly caressing the green grass.

Although he did not have a sweet tooth he was very partial to blackberries. I quickly acquired this taste, but reaching for the most luscious blackberries was a hazardous experience when they were shielded by an almost impenetrable fortress of briars. The price for my snacks were a few scratches on my hand and quite a few tears on my clothing, a tendency which did not endear me to my mother.

A farmer's *place* was his castle. It was a sacrilege to ravage another farmer's 'place'. The 'place' was comprised of a house, land, animals and possessions. It was not just a physical or geographical entity but defined a person and their life's work. It was a statement of who and what one was, is and would be. After my father's death my grandfather's toil had one purpose: to have our place fit to hand over to me. It took me a long time to understand why he put himself through so many hours of backbreaking work.

I was the son he never had. I went everywhere with him when I was not in school. Often when we travelled to the sheepfair people would ask him, 'Is he the youngest?' 'No. He's the oldest grandson. ' 'God you are a fresh-looking man to be a grandfather. 'Although he was in his seventies I never thought of him as an old man. He would have passed for a man twenty years younger.

After eating my dinner when I came home from school I would take out my tricycle to work with him in the fields. In autumn as it snowed yellow leaves I would pick the potatoes for him and my mother. I wore an old pair of stockings on my hands to keep me warm. In June I would help him round up the sheep for the shearing. His life was marked by great simplicity yet also by extraordinary beauty.

From my earliest days I never doubted his love. We slept in the same room and he would tuck me in at night when I was small. In later years as Father Time caught up with him the roles were reversed.

I hated to see him out on bitterly cold days after he turned eighty, though I knew he needed exercise, otherwise his arthritis would have crippled him.

I remember when I was seven he had gone to my aunt's house to help them save the hay. With little warning a violent thunderstorm broke out. I was safely inside the house as my mother lit the blessed candle to protect us all. The lightning was dancing jigs and reels on the floor. It was petrifying. I knew my grandfather would have been out in the hayfield when the storm started and that there was no way he could survive in the deadly lightning. Despite my mother's assurances that he would have been inside, my fears were unabated. Between my tears I prayed harder than ever before that God would envelop him in a protecting veil. My heartbeat returned to normal three hours later when I heard the car outside and rushed to the window to see that he was still in good order.

He was very proud of me, though I never really did anything to arouse such an emotion apart from one day outsmarting my uncle-in-law. Uncle Michael was a farmer and cattle dealer. The greatest professional compliment he could pay to anybody was to say: 'He is a great judge of a bullock'. One day we were walking our one bullock to the cattlemart with his eight cattle. My grandfather asked which of the nine was the heaviest. It was a serious question and I answered dispassionately: 'Ours'. Uncle Michael laughed. I countered defensively, 'Ours is ten-and-a-half hundred weight. None of yours is more than ten hundredweight'. 'Would you like to bet on that?' Michael asked with a laugh. I shook my head reluctantly. I believed I was right but he had a life's experience behind him and I had not even begun my novitiate as a cattle dealer. To my astonishment my grandfather interjected: 'I bet you half a crown Dermot is right'. Though equally surprised my uncle said 'Done'. The weighing scales, like the camera never lies. My analysis was vindicated. My grandfather insisted that Michael give me the half crown. I knew he thought nothing of losing the money, but the blow to his ego was enormous. My grandfather never allowed him to live it down and my fledgling farming career ascended new heights.

If there was one reason why I loved my grandfather so much it was that he always listened to me. He never cut me off in midstream. I always felt that he valued my opinion, even when my ideas were totally harebrained. I was deeply grateful that he was living with us, otherwise I would just have been a 'Mammy's boy', without a dominant male in my life.

Although I was physically like my father, I inherited many of my grandfather's characterstics and qualities: fierce independence, a near obsession with punctuality, a concern to use money judiciously, a deep attraction to privacy and a belief that a promise made should not be broken. The gap of two generations between us did not seem to matter. Whenever it was necessary he had no hesitation in bringing me down a peg or two, but criticism was always tactfully offered. In the cossetted comfort of his presence I learned much about patience, kindness, and selflessness. The pity was I seldom put these lessons into practice.

Frank Galligan

UNIFORMS

The night they wrecked the North Star
Ballroom, I listened to the sounds
Of pitched battle from my window,
And thought of a man gone to war,
Heavily outnumbered by Teds
Home for the summer from Glasgow.

I had watched them march that tense
Evening, forearms encased
in Plaster of Paris, scout knives slung
In scabbards from their studded belts.
My father searched for his baton,
Under the stairs where it had hung

Amidst wire hangers of bills paid
And family coats, for as long
As anyone could remember.
An hour before the dance, he said
Goodbye, the peaked cap shading
His wet brow; he stepped through the door.

Next morning, I crept into his
Bedroom to find the uniform
Crumpled in a heap, his off-duty
Face puffed against the sheets
Like a gaudy bolster, torn
Lips smiling, as I reached for my holster.

II

When they played the National Anthem
At the end of the dances, I watched
My father clip himself to attention
And wondered if he'd walk me home.

Perfume didn't hang as well
As the damp of a greatcoat
On the Umlagh road.

High on brilliantine and bottle,
The boys who fell during the Soldier's Song,
Rose up rejuvenated, now hard men.
Thick in our fear, we'd watch them gather
'Fuck you, and your Guard of a father!'

Some Easters later, I watched them
Play at soldiers, where once
 I'd fought the great Sioux nation,
And wondered at their sudden
Sober grasp of strut and ceremony.

I remembered the night, or was it nights
Outside the John the Baptist hall,
His gloved hand on my elbow,
Eyes nodding me for home,
Where one day in a confidence of beer,
He will speak to me of fear, pure fear.

Jack Houlahan

'ME OWN'

I'm five years old. Each new word is a mystery. Words are sounds and pictures. Stringing them together is a game like doing a jigsaw. I prefer cartoons to photographs. Words are cartoons.

'Who is God, Jack?', asks Miss Smith.

'God is a ternity of three divine parsons who really are a stink.' ('God is a Trinity of three Divine Persons who are really distinct.')

I'm five years old and the really important meanings don't come from words at all. A look, the tone of a voice, the length of a caress, the precise weight of a slap — these tell me more than the words I play with.

Five years old. Not young. A part of my life has already been wiped from my memory. Down through the years others will remember it for me from time to time. A succession of dangerous fevers, bouts of convulsions; but I'll have no memory of words of comfort whispered in the dark.

I have four sisters and one brother, all older than me. Sometimes — when they hate me for a minute or two — they taunt me with a name. 'ME OWN', they call me. It sounds like the cry of a tone-deaf cat. I don't know what it means — but their angry, teasing tones, and the scared shamed feeling that rises in me when I hear it, leave me in no doubt it's a serious name. They heard it from my mother, of course — 'My own, My own', as she stroked my face with a damp towel. But I don't know that now; I only know I've stolen her from them, and that I did it by playing dirty, by some shameful weakness.

'That's enough', Mammy says, if the teasing goes too far. She chases them out to play and comforts me, but I feel uneasy, as if her comfort proves the truth of their accusation. Fortunately, my brother and sisters don't hate me very often.

Now I'm eight. Everyone says I'm the spitting image of my father. I don't know what to make of this. I've only ever seen him from behind my mother's hip: he's awful big; he drinks; when he drinks he gets angry and when he's sober he reads the paper a lot.

Every year he goes to the races at Fairyhouse. (There's a word for you: horses galloping, elves and pixies dancing in the air). There's a place on the way home where the men stop to drink. They call it a 'bona fide'. I've only ever seen it in my mind's eye, but it's a kind of shop with huge sides of bacon hanging from a rack and a fat bald man in an apron handing out bottles of Guinness. Daddy buys our sweets when he's leaving — six packets of Rolo or whatever's handy.

We're all in the sitting-room when he comes in, us and Mammy and the new baby. He's happy drunk. His collar is open and there's a brown stain on his upper lip. He has a rolled-up newspaper in one hand and he's reaching in his overcoat pocket with the other for the sweets.

The others run to him. I wait by the fire with Mammy. I want to run to him and I don't know what's holding me back.

He looks down the room at her. The happy light goes out of him. He stares at me.

'Come on for your sweets, son', his voice says, while his eyes turn it into a challenge.

'Come on to hell', when I don't move. 'What's the matter with you?'

I go. My legs are trembling. The tears that always come too easily are in my eyes. He holds out the Rolo. My arm won't move. His big face comes down to mine. I can smell stout and fags.

'What sort of man are you? Afraid of your father? A wee Mammy's boy? Away to hell, ME OWN' — and he cuffs me on the cheek with the rolled-up paper.

I hear her call out and suddenly I'm swept by a rush of the purest hatred for her. I grab hold — I cling to the strength of it and run out of the room.

His or Hers? The fence I climbed that day still cuts me like a two-edged sword from time to time.

John O'Donoghue

IN A STRANGE LAND

Brian! Brian! — shouts my father. 'The cows are at the gap. Get up and see after things while I go out and tie them in. The morning's fine. Don't be wasting it lying there all day. '

I twist about in the blankets and look through the window at the purple mountains in front and the clear blue sky beyond.

'Tis nice to get up in the morning', said I to myself, re-echoing the words of a popular song, 'but 'tis nicer to stay in bed!' so I get into a more comfortable position so as to enjoy a few more minutes before getting up.

I hear a creaking sound in the yard. 'That's my father bringing in the donkey and car he's after borrowing from Barney O'Loughlin, as sure as you're there', said I in my own mind.

'Brian! Brian!' goes the voice again. 'Brian, leave that!' warning me to leave the bed, and then: 'What in the name of goodness is Barney after doing?He never put the kippen on to secure the gate of the rail, and I'm after losing it on the road. Get up out of that and go west to see if you can find it. '

I make a move to rise and look once more through the window at the old familiar sight of the mountain that showed between the trees at my old home in Coomlaegill, but the scene changes slowly as I open my eyes. The trees become the painted curtains of the window in a little Dublin hotel, and the mountains I'm after seeing in the blinking of my waking is only the brown slated roof of a house on the opposite side of the street.

My father had been dead for nearly a year at the time, God rest him and the voice I was after hearing was not his , but that of a neighbour, Dansey O'Grady, who was on his way to England with me. The creaking noise I had mistaken for a donkey car coming into the yard was made by the beds of my companions lying close around me in the room as they got out to dress themselves and prepare for breakfast. Dansel was calling me to get ready for him. What a shock I was after getting , to wake up from my pleasant dream of home, and to realise that, alas, that scene of the donkey and cart coming into the yard in readiness for going to the bog to draw out the turf would never again be a reality for me!

Michael Longley

TUPPENNY STUNG

I began by loving the wrong woman.

In 1936, when she was seventeen, Lena came from County Fermanagh to work for my parents as a maid. At approximately 4 pm on 27 July 1939 I was born, followed half an hour later by my twin Peter. My sister Wendy was nine when we arrived. According to her we were cranky babies, victims of the now discredited Truby King method of feeding by strict regime rather than demand. We did not get enough milk and because we yelled day and night were kept in separate rooms and prams — one at the back of the house, the other in the porch at the front. My mother concentrated on Peter, the slightly more difficult child. Lena looked after me and turned into my mother. She exchanged the uniform of a maid for that of a nurse, but this was for her much more than a promotion. She was a natural and devoted surrogate mother: the two of us became inseparable.

The Second World War began in September. My father who had survived the trenches enlisted again and was posted to England where he remained for two years. My mother, Lena and a succession of wayward maids looked after Wendy and 'the Twins' (as we were called until puberty, when we changed to 'the Boys'). The crying stopped as soon as we graduated to solids; and some photographs show us peacefully sharing a large black pram. Because those years are mostly beyond my recall, I have to borrow Wendy's memories of the air-raids on Belfast, the search-lights, the hand-bells and whistles, the gas-mask into which Peter and I were inserted, the perspex visors through which we peered and tried to make sense of the huddle under the stairs. There survive in my mind the rough feel of khaki as I climbed over a soldier's knee, the coolness of the brass buttons, the kitchen light reflected in the polished toecap of an army boot. Had the maid been bringing her soldier boyfriend home?

Just down the road from our house the King's Hall, a huge Art Deco concrete and glass barn, was converted into a barracks for the troops. One of them, Bill Hardy, married Lena, and they left Belfast for Nottingham in 1941. I was inconsolable and for weeks afterwards toddled to the front door when the bell rang, expecting Lena to be there. The marriage was not a success. With her daughter Paddy, Lena returned in 1945 to live with us for a few more years. The three of us accepted Paddy as a sister and I liked it when she called *our* father Daddy. As my love for Lena deepened, my relationship with my mother grew more tense and complicated.

I last met Lena in 1967 when, on her way to visit relations in Fermanagh, she called briefly to meet my wife and our first child. My arms melted around her in acceptance and surrender. She was (and, so far as I know, still is) working as a priest's housekeeper in New York. A few years ago Paul Muldoon and I gave a reading there in the Public Theatre. I had thought of contacting Lena, but was anxious that no audience would turn up and that she would be upset and embarrassed on my behalf. The evening turned out to be a considerable success. Lena should be have been sitting in the middle of the front row.

My parents came from Clapham Common to live in Belfast in 1927. My father was a commercial traveller for an English firm of furniture manufacturers, Harris Lebus. Before the war his territory was the whole of Ireland, and the family album is full of his photographs — Antrim, Donegal, Kerry: he seems quickly to have fallen in love with the island. Business did not resume until well into the fifties; so on leaving the army my father for several years scraped a living as a professional fundraiser — for the Ulster Hospital for Women and Children and, when the introduction of the National Health Scheme rendered him redundant, for the War Memorial Rebuilding Fund. The inventiveness and panache of his schemes were a minor talking-point in the community. Photographs of him receiving cheques and smiling at Ulster's grandees appeared regularly in the local press. He was always referred to as Major R. C. Longley, M. C., a billing he disliked. The war was over, he used to insist. But Ulstermen adore military titles and my father's, with its aura of courage as well as authority, endured stubbornly. To this day when certain people hear my surname, which is unusual in Northern Ireland, they ask 'Any relation to the Major?'

As a commercial traveller my father did as little travelling as possible. In no time at all he had sewn up the smaller territory of the Six Counties. Rising late and after a breakfast of tea and Woodbines, he would accumulate the day's orders over the telephone. 'I've got a lovely little number here, Mr Gillespie. Only £200. No, you won't be disappointed.' He was that rare thing, an Englishman accepted and trusted by Ulstermen. Handsome, charming, deft with people, he could have gone far in public life, I believe. He had enjoyed his charismatic fundraising days, but now preferred to stay at home, in retreat. I picture him chainsmoking in his dressing-gown and giving the fire a last poke before strolling to the telephone with his bundle of catalogues.

Having lived through so much by the time he was thirty, perhaps my father deserved his early partial retirement. At the age of seventeen he had enlisted in 1914, one of thousands queuing up outside Buckingham Palace. He joined the London-Scottish by mistake and went into battle wearing an unwarranted kilt. A Lady from Hell. Like so many survivors he seldom talked about his experiences, reluctant to relive the nightmare. But not long before he died, we sat up late one night and he reminisced. He had won the Military Cross for knocking out single-handed a German machine-gun post and, later, the Royal Humane Society's medal for gallantry: he had saved two nurses from drowning. By the time he was twenty he had risen to the rank of Captain, in charge of a company known as 'Longley's Babies' because many of them were not yet regular shavers. He recalled the lice, the rats, the mud, the tedium, the terror. Yes, he had bayoneted men and still dreamed about a tubby little German who 'couldn't run fast enough. He turned around to face me and burst into tears.' My father was nicknamed Squib in the trenches. For the rest of his life no-one ever called him Richard.

After the war he travelled through Europe as part of an anti-German propaganda mission, which he found distasteful. ('Goebbels learnt a lot from us.') He also disliked the snobbery of the officers' mess where he was dismissed as a 'trench officer', his medals failing to outweigh the fact that he had not attended public school or Sandhurst. But for this he might have become a career soldier. Instead he vanished to West Africa and mined tin and gold there until he was thirty. In the photographs from Europe and Africa he is often accompanied by beautiful women. As I grew older, I noticed that he behaved most vitally in women's company, and most peacefully as well. For him a sense of unexpected bonus pervaded all the ordinary aspects of life: he could not take being alive for granted. He once showed me the gas-burns like birth-marks on his shoulder, the scars on his legs. Running away from a successful German offensive, he had been wounded by shrapnel without feeling any pain. Back in his dug-out he discovered that he had been shot through his scrotum, that the top of his penis had been severed. His children owe their existence to skilled medical orderlies. We were three further bonuses whom he enjoyed deeply and with as little fuss as possible

To use a geological metaphor, my father's personality was sedimentary, my mother's volcanic. She had been born with a congenital hip malformation and walked with a severe limp. My grandmother, a beautiful Jewess called Jessica Braham, died at the age of twenty when my mother was still a baby. My Grandpa George, a man of limited sensibility, then married his housekeeper Maud who was insanely jealous of her step-child. My mother's childhood was an unrelieved misery: daily humiliations, mental and physical cruelty. My heart goes out to the little girl cowering in a corner, sobbing at the top of the dark stairs. My father told me of the first time he visited his future in-laws. Maud rushed at the young couple sitting nervously on the sofa, scrabbed her nails down my mother's face and ran out of the room screaming. When my parents had departed on their honeymoon, Maud took the wedding guests up to my mother's bedroom to show them the mess she had left it in (after working overtime the night before at her job in a record shop). My father's mother, by all accounts a saintly women, said to the embarrassed assembly, 'You know the trouble with Maud? She's jealous!' Everytime I remember that story I savour the release of vengeance.

When they married, my mother was not yet twenty and my father thirty. She told me several times of their first meeting. 'He was just back from Nigeria, tanned, a bit overweight but terribly dashing. I stopped to admire his red setter and he invited me to meet him in a tearoom the following week. He was something of a local hero in Clapham. Could have had any girl he wanted. Why did he choose me with my dot-and-carry walk? I still wonder. In the tearoom he said, as bold as brass, "We're going to have wallpaper like that when we get married." Soon they were living in Belfast and Clapham shrank to a yearly phone-call to Grandpa George on Christmas Day, birthday cards from Auntie Daisy. I visited Daisy and two of my father's brothers, Maurice and Charlie, when I was sixteen and on holiday in London. I never met Uncle Hugh, nor my paternal grandparents (he was a journeyman carpenter, she the possessor of second sight). Because my mother's retarded brother had molested her, Grandpa George threw him out of the house. He was last heard of following the stretcher parties across No Man's land with a sack into which he was putting bits and pieces of soldiers.

So there was no hinterland of aunts, uncles and cousins to which Wendy, Peter and I could escape and still feel at home. Perhaps because of my father's passivity, her children became the main outlet for my mother's emotions. Her moods changed unpredictably. It has taken me a long time to forgive her that atmosphere of uncertainty, its anxieties, even fears. I appreciate now that somewhere inside her intelligent humorous personality crouched the tormented child. Perhaps I was responding to this even as a boy when I would bring her sticky little bags of sweets as peace-offerings. My father sat quietly until the storm clouds passed. If this was taking too long, he would venture, 'A little gin and orange, Connie?' Out of sight in the kitchen he would take a long swig of neat gin before presenting the drinks with ostentatious ceremony.'There we are, dear.' Occasionally, if he realised Peter and I had been really disturbed by the climactic changes, he would say, 'Your mum may walk a little funny, but she's a marvellous woman all the same'. A well-meant but patronising simplification.

I remember her solving crosswords swiftly in ink. She was a first-class bridge player. My parents did not engage in any regular social intercourse except for bridge parties. Where were their close friends? My mother's good moods could be a firework display of wit and surreal invention. She would laugh for minutes at a time, her eyes watering, so that even when Peter and I were too young to understand the joke we would join in. Though her bad moods meant perhaps that the child in her was competing with us, her generosities as a mother could be bottomless. During the war she limped down many streets to buy us second-hand tricycles and other toys. Despite rationing, powdered eggs, Oxo cubes, parsnip disguised as banana, we looked forward to her carefully prepared meals. Like my father, she was depressive, and the latter part of Peter's and my childhood probably coincided with her menopause. By that time she would have been well into her forties, my father in his mid-fifties. They withdrew into themselves still further, and Wendy, a maturing teenager who at sixteen had already fallen in love with her future husband, Ernie Clegg, started to fill the emotional gaps. She became my second surrogate mother.

Grandpa George was the only relative who crossed the water to visit us. He took the train to Stranraer, then the boat to Larne — an ordeal for a man in his eighties. On arrival he would claim that his journey had been 'in the lap of the gods', a phrase I pretended to understand. Grandpa had been a teacher of ballroom dancing in Clapham. Top hat and tails, sequins and swirling tulle. He liked to dress up and hold centre stage, a natural master of ceremonies. His chief ambition, to be Mayor of Battersea, was never realised, despite his masonic connections (he had risen as high as Worshipful Master). I realise now that he could be vulgar and pompous, but at the time I found his Cockney accent with its genteel adjustments, his taste for polysyllables and periphrases really exotic. A good meal was always 'a highly satisfactory repast'. Inclined to choke at the dinner table, he would declare, 'A particle of food would appear to have lodged itself against my uvula'. Every morning he would give us a full account of his 'motions' (I guessed what that word meant). Laxatives, All-Bran, elastic stockings, Vic, Thermogene, long johns: these were his obsessions. At the seaside he would roll up his trousers and rub seaweed on his white shins.'Iodine, Michael. Good for the pores.' On a calm day he would lie at the water's edge and siphon the sea through his long nose. Legs astride, bending over, he would then snort out a stream of snot.'Salt water, Michael. Very good for the tubes.'

Grandpa taught me cribbage, a card game not much played in Ireland. I was happy to listen to his endless monologues and fantasies as we pegged up and down the board: he needed an audience. Rickets had left him with bow-legs.'Got those riding horses. The calvary. Tipperary, 1916.' Sometimes it was the Boer War (he was jealous of my father's military record). He never mentioned his retarded son, and found it impossible to accept that he had fathered a physically imperfect daughter. 'A nurse dropped little Connie on the floor when she was delivered.' He referred once or twice, tearfully, to Jessica Braham and seemed after all those years to be in love with her still. He also passed on to me an interest in good food and drink, about which he knew a great deal. I owe to him my first taste of pheasant, hare, smoked salmon, tripe and onions, lambs' kidneys. He allowed me to sip his Guinness.

Towards the end of his life I visited Grandpa George and Maud in London. They had rented out the rest of their house and were living in the ballroom in a maze of screens and curtains. Grandpa wept then, partly because I could not stay, partly because of the pain a catheter was causing him.'The waterworks, Michael. The waterworks.' Maud burst out laughing. She may have been embarrassed, but I still hate those giggles. When he died in 1958 I was the only member of our family able to attend the funeral. A few of his old cronies turned up and went to the house afterwards.'I need a whiskey', Maud said. 'I've a bottle in the cabinet over there, but I'm not giving any of it to you lot.' This saddened rather than shocked me, because at the crematorium her tears had made on the linoleum circles the size of half-crowns. And she had sighed again and again, 'Poor George. Poor George. Poor George.'...

~

My father died in 1960 when I was twenty and too young to appreciate his strengths or understand his weaknesses. My mother died in April 1979. For about a year beforehand we both knew that she was going to die. I wanted to feel free to embrace her as I had embraced Lena, and agreed to call with her every day for five minutes or five hours — for as long as both of us could stand it. Over several tumultuous months we lived out her childhood and mine. She gave me X-ray pictures in which the shadowy shapes of Peter and me curl up and tangle about five months after conception. ('Tuppenny Stung for a penny bung', my father had said.) She confessed that in the early days of the pregnancy she had attempted in an amateurish way to abort us — or 'it' as we then were. I registered neither shock nor pain. Somehow this knowledge made it easier for me to hug her dying lopsided body. It was like a courtship, and I accompanied her on my arm to death's door.

Since April 1979 I have been promising myself that some day I shall phone New York and talk across the Atlantic with Lena.

Fred Johnston

STAMP COLLECTING

It was what he did to forget her,
to forget them together
in that house
that contained, now, no one he knew
(certainly not me)
and he set to it with his old strict-
ness, annotating, listing, wearing
her memory and his eyes away

I have them now, both collections,
two slim volumes, every stamp
priced in shillings and pence
(I left him to eat his Christmas
dinner alone in a Dublin hotel)
they're in a drawer, gathering time —

and I shouldn't wonder why
there are bad nights
and I wake up feeling abandoned
as if my life were a foreign country
and I'd been sent here, marked
'Postage Unpaid'.

ACKNOWLEDGEMENTS

For permission to reprint extracts and poems we would like to acknowledge with thanks (in the order they appear in the book):

My Dark Fathers, Brendan Kennelly, Bloodaxe Books Ltd.
A Stroke of a Pen, © Hugh Leonard
My Father and I, © Brian Smeaton
Field of Battle, William Trevor, from *Excursions in the Real World*, Hutchinson, 1993
The Betrayal, Michael D. Higgins
All in a Life, Garret Fitzgerald, Gill & Macmillan
Brendan's Wedding Day, Peter Sheridan
My Father and I, © John D. Nugent
Father's Christmas Party, from *Belfast Stories*, Sam McAughtry, Blackstaff Press, 1981
I See You Dancing, Father, Brendan Kennelly, Bloodaxe Books Ltd.
My Father, © Des Wilson
My Father: CJH, © Sean Haughey
The Time of My Life, Gay Byrne, Gill & Macmillan.
A Song for My Father, Desmond Egan, Peterloo Poets, The Kavanagh Press Ltd., 1989
Childhood Days, Patrick Moloney, Merlin Books, 1987
House, Pat Boran
My Story, Paddy the Cope
Malachi Horan Remembers, George A. Little, M.H. Gill, 1943
My Life and Easy Times, Patrick Campbell, Anthony Blond Ltd, 1967
Pieta, Gerry McDonnell
The Sweet Sorrow, David Hanly, *The Sunday Tribune*, 1991
Medicine Man, Mick Hanly
A Letter, © Kieran McKeown
The Prodigal Son, Saint Luke
Digging, Seamus Heaney, *from Death of a Naturalist*, Faber & Faber Ltd
Vive Moi, Sean O'Faolain, Sinclair Stevenson, 1963,'64 & '93 reproduced by permission of the Estate of Sean O'Faolain, c/o Rogers, Coleridge & White Ltd., 20 Powis Mews, London W11 1JN
Speaking to My Father, Theo Dorgan
Out of My Class, © John Boyd, Blackstaff Press, 1985
In The Hands of My Father, © Harry Ferguson
I Believe In The Father, © Keith O'Flaherty
Desperadoes, Joseph O'Connor, Flamingo, 1994
Father's Legacy, © Niall Kelly
My Father, © Derek Shiel
The Story-Teller, © John Creedon

An Autobiography, James Galway, Chappell & Co Ltd/Elm Tree Books
  Ltd., 1978
Ulysses, My Father, Fred Johnston, from *Measuring Angles*, Cló Iar-
  Chonnachta Teo, 1993
Our Apprenticeship, Jim and Peter Sheridan
My Father, © Michael Conboy
Birthday Walk With Father, Eamonn Grennan, Gallery Press
A Father's Death, © T. M. R. Jackson
My Father, © Billy McKee
One Man and His Donkey, John Scally, RTE Radio
Uniforms, Frank Galligan
'Me Own', Jack Houlahan, Radio Ulster, 1988
In A Strange Land, John O'Donoghue
Tuppenny Stung, Michael Longley, Lagan Press, 1994
Stamp Collecting, Fred Johnston, from *Measuring Angles*, Cló Iar-
  Chonnachta Teo, 1993

*Every effort has been made by the publishers to contact the copyright holders of
the material published in this book and any omissions will be rectified at the
earliest opportunity.*

FROM MY SHELF

Books:

A Little Book on the Human Shadow by Robert Bly — Harper & Row, 1988

At My Father's Wedding by John Lee — Judy Piatkus (Publishers) Ltd. , 1992

Catching Fire: Men's Renewal and Recovery Through Crisis by Merle Fossum — Hazelden Foundation, 1989

Fathers, Sons and Daughters — Exploring Fatherhood, Renewing the Bond edited by Charles S Schull — Jeremy P. Tarcher, 1992

Finding Our Fathers: How a Man's Life is Shaped by His Relationship with His Father by Samuel Osherson — a Fawcett Columbine book, 1986

Fire in the Belly — On Being a Man by Sam Keen — Judy Piatkus (Publishers) Ltd. , 1992

HE — Understanding Masculine Psychology by Robert A Johnson — Harper & Row, 1989

Iron John by Robert Bly — Element Books, 1991

Men and the Water of Life by Michael Meade — Harper Collins, 1993

Men Speak Out: In the Heart of Men's Recovery by David Lenfest — Health Communications Inc, 1991

Of Water and the Spirit by Malidoma Somé — Jeremy P. Tarcher, 1994

Ritual: Power, Healing and Community by Malidoma Somé — Swan Raven & Co, 1993

The Flying Boy: Healing the Wounded Man by John Lee — Health Communications Inc, 1987

The Grown-Up Man: Heroes, Healing, Honor, Hurt, Hope by John Friel — Health Communications Inc, 1991

The Rag and Bone Shop of the Heart by Robert Bly, James Hillman and Michael Meade — Harper Collins, 1992

Tracing Your Irish Ancestors by John Grenham — Gill & Macmillan, 1992

Audio-tapes:

The Dance Of Gender: when the women went one way and the men went the other — Michael Meade

The Great Self Within: Men and the Quest for Significance — Robert Moore & Michael Meade

Images of Initiation — James Hillman, Michael Meade & Malidoma Somé

Middle Tales: Fairy Tales and the Psychology of Women and Men at Mid-Life — Allan Chinen

Men and the Life of Desire — Robert Bly, James Hillman & Michael Meade

Men and the Water of Life — Michael Meade

Thresholds of Change: Finding Purpose and Inner Authority in Troubled Times — Michael Meade

Author's Leaflet

On Father ...

Father or Dada, God, Daddy, Dad, Da, 'the Ould Fella', 'The . . . .'

The father is the initiating priest through whom the young being passes into the larger world.

Joseph Campbell

The father is the most powerful incarnation of the archetypal.

- Carl Jung

We are missing a fundamental dilemma of the times if we don't pay attention to the fact that the women's movement intensifies men's sadness and terror at the loss of their fathers.

Samuel Osherson

There is no good father, that's the rule. Don't lay the blame on men but on the bond of paternity which is rotten.

J P Sartre

Father and son form the most dangerous and critical animal relationship on earth.

W Labarre

Father! Father! Where are you going? Oh do not walk so fast.
Speak, father, speak to your little boy or else I shall be lost.

William Blake

The missing father is the dead God who offered a focus for spiritual things.

James Hillman

You have to dig deep to bury your father.

Gipsy Proverb

Fatherhood is about being who you are and revealing that to those you love.

Charles Scholl

Some sons wait eternally for their dads to become the dad they never had.

John Lee

The journey to become true men requires that we demythologise our fathers.

John Friel

This is not princely, to be swept away by wonder at your father's presence.

Odysseus

We may identify with a deeply unhappy father too 'good' to be selfishly happy in life, so loving and suffering become confused.

Samuel Osherson

In more than 95% of cases fathers were either cited as negative examples or were mentioned as people who were not influences.

The Grant Study

While the traditional family often seems to glorify father, it also secretly degrades and undercuts the son's sense of masculinity.

Samuel Osherson

The powerful father knows: that we all lose some of life's battles, that the real skill is knowing which ones to fight and which ones to release; how to pray — to humble himself before God, nature, the universe or whatever he defines as his Higher Power.

John Friel

We need the father who helps us define masculine strength in a changing world.

Samuel Osherson

What a father says to his children is not heard by the world, it will be heard by posterity.

J P Richter

If a father is healthy enough to choose to let his son win just once at the right moment, his son will feel full and whole.

John Lee

FAMILIAR WORDS

'Father, Father why have you forsaken me?'

'My father? He was the parent who made home uncomfortable by his presence.'

'He was just like an extra child — always being coddled by my mother. I hated to see it.'

'You're just like your father.'

'If my father did cry, he never let me see it. So I became determined to be a man, if it killed me.'

'I'd always wish I hadn't taken a penny from him and vow never to do so again.'

'Fighting with him is easy — I don't know how to just love him.'

'It's embarrassing to be alone with my father, we don't know what to say to each other.'

'Today, I wonder if my Dad missed seeing me with his own eyes, if he missed telling me stories, holding me in his lap?'

'I've begun to see him more as a man in a complicated situation.'

The **Limbus** mail-order catalogue carries hundreds of books and tapes titles on gender, mythology, psychology, poetry and world music.
Purchases through limbus benefit Mosaic — a non-profit foundation that produces conferences bringing together people from various economic, racial and cultural backgrounds.
For more information write:
Mosaic, P.O. Box 364 Vashon, WA 98070. Fax: 1-206-463-9236

CONTRIBUTORS AND COPYRIGHTS

BORAN, Pat. Has facilitated writing groups throughout Ireland and has worked with the Eastern Washington University Summer Writing Programme. He has published two collections of poetry, *The Unwound Clock* and *Familiar Things* as well as a volume of short stories, *Strange Bedfellows*. In 1993 he was the editor of *Poetry Ireland Review*.

BOYD, John. Born in working-class Belfast in 1912, he worked as a teacher, lecturer and a BBC radio and television producer and on retirement began a new career as a dramatist. His *Collected Plays* Vols I and II are published by Blackstaff Press.

BYRNE, Gay. Broadcaster extrordinaire for over three decades on radio and television, he has 'aired' topics for conversation and debate which changed not only the way Irish people look at social issues, but possibly Irish society itself — certainly, as he might say himself, he is blamed for everything by opponents of change whatever the change! I, like many, many people, over the years, am indebted to him: one of his Late Late Show Specials — on alcoholism — left me in no doubt about my own drinking behaviour and how I could get help successfully for it, if that was what I really wanted. 'Thank You, Gay. '

CAMPBELL, Patrick. Known to most people for his impish wit, his agonised stutter and his irrelevant interruptions as a much loved television personality and journalist. His autobiography is a delight and includes not only the hilarious, diffident account of his succession to the Lordship, but also an interesting description of the mentorship he received from the legendary R.M. Smyllie of *The Irish Times*.

CONBOY, Michael. A chef working in Dublin whom I met on a Sufi Meditation Week-end for men soon after I decided to abandon the retraining opportunity following my last experience of 'redundancy'.

CREEDON, John. One of the younger, i.e., younger-than-Gay, broadcasters, whose station-opening radio programme was an integral part of my days during the period in which I worked on changing the habits of a lifetime. His anarchic comedy routine on another programme later some mornings was obligatory listening during my time-out in Clare.

DORGAN, Theo. A Cork-born poet whose immediate response to my first request for items on the subject was the beginning of a number of encouragements which I received from this man, previously a stranger. His works include: *Rosa Mundi* and *Kavanagh and After* (Ed.), 1995.

EGAN, Desmond. Another 'previously a stranger' whose response to my request to include something from his extraordinary *A Song For My Father* was generous and instant — and I have yet to meet him! His other work includes: *Midlands, Leaves, Siege!, Poems for Peace.*

FERGUSON, Harry. By chance sat beside me at the '92 Mens' Gathering, then we found ourselves together in the same small group and went on to share two years together in the Mens' Group to which I traveled from Clare to attend during my time-out. He has recently begun teaching as a Senior Lecturer in the Department of Applied Social Studies in UCC.

FITZGERALD, Garret. Born to Catholic father and Protestant mother in Dublin he was an economist, statistician, journalist and lecturer before entering politics. He became Party Leader in opposition and subsequently was elected to lead the country. Having been a student of his in UCD, and his father's reply to a heckler while campaigning in Cork having been one of Dad's oft-repeated stories, I was delighted to read the comprehensive account of his early years in his autobiography — the only one to have been written by a Taoiseach.

GALLAGHER, Patrick The Cope. Became a major community leader in Donegal, to which he returned, as described, through his father's concern and served in Dail Eireann for many years. His grandson now represents Donegal (and the Northwest region) in the European Parliament.

GALLIGAN, Frank. Born and brought up in Co. Donegal and now lives and works in Derry. He has won numerous literary awards and Bursaries. In addition to his book of poetry, *A Cold Forbidding Irish Green*, he has published a short novel, *Out Of The Blue*.

GALWAY, James. Is recognised throughout the world as a superstar of music.

GRENNAN, Eamonn. One of the poets who seemed to be more numerous among the student population when I first came to Dublin and though we'd not set eyes on each other for probably three decades I was delighted to receive the *Birthday Walk With Father* from him in America where he's been since we shared coffee in the Annex that long ago. His other work includes: *What Light There Is* and *As If It Matters*.

HANLY, David. Born in Limerick,1944, he first worked with RTE for seven years, then Bord Failte before becoming a full-time writer publishing *In Guilt and Glory*, 1976. He returned to RTE and has for years now been the presenter of *Morning Ireland* which accompanies most Irish family breakfasts, as well as presenting a number of television series.

HANLY, Mick. A musician and songwriter at the forefront of the development of expression of traditional Irish music and sound and most recently was one of the Four for the Road tour which so successfully demonstrated the range of talents of four Irish musicians.

HAUGHEY, Sean. As son of one of the most prominent political leaders since I became a voter he was an automatic 'target' for my curiosity about a father/son in politics. That he was the only one to provide me with an original account of his experience for inclusion here is, to my mind, an expression of his courage and that he is very much a son of his father. Sean has been Lord Mayor of his native Dublin and is a T. D.

HEANEY, Seamus. Born in Co. Derry in 1939 he was first a teacher and then a lecturer in QUB. His first book of poetry, *Eleven Poems*, was published in 1965, after which he was soon recognised as one of Ireland's major poets and has, since the early seventies, been a poet, broadcaster and Visiting Lecturer in different countries and won numerous awards. His other published work includes *Preoccupations: Selected Poems 1968-1978*, and *Station Island, 1984.*

HIGGINS, Michael D. A teacher and prominent Labour Party activist in Galway from the 1970s. Is a member of Dail Eireann and is currently Minister for Arts, Culture and the Gaeltacht for the second time.

HORAN, Malachi (1847 — 1945). Was four years old when my grandfather was born and out-lived him by thirteen years. So, though living in different counties and circumstances, I was very interested to find *Malachi Horan Remembers* by Dr. George A. Little, and his story of his father's experience of the punishment squad of four or five generations ago, apparently a recurring theme for Irishmen — whether fathers or sons.

HOULAHAN, Jack. Writer of essays, poems, short stories and drama. Now living in Derry. His work has been widely translated and includes the BBC Radio plays *Maiden City Magic* and *One Winter by the Foyle.*

JACKSON, Tim. My oldest friend — not by age, but in the length of our friendship. Though we see each other rarely — he being a public health specialist based in Tralee and I somewhat of an itinerant — his intelligence, sensitivity, integrity and enormous love places him at the top of my 'Men I Admire' list.

JOHNSTON, Fred. Born in Belfast in 1951, he now lives in Galway. His published poetry includes *Song at the Edge of the World*, *A Scarce Light* and *Measuring Angles* which has also been produced on audio-cassette.

KEARNEY, Philip. One of the organisers of the '92 Men's Gathering and two years later participated in the second one in the same small group as my youger son David. I am really pleased to have thought of him 'at the twelfth hour' and grateful to him for his immediate willingness to write the Foreword. He is a family therapist and co-founder of the Clanwilliam Institute in Dublin where he is director of professional training.

KELLY, Niall. An independent Human Resources Management Consultant based in the Mid-West. Professionally our paths crossed over the decades but during my year in Co. Clare we never met. My first day back in Dublin we met accidently and he volunteered that he had 'something which might be of interest' and sent me his poem!

KENNELLY, Brendan. Born in Kerry in 1936 he has been Professor of Modern Literature in TCD since 1973 and has been an indefatigable mentor to practically every poet in the country over the past three decades. His published work of more than twenty books includes *The Crooked Cross*, *Let Fall No Burning Leaves*, *Between Innocence and Peace* (an anthology), *Cromwell* and *The Judas Book.*

LEONARD, Hugh. Born in Dublin in 1926 he first worked as a civil servant but with the success of his first plays became a professional writer in the late 1950s. His work incudes television and film scripts and he is a regular newspaper columnist. His books include: *Leonard's Last Book*, *Home Before Night* and *A Life*, which won a Harvey Award; his plays include *Stephen D*, *Irishmen* and the copiously awarded *Da.*

LONGLEY, Michael. Born in Belfast in 1939. He was one of the 'student poets' in Dublin in the early sixties — but he was in 'the other place' (Trinity, not UCD where I got 'lost'). Collecting these recollections from other sons awakened many memories for me and just as I was wondering about contacting Molly — after nearly fifty years! — I read Michael's opening line in *Tuppenny Stung*. His other published work includes: *An Exploded View, Selected Poems 1963-1980* and most recently, *The Ghost Orchard 1995*.

McAUGHTRY, Sam. Born in Belfast in 1921. Joined the RAF in 1940 and subsequently the Ministry of Agriculture in Belfast. He is a regular newspaper columnist and his books include: *The Sinking of the Kenbane Head*, *Play It Again, Sam* and *Blind Spot and Other Stories*.

McDONNELL, Gerry. One of the first contributors to this book because he has been a friend since long before he published *From the Shelf of Unknowning*. His *The Dream of James Clarence Mangan* has been broadcast on RTE Radio and he has also written the libretto for a chamber opera *The Poet and the Music*, music by John Byrne. He is currently working on *Glimpsed Lives*.

McKEE, Billy. We became friends when he was exploring the difference between alcoholism and being 'just neurotic'. Since then he has begun to earn his living with increasing success from the words he writes for publication and broadcasting media.

McKEOWN, Kieran. I met Kieran at the 1992 Men's Gathering. He works in Dublin as an independent social and economic researcher and is a quiet, dedicated admirable man in every way and a caring friend.

MOLONEY, Patrick. Born in 1925 in rural Ireland, he joined the Irish Army during the Emergency, as the second World War was known in Ireland and had an outstanding athletics career with his three brothers. Thereafter he spent thirty-five years in the RAF in various capacities but always with a reputation for physical fitness, especially during his record-setting long-distance walking challenges in the early 1960's.

NUGENT, John A. A solicitor by profession. Has published authoritively on addictions, notably alcoholism. Has also recently published a hilariously irreverent novel entitled *The Fat Cat Fiddler at the Vatican Ball*.

O'CONNOR, Joseph. Born in Dublin in 1963. Early became a full-time writer, with obvious success. His first novel, *Cowboys and Indians* was shortlisted for the Whitbread Prize, and his first collection of short stories, *True Believers*, received widespread acclaim. He has written film and television scripts and as a journalist his regular features on Irish society are incisive and very humorous.

O'DONOGHUE, John (1900 — 1964). Served in the unarmed Garda Siochana immediatly after the Civil War, left to spend some time in a monastery, then emigrated to England where, working as a labourer, he wrote: *In A Quiet Land*, *In A Strange Land* and *In Kerry Long Ago*.

O'FAOLAIN, Sean (1900 -1990). Was the author of four novels, numerous short stories, a number of biographies, travel books and works of literary criticism. During the first half of the 1940's he edited the distinguished literary magazine *The Bell*. Although some of his early work suffered at the hands of the censors, in 1989 he became a Freeman of his birthplace, Cork city.

O'FLAHERTY, Keith. Was reared in London to a Kerry-born father whose recent death had caused me to visit Keith's mother soon after I began my father-son collecting. Almost flippantly I had invited him to contribute his experience — as I tended with all men at the time — and was more than surprised and humbled to later receive his poem.

SCALLY, John. Just when I thought I had finished collecting for this book, RTE Radio 1 broadcast *The Primrose* and *The Blue*, John's autobiographical drama-documentary from which I had to have an extract for a number of reasons: however unhappy father-son relationships may be, here was an example of a just as important inter-generational male relationship — and one which perhaps may become even more common with the increase in the number of female-parent-only families. Meeting John so opportunely was the last happy coincidence of making this book for me.

SHERIDAN, Jim and Peter. Graduated from their father's Oriel Players to set up the Project Theatre about which Gabriel Byrne wrote: 'It was in a way the begining of an artistic explosion that gave rise to a great deal of what has happened in theatre and film in Ireland over the last twenty years'. Before begining the search which produced this book I had never met either of these men. Now I am pleased to regard Peter as a friend.

SHIEL, Derek. Born in Dublin but has lived in London since the 1960s. He is a painter, sculptor and writer, committed to the men's movement since 1988 and has recently founded a Mens' Databank in Britain and Ireland. What he has written here is condensed from a long interview he gave some time ago.

SMEATON, Brian. A Church of Ireland clergyman in Donegal where his community activities include organising a Writers' Group. We met once in the hospitality room of a television production set.

TREVOR, William. Born in Co. Cork in 1928; practised as a sculptor before turning to writing. His first novel was *A Standard of Behaviour*, 1958 and he is the only wrtier to twice win the Whitbread Prize. His published short stories include *The Ballroom of Romance*, 1972.

WILSON, Des. Belfast-born he has spent his working life there as a Roman Catholic priest. Challenged as a priest by the horrific events of 'normal' life there in recent decades he took a very individual course of action, which I admired. He works today in independent education.